Springer Texts in Business and Economics

For further volumes:
http://www.springer.com/series/10099

Volker Eric Amelung

Healthcare Management

Managed Care Organisations and Instruments

With collaboration of Mirella Cacace, Axel Mühlbacher,
Ulla Tangermann, Anika Brümmer, Andreas Domdey,
Christian Krauth, Susanne Bethge, Peter Berchtold,
Christoph Wagner and Urs Zanoni

 Springer

Volker Eric Amelung
Institute for Epidemiology, Social Medicine and Health
    Systems Research
Hannover Medical School
Hanover
Germany

Original German edition published by Springer Fachmedien with the title "Managed Care:
Neue Wege im Gesundheitsmanagement".

ISSN 2192-4333   ISSN 2192-4341 (electronic)
ISBN 978-3-662-52459-6   ISBN 978-3-642-38712-8 (eBook)
DOI 10.1007/978-3-642-38712-8
Springer Heidelberg New York Dordrecht London

Foreword

Not long ago, "management" of healthcare seemed pretty much to begin and end with hospital administration. In the last four decades the situation has changed dramatically, and for three main reasons. First, healthcare costs that rise steadily as a share of stagnant national economies call attention to who is running the show and to the importance of getting "provider dominance" and "professional sovereignty" under control. Second, accumulating research and evidence that disclose mysteries and dysfunctions (for instance, practice variations among small areas) show that caregiving is not simply a matter of pristine professional judgment but rather can be not only costly but also inexplicable, indeed indefensible and dangerous. Third, the rise of consumerism, the advance of patients' rights, and scepticism about the wisdom of deference to professional monopolies and guilds have fuelled determination in many quarters to redress the balance of power between providers and the patients and payers they serve. These three complementary and converging forces have sent to policymakers a message both consistent and insistent, namely, it is long past time to learn to "manage care", to seek to redesign the structures, processes, and outcomes of care by the light of evidence about effectiveness and efficiency.

The organisational structures and processes that came to be called managed care have venerable roots in prepaid group practices (PGP) such as the Kaiser-Permanente plans that won heavy market penetration in California after World War II. PGPs proceed on the premise that achieving healthcare that is at once accessible, of high quality, and reasonably priced requires sound management of systems that integrate the delivery and financing of care, functions usually separated in traditional systems. Before 1970, PGPs were important players in California and in a few other US venues, but remained idiosyncratic and underdeveloped in the US system at large. In Western Europe, meanwhile, a kind of social contract within national systems of universal coverage held that providers who agreed to bargain over the price term in the equation "cost = price × volume" would be spared extra-professional interference in their management of the volume term.

In 1970 the US picture began to change. The enactment of Medicare and Medicaid in 1965 thrust the US federal government into the health financing "game" in a big way and for the first time. As the Nixon administration brooded on its options for addressing the "soaring" costs of the new programs, a policy entrepreneur, Paul Ellwood, pinpointed the purported essence of the problem – the unmanaged conjunction of fee-for-service medical practice and third party payment for medical care assured fiscal disaster – and identified the antidote, namely, the PGP model, which integrated financing and delivery in a unified organisational framework and thereby reversed the faculty incentives of the traditional system. The Nixonians embraced this reasoning and PGPs were born again, as it were, this time as "Health Maintenance Organisations." After a slow start, this organisational type diffused rapidly, though the dilution of strong management structures that was the price of this diffusion meant that most of the "managed care organisations" that had become mainstream in the US by the end of the 1980s bore but a weak resemblance to the Kaiser-Permanente plans that had inspired the government's policy innovation in 1970.

In Europe too, the widening gap between the growth of healthcare costs and that of GDP, the stream of studies suggesting that those costs sustained no small measure of excessive (anyway questionable) use, and declining deference to the autonomy of the judgements of medical professionals combined to argue that allowing the "v" term in the cost equation to continue to go largely unconstrained was bad public policy. Health experts from several European nations visited the United States to learn what "managed care" was all about, and although few returned home enthralled with the US system as a whole, many selectively imported specific managerial strategies that, they hoped, would enhance the efficiency of their systems without damaging the impressive access, quality, equity, and solidarity these systems of affordable and universal coverage cherished. Some nations (Germany, for example) went beyond ad hoc picking and choosing of managerial tools to legislation that promoted competition among payers as a vehicle to encourage managerial efficiency. Others (the Netherlands and Switzerland, for instance), wary of the risks that accompanied unmanaged competition among health plans (managed care or other) raised the ante to rigorously managed competition: within a firm framework of government rules, purchasers would bargain hard with health plans which, eager to preserve or expand market share, could satisfy the purchasers' requirements only by ensuring strong management of the providers who supplied the care.

Since the second decade of the twenty-first century, then, managed care is both a fait accompli and a work in progress on both sides of the Atlantic. Variations on the managed care theme abound: how to define "it," how to set priorities among its myriad managerial elements; how to adjust and adapt strategies in the light of experience and evidence; how better to manage healthcare systems that perpetually overflow their existing boundaries as innovations in technology, organisation, and payment methods advance. The sheer scope of managed care and the multiplicity of its strategic components can be dizzying to those who seek to make sense of, not to mention work successfully within, this "field."

No scholar is better suited to illuminate these challenges than Volker Amelung, and those in search of essential information and sound theoretical grounding, whatever their orientation and piece of the healthcare action, can do no better than to consult this, the first English edition of a book already established in the German market.

The book has carefully kept pace with both continuities and innovations in managed care and with evidence on how managed care works in an impressive range of national healthcare systems. Well before the sharp economic downturn that arrived in 2008, leaders in Western nations had come to view managerial improvements in healthcare as nothing less than imperative. Volker Amelung's learned, meticulous, and sophisticated exploration of the ever-widening world of managed care – from utilisation review to integrated systems with much in between – remains indispensible to scholars and practitioners of healthcare policy and management.

Columbia University   Prof. Dr. Lawrence D. Brown
New York, USA
April 2013

Preface

Within the international discussion on the structure of healthcare systems, managed care is an increasingly important topic. Over more than 20 years, managed care approaches have fundamentally influenced healthcare systems in terms of patient orientation, efficiency, and quality. Experts assume that up to 20 % of healthcare expenses can be saved by applying high-quality managed care approaches. By using suitable organisational forms and management principles, not only can costs be reduced, but the quality of medical service provision can be augmented. Managed care is therefore much more than a cost-cutting strategy. The goal of this book is to offer a systematic overview of the organisational forms and management instruments implemented in managed care.

But there are few terms in healthcare which have been as controversially discussed as that of managed care. Some consider managed care to be the "downfall of healthcare" and pure commercialisation. This unfairly equates managed care with striving for profit, two-class or multi-class medicine, and diminishing solidarity.

Advocates consider managed care to be a logical and necessary developmental step in modern healthcare systems. They call for the breaking out of stagnated structures and they recognise the central problem of the fragmentation of supply structures. An increase in quality and at the same time a reduction of costs is not seen as contradictory but rather as consistent. Therefore, managed care is a response to changed challenges in the provision of healthcare.

As is often the case, reality is more complex. Managed care is not a self-contained theory but rather a bundle of widely differing organisational models and management instruments which can be used in different combinations. Thus, it is not possible to be "in favour" or "against" managed care; instead, one has to scrutinise organisational forms or management instruments individually.

It is particularly fascinating that the general attitude towards managed care is often negative, while classic managed care institutions and instruments are widely accepted. The best example of this is integrated care, a core concept of managed care. There are no voices that speak against integrated care which can be taken seriously. Although all players recognise the necessity for more cross-sectoral and interdisciplinary care concepts, their implementation often lacks continuity, professionalism, and evaluation. The same is true for a number of other managed care instruments and institutions.

Over the last years, there has been a significant increase in the international orientation of healthcare systems. However, the focus is not on the classic question "Is the German or the British healthcare system better?" but rather on individual institutions. What can we learn from the Dutch experience, how does pay-for-performance work in the United States or in Great Britain, and which risk management instruments have proven valuable in Switzerland? There is a much higher potential to learn from comparisons on the micro level (e.g., best practices) than to comparatively examine whole systems. We have thus included a number of case studies from different countries.

This book is directed at a very broad and heterogeneous target audience. On the one hand, we want to address students from different courses of study who deal with health economics and healthcare management, while on the other hand, the book is also directed at practitioners from various fields. These include interested physicians as well as representatives of health insurances and politics. Due to the broad spectrum of the addressees, we have tried not to presuppose a certain background knowledge of our readers. This book should be understandable for economists, sociologists, and physicians as well as for political scientists. We are convinced that the challenges in our healthcare system can only be overcome together, whereas a "solo effort" is counterproductive and doomed to failure.

The original German version of our textbook has been on the market for twelve years. The following people contributed to this or previous editions: PD Dr. Peter Berchtold, Anika Brümmer, Susanne Bethge, Prof. Dr. Mirella Cacace, Dr. Andreas Domdey, Joy Hawley, Prof. Dr. Katharina Janus, PD Dr. Christian Krauth, Prof. Axel Mühlbacher, Ulla Tangermann, Christoph Wagner, and Urs Zanoni.

I would like to thank Dr. Martina Bihn from Springer, who very patiently assisted us in the creation of this new edition. Without her continual support, we would not have been able to complete this edition so successfully. For the translation of the German edition and the revision of the document special thanks are due to Joy Hawley, Courtney Metz, Ulla Tangermann and Dr. Florian Stache.

I naturally take responsibility for all of the remaining deficiencies in the content and form of this book. Accordingly, I gladly welcome responses and suggestions from our readers. I can be contacted in the Department of Epidemiology, Social Medicine and Health Systems Research at the Hannover Medical School or directly via email (amelung@berlin.de).

Berlin, Germany   Prof. Dr. Volker Eric Amelung
September 2013

Contents

Part I

Basic Ideas of Managed Care

Definitions and Concepts

1

In this introduction, the development tendencies that aid and impede managed care will first be discussed. Subsequently a definition framework will be developed which will address the instruments and organisational forms in more detail, as well as the consequences that result. The consideration of inhibiting factors is necessary because, after a period of massive growth at the beginning of the decade, managed care is seen increasingly critically – sometimes even with hostility – and certain market segments have proven to be unsustainable and have since disappeared. Despite all critique, including partly justified criticisms (see Cooper et al. 2006; Rechovsky and Hargraves 2002; Draper et al. 2002; Landon et al. 2001; Mechanic 2000 or Havighurst 2001; Berchtold and Hess 2006), there is no doubt that substantial elements have become indispensable to our healthcare systems and are now considered givens. In most cases the critique is not directed against managed care instruments (e.g. Disease Management Programmes), but rather against the behaviour of the programme participants (inappropriate exclusion from services, risk selection and/or excessive pressure on the service providers). Accordingly, managed care has a substantial image problem, at least in the United States. However, due to the obvious deficits of "unmanaged care" and increasing financial pressure to act, managed care has experienced a renaissance. A number of pilot projects have shown that higher quality and at the same time lower costs are not necessarily a contradiction. The belief that there is nothing more expensive than poor quality care is increasingly prevalent as well as vice versa, that quality care is the most affordable form of care.

In the second part of this chapter, we portray the essential characteristics of the structure of the American healthcare system which are necessary to understand the organisational forms. In the third section, two theoretical concepts will be introduced for the analysis of managed care instruments and institutions. This section is primarily aimed at readers interested in theory and can easily be skipped.

V.E. Amelung, *Healthcare Management*, Springer Texts in Business and Economics,
DOI 10.1007/978-3-642-38712-8_1, © Springer-Verlag Berlin Heidelberg 2013

1.1   Supporting and Inhibiting Factors of Managed Care

The development of managed care has been significantly shaped by changes in the general condition of healthcare systems. The central aspects will be briefly outlined below:
1. Shortage of resources and mixed financing,
2. Competition as target dimension of economic policy,
3. Healthcare as a significant individual branch in the service-based society,
4. Changes in the illness spectrum and demographic change,
5. Changing role of medicine in society and
6. New technologies.

Healthcare – like all social security systems – is being confronted with an increasing shortage of resources. Regardless of whether the system is organised in a way which is more oriented towards market economy or planned economy, or whether it is more corporately organised, the gap between what can be financed and what is medically possible is growing. Limited financial resources increasingly dominate the decisions in healthcare. Hence, this means that not only medically feasible services should be taken into account but solutions considering economic objectives are sought as well. In addition, in nearly all industrial nations dual financing systems are being increasingly used. Along with traditional forms of financing, components from the private sector are gaining significance. In Switzerland, the amount of expenditures on healthcare directly paid by patients constitutes 25.1 % of the total healthcare expenses (OECD 2012). With this background, it can be assumed that so-called "basic benefit packages" will become increasingly important.

One essential aspect also is the demand for more competition in all sectors of economy and, in turn, also in healthcare, which has been expressed in most Western industrial countries since the mid-1970s (Brown and Amelung 1999). According to Reaganomics and Thatcherism, for example, competition was seen as a goal in itself and was indiscriminately accepted. Thus, the American Supreme Court determined early on that the profession of medicine is not free from the law of competition, but that it is rather a business (Light 1997, p. 41). This is associated with a shift from a macro-political to a micro-political perspective (Schumacher 1996) which places an emphasis on the efficiency of individual institutions within the healthcare system. The institutions and instruments that resulted are to a certain extent not innovations, but rather a return to and a further development of familiar forms which are now implemented under other conditions. In addition, it must be taken into account that healthcare makes up the largest single branch in all Western industrial countries (OECD 2012). For example, in Germany there are more than 4.8 million people employed in the healthcare sector (Statistisches Bundesamt 2013). Healthcare and economic policy increasingly overlap (Amelung 2011). In addition to the Ministry of Health, further ministries typically responsible for finances, the economy, the labour market, education, research, families, consumer protection, and social policy are beginning to feel partly responsible for healthcare policy.

Changes in the group of insured – i.e. shifts in the illness spectrum – are widely discussed in managed care. Key aspects of this include increasing multimorbidity as well as the growing significance of chronic illnesses (Amelung 2011; Scheidt-Nave et al. 2010; WHO 2008; Schlette et al. 2005). More than 62 % of all deaths worldwide in 2009 and 43 % of the global burden of disease can be attributed to chronic conditions. By 2020, the deaths due to chronic diseases are expected to increase to 73 % of all deaths (Harris 2012). In this context, there is not only a focus on the effects of the total costs of healthcare, the different treatment requirements are equally important. Particularly the chronically ill are in a poor position in a fragmented healthcare system strongly dominated by acute care (Kane et al. 2005). In Medicare, the social insurance programme for Americans over 65 years old, more than two thirds of the beneficiaries had at least two chronic diseases in 2010. Fifty-five percent of Medicare's spending on hospitalisation can be attributed to the 14 % of Medicare beneficiaries with six or more chronic conditions. Ninety-three percent of the Medicare's entire expenses stem from patients with at least two chronic conditions (CMS 2012). Managed care methods, which focus on the integration of service levels, are clearly more suitable and are able to better conform to the overall goals – both by increasing quality and lowering costs. In addition, the demographic shift should not be ignored since it not only includes aspects of financing, which are less relevant here, but also equally results in shifts in the structure of demand (e.g. optimisation of the interface of acute care and nursing care).

The relationship between society and healthcare also plays a significant role. Healthcare providers and particularly medical professionals sense increasing pressure to hinder increasing costs and justify their provision of services. The cliché of physicians as "half-gods in white" is crumbling more and more. To put it bluntly, this development is similar to a transformation from a strong authority-based seller's market to a customer-orientated buyer's market in which consumers are becoming increasingly confident, critical and discerning (SVR 2003, p. 181ff.). Thus, people are referring more and more to the "empowered customer" in this context. This inevitably leads to a high level of insecurity and even defensive attitudes among service providers who have to redefine their roles. The changed structure of the medical profession also plays a significant role. While men dominated the physician's profession in the past, today women make up the greatest part of the graduates in medicine. In the long run, this will have a massive influence on the nature of the provision of services.

The final aspect concerns technological changes. Nearly all of the methods in managed care are based on optimising information processes (Kongstvedt 2013). Having comprehensive patient information "online" at every point of integrated care is a major element of this concept. This goal is facilitated by the fact that new technology for information processing and storage has not only become much more affordable, it also enables a completely different form of networking. Even x-ray images, which require a large memory capacity, can be collectively used today without a loss in quality. Furthermore, all essential information about a patient can be saved on a chip card today. Thus, it is no longer the technological problems but rather data protection issues which now pose limitations in many countries.

Alongside these supporting functions, whose significance and relevance has not diminished after the so-called "managed care backlash", there are also two important, strongly interdependent inhibiting factors. First, there is the question of confidence in managed care in general and particularly in for-profit organisations. Although managed care is well received as long as a person is healthy (since it is associated with lower premiums), there are also great fears that services will be withheld or ones options will be restricted. The same is true of the deep distrust of for-profit organisations in healthcare. Both have not been proven, but they lead to a latent rejection in the negative perception and the demand for stronger patients' rights (Reschovsky et al. 2002). Up to a certain point, this is a conflict which cannot be solved. Patients will always be critical of the increasing commercialisation of their healthcare and – also in part justifiably – be distrusting. For this reason, the main focus of managed care organisations should be building up trust. Trust can be primarily built up through continuity, positive experiences and corresponding public relations work. It is precisely in the aforementioned areas that American managed care organisations have often failed and underestimated their significance. Likewise, Germany's primary problems concerning integrated care concepts are rather a result of communication problems than a performance issue (Weatherly et al. 2007; Amelung 2011). Evaluation is particularly significant here. It is still the case that only a few models are scientifically evaluated. There are many service promises, but few reliable studies that substantiate them. However, managed care can only become established in the long term when organisations majorly invest in health services research.

1.2 Definitions of Managed Care

As with all new management concepts, managed care also has a wealth of definitions. The following list represents a small selection of definitions and descriptions of terms.

Selected Definitions of Managed Care in the American Literature . . .

"When one thinks about managed care, one should distinguish between the techniques of managed care and the organisations that perform the various functions. Managed care can embody a wide variety of techniques, . . . These include various forms of financial incentives for providers, promotion of wellness, early identification of disease, patient education, self-care, and all aspects of utilisation management." (Fox 2001, p. 3)

"Managed care is a system that integrates the efficient delivery of your medical care with payment for the care. In other words, managed care includes both the purchasing and delivering of care." (Cafferky et al. 1997, p. 3f.)

(continued)

Selected Definitions of Managed Care in the American Literature . . . (continued)

"The original idea of 'managed care' was simple and elegant – a primary care physician close to the patient would ensure that the care delivered was neither too much not too little, involved appropriate specialists, and reflected the individual patient's needs and values." (Porter et al. 2006, p. 76)

"Managed care, in the broadest sense, encompasses a range of activities, organizational structures, and financial incentives designed to better integrate health insurance and health care delivery in order to more effectively "manage" the delivery of health care and achieve goals such as lower costs, increased quality and improved efficiency." (Baker 2011, p. 405)

"The term managed care encompasses a diverse array of institutional arrangements. (. . .) Many definitions of managed care focus on the nature of contract, arguing, in effect, that managed care contracts are more complete contingent claims contracts than traditional health insurance contracts. For example, managed care organizations may intervene in the relationship between the provider and the insured individual, limiting service use in particular circumstances, or they may selectively contract with a defined set of providers, limiting choice of provider." (Glied 1999)

. . . and in the European Literature

"The concept of managed care describes a principle of care which strives towards an efficient allocation of funds and resources so that every patient receives the 'right' type and amount of preventive and curative medical services. Unnecessary and disputable services are excluded from this process. Managed care is offered in a multitude of very different organisational forms.[1]" (Schwartz and Wismar 2003, p. 571)

"In turn, managed care means on one hand the application of management principles in medical care, particularly in medical and nursing services and the patient's utilisation of healthcare, on the other hand it means the integration of insurance and care." (Kühn 1997, p. 7)

In the scope of this study, managed care should not be seen as a closed theory, but rather as a bundle of management instruments and forms of organisations which intend to increase efficiency in healthcare.

Managed Care Definition Which Underlies This Book

Managed care is the application of general management principles and at least partially the integration of the purchasing and the provision of services as well as the selective contracting with chosen service providers. It aims to efficiently manage the costs and quality of healthcare. Managed care includes models of organisation and control instruments which improve the structures of care from the perspective of the patient. Thus, the approach is a consistent optimisation of the value chain from the patient perspective.

---

[1] Translated by the author.

Through the service purchaser's direct exertion of influence on the service provider as well as the insured, both goals should be made compatible. This is also the reason for the concept's high appeal. Managed care thus leads to "better" care – in terms of costs as well as in quality.

That being said, the assumption that managed care can be equated with reducing costs is far too narrow. For example, rebate contracts or discounted fee-for-service contracts alone do not constitute managed care methods.

Managed care is not synonymous with American healthcare (see Chap. 2). Even though many instruments and organisational forms of managed care were indeed developed there, one must very clearly distinguish between the entire system and its goals as well as between the instruments and organisational forms used. Through this book we particularly aim to demonstrate that managed care can be compatible with the goals of other healthcare systems such as the Bismarck models in Germany, France or Austria, or the Beveridge models in the United Kingdom or Denmark after all, since it is primarily a tool comprised of instruments and organisational forms for management on the level of individual organisations.

It should therefore be emphasized that managed care is not a method for designing an entire healthcare system, and it does not require any specific basic conditions. Managed care instruments have also been introduced in the public healthcare system in Great Britain as well as in Scandinavian countries (Amelung et al. 2008). Competition can also be implemented using so-called "internal markets" in what is more or less a regulatory system (Jérome-Forgot et al. 1995). In Europe, Switzerland can be considered the pioneer of managed care. Results from Switzerland, which are often used as examples in this book, are of particular interest due to the cultural similarities to other European countries and the excellent evaluations (regarding Switzerland, see Baumberger 2001; Lehmann 2003; Gerlinger 2003; Berchtold and Hess 2006; Berchtold and Huber 2011).

The fact that healthcare systems are highly dependent upon culture (Payer 1996) should not be questioned. Management instruments that work in country-specific healthcare systems (or which do not work) do not necessarily lead to the same results in another country. For this reason, in this book we will mainly concentrate on the ways in which instruments and organisational forms function and not primarily on concrete, empirical results and anecdotal evidence.

1.3 Which Instruments and Organisational Forms Belong to Managed Care?

Managed care leads to a strong differentiation of organisational forms as well as between the management instruments that are implemented (Fig. 1.1).

A heterogeneous system with strong differentiation and a corresponding lack of transparency resulted from the former, clearly structured system. This differentiation not only takes place between organisational forms and management instruments, but also in the manner in which they are structured. For example, it is exceptionally difficult to compare HMOs or physician networks since every

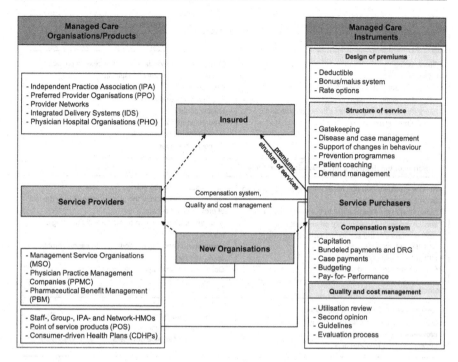

Fig. 1.1 Institutions and instruments in managed care (selection)

HMO or network of doctors uses different structures and competition strategies – which is only logical in a context of competition – which makes it almost impossible to compare complete organisations.

Many instruments and organisational forms discussed in managed care constitute no real innovations in European healthcare, but rather a return to tried and tested instruments. As previously mentioned, it is sometimes only the American terms that are new, rather than the instruments themselves.

1.4 What Changes for Those Involved in the Managed Care Context?

Before specifically addressing the individual instruments and organisational forms in the next chapter, the following table will highlight some typical central changes regarding the managed care concept (Fig. 1.2).

For the insured, managed care means first and foremost that the market for health services becomes less transparent, but still provides considerably more consumer sovereignty at the same time. Instead of "one-size-fits-all" solutions, there are differentiated services; they are, however, faced with high information costs regarding the suitable insurance protection. The insured must now determine their

Managed Care Context	Traditional System
Mananged care instruments	
– Gatekeeping – Utilisation review – Prevention orientation regarding guidelines – Integrated quality management – Integrated treatment processes through case and disease management – Outcome orientation	– Free choice of physicians, direct access to physicians – Controls only in cases of suspicion – Cure orientation – Far-reaching freedom in therapy – Quality control – Fragmented treatment processes with losses of information at the interface – Process orientation
Integration of the financing and provision of services	
– Service providers and purchasers share the risk sharing as well as gain sharing – Delegation of the financial risk to the lowest level of service provision (primary care phyicians) – Own resources of the service purchasers for the provision of services – Integrated healthcare systems – Benefits/service in kind principle	– Risk is solely with the service purchaser – No financial inclusion of the primary physician in the risk of providing the service – Strict separation between provision and financing of services – Fragmented financing of services with serious problems at the interfaces – Cost reimbursement principle
Selective transaction	
– Specific selection of service providers – Differentiated systems for the selection of service providers – Limitation of the freedom of choice	– Transaction obligation – No instruments for the assessment of service providers – Free choice of service providers

Fig. 1.2 Comparison of managed care and traditional fee-for-service

current and future needs – therein lies one of the central difficulties – and search for suitable offers. The deciding change, however, is the relationship with the service provider, the physician. Instead of only being the representative of the interests of the insured, the physician is now a service provider who increasingly also represents other interests than those of the insured, namely those of the service purchasers (which are indirectly their own interests).

Managed care assumes a considerably more active role for service purchasers. From the "money collection points" management-orientated service purchasers have emerged who directly intervene in order to control the provision of services and transact selectively. New freedom in structuring leads to more flexibility on the one hand, but it can also result in cut-throat competition.

Some service providers can surely be seen as losers in terms of the managed care concept. The market, which was dominated by service providers for many years, is shifting to a "consumer" and service purchaser dominance. The service providers are increasingly adapting to the market and see themselves faced with cut-throat competition as well as new challenges. Particularly painful is the occasional restriction in decision-making. It is no longer only the physician who decides which services may be provided and how these should be carried out, but also the service purchaser. Strategic alliances among service providers can be used as a defence strategy meant to develop a market power and create room for discretion.

However, it must be emphasised that it is up to the service providers to a large extent as to whether they see managed care as a threat or as an opportunity.

One winning element in the managed care concept are the new forms of organisations, for which new markets have emerged. These predominantly take the form of management-orientated consultations which assume individual functions in the provision of services. These can be services in the medical process, for example → utilisation review or → disease management, as well as in the classic management sector, such as the management of a network. However, after the great euphoria in the mid to late 1990s, disillusionment was widespread particularly in this segment and many business models failed miserably. This was particularly the case with internet-oriented business models, which have for the most part disappeared again. The deciding factor was that many of these companies did not possess enough medical expertise and underestimated how long it would take to fully establish themselves on the market – thus, the business plans were constructed in a manner that was far too short-term. However, the concepts which so magnificently failed ten years ago are experiencing a renaissance today, as the market is now ready for such concepts.

The associations and professional associations covering entire professional groups are becoming less and less significant. Selective contracting and competition stand in opposition to consensual negotiations. Thus, it is no wonder that the bulk of criticism of managed care comes from this sector. Professional associations will also gain importance in a managed care context. The tasks and areas of competence of professional associations, however, are drastically changing, and a much greater diversity among representative groups will ensue.

The role of the state is also undergoing long-term changes. Instead of directly intervening in activities, the state has reduced its role to the establishment of competitive conditions and the establishment of external quality control (Knight 1998, p. 227ff.). We must again point out here that most managed care methods can also be introduced (sometimes even in better ways) in public healthcare systems such as in Great Britain or Denmark. Thus, pay-for-performance compensation is currently widely implemented in Great Britain – at least among general practitioners.

Before going into detail about the organisational forms and management instruments in managed care, in the following chapters the American healthcare system will first be examined and subsequently two theoretical concepts will be outlined for the evaluation of managed care.

Literature

Amelung, V. E., Weatherly, J. N., Deimel, D., Reuter, W., & Van Rooij, N. (2008). *Managed Care in Europa*. Medizinisch Wissenschaftliche Verlagsgesellschaft, Berlin.

Amelung, V. E., Meyer-Lutterloh, K., Schmid, E., Seiler, R., & Weatherly, J. N. (2009). *Integrierte Versorgung und Medizinische Versorgungszentren – Von der Idee zur Umsetzung* (2nd ed.). Medizinisch Wissenschaftliche Verlagsgesellschaft.

Amelung, V. E., Eble, S., & Hildebrandt, H. (2011). *Innovatives Versorgungsmanagement, Neue Versorgungsformen auf dem Prüfstand*. Medizinisch Wissenschaftliche Verlagsgesellschaft, Berlin.

Baker, L. (2011). Managed care. In S. Glied & P. C. Smith (Eds.), *The Oxford handbook of health economics*. Oxford: Oxford University Press.

Baumberger, J. (2001). *So funktioniert Managed Care. Anspruch und Wirklichkeit der integrierten Gesundheitsversorgung in Europa*. Stuttgart: Thieme.

Berchtold, P., & Hess, K. (2006). *Evidenz für Managed Care – Europäische Literaturanalyse unter besonderer Berücksichtigung der Schweiz: Wirkung von Versorgungssteuerung auf Qualität und Kosteneffektivität* (Arbeitsdokument 16). Schweizerisches Gesundheits–observatorium, Obsan Zollikofen.

Berchtold, P., & Huber, F. (2011). Schweitzer Ärztenetze: ein Beitrag zur Integrierten Versorgung. In V. E. Amelung, S. Eble, & H. Hildebrandt (Eds.), *Innovatives Versorgungsmanagement, Neue Versorgungsformen auf dem Prüfstand*. Medizinisch Wissenschaftliche Verlagsgesellschaft.

Brown, L. D., & Amelung, V. E. (1999, May/June). "Manacled" competition in the German health insurance market. *Health Affairs, 18*(3), 76–91.

Cafferky, M. E. (1997). *Managed care & you – The consumer guide to managing your health care*. Los Angeles: Practice Management Information Corp.

CMS [Centers for Medicare and Medicaid Services]. (2012). *Chronic conditions among Medicare beneficiaries*. Chartbook: 2012 Edition, Baltimore.

Cooper, P., Simon, K., & Vistness, J. (2006). A closer look at the managed care backlash. *Medical Care, 44*(5), I-4–I-11.

Draper, D., Hurley, R. E., Lesser, C. S., et al. (2002, January–February). The changing face of managed care. *Health Affairs, 21*(1), 11–23.

Fox, P. (2001). An overview of managed care. In P. R. Kongstvedt (Ed.), *The managed health care handbook* (pp. 3–15). Gaithersburg: Aspen.

Gerlinger, T. (2003). Gesundheitsreform in der Schweiz – ein Modell für die Reform der Gesetzlichen Krankenversicherung. *Jahrbuch für kritische Medizin, 38*, 10–30.

Glied, S. (1999). *Managed care* (NBER Working Paper Series). Cambridge: National Bureau of Economic Research.

Harris, R. E. (2012). *Epidemiology of chronic disease: Global perspectives*. Burlington: Jones & Bartlett Learning.

Havighurst, C. (2001, July–August). Consumers versus managed care: The new class actions. *Health Affairs, 20*(4), 8–27.

Jérome-Forgot, M., White, J., & Wiener, J. (1995). *Health care reform through internal markets*. Montreal: Institute for Research on Public Policy.

Kane, R. L., Priester, R., & Totten, A. M. (2005). *Meeting the challenge of chronic illness*. Baltimore: The Johns Hopkins University Press.

Knight, W. (1998). *Managed care – What it is and how it works*. Gaithersburg: Aspen.

Kongstvedt, P. R. (2013). *Essentials of managed health care* (6th ed.). Burlington: Jones & Bartlett Learning.

Kühn, H. (1997). *Managed care* (Discussion Paper). Berlin: Wissenschaftszentrum.

Landon, B. E., Zaslavsky, A. M., Beaulieu, N. D., et al. (2001, March/April). Health plan characteristics and consumers' assessment of quality. *Health Affairs, 20*(2), 274–286.

Lehmann, H. (2003). *Managed care. Kosten senken mit alternativen Versicherungsformen*. Zürich: Rüegger.

Light, D. W. (1997). Gründe für den Kostenanstieg und Kostenkontrolle im Gesundheits–wesen: Die Vereinigten Staaten. In M. Arnold, K. W. Lauterbach, & K.-J. Preuß (Eds.), *Managed care*. Stuttgart: DUV Gabler Edition Wissenschaft.

Mechanic, D. (2000, September–October). Managed care and the imperative for a new professional ethic. *Health Affairs (Millwood), 19*(5), 100–111.

OECD [Organisation for Economic Cooperation and Development]. (2012). *OECD health data 2010*. http://stats.oecd.org/index.aspx?DataSetCode=HEALTH_STAT. Accessed 31 Jan 2013.

Payer, L. (1996). *Medicine and culture* (2nd ed.). New York: Holt.

Porter, M., & Teisberg, E. (2006). *Redefining health care – Creating value-based competition on results*. Boston: Harvard Business School Press.

Reschovsky, J., Hargraves, L., & Smith, A. (2002). Consumer beliefs and health plan performance: It is not whether you are in an HMO but whether you think you are. *Journal of Health Politics, Policy and Law, 27*(3), 353–377.

Scheidt-Nave, C., Richter, S., Fuchs, J., et al. (2010). Herausforderungen an die Gesundheitsforschung für eine alternde Gesellschaft am Beispiel "Multimorbidität". *Bundesgesundheitsblatt, 53*, 441–450.

Schlette, S., Knieps, F., & Amelung, V. E. (2005). *Versorgungsmanagement für chronisch Kranke*. Bonn: Kompart.

Schumacher, H. (1996). Die Leistungsfähigkeit von Gesundheitssystemen im Vergleich. In *Hamburger Jahrbuch für Wirtschafts- und Gesundheitspolitik* (pp. 189–215), 41. Year, Hamburg.

Schwartz, F. W., & Wismar, M. (2003). Planung und Management. In F. W. Schwartz et al. (Eds.), *Das Public Health Buch* (2nd ed., pp. 558–573). Munich: Urban und Fischer.

Statistisches Bundesamt. (2013). *Gesundheitspersonalrechnung*. https://www-genesis.destatis.de. Accessed 31 Jan 2013.

SVR [Sachverständigenrat für die Konzertierte Aktion im Gesundheitswesen]. (2003). *Finanzierung, Nutzerorientierung und Qualität*, Gutachten 2003, Bonn.

Weatherly, J. N., Seiler, R., Meyer-Lutterloh, K., Schmid, E., Lägel, R., & Amelung, V. E. (2007). *Leuchtturmprojekte Integrierter Versorgung und Medizinischer Versorgungszentren – Innovative Modelle der Praxis*. Medizinisch Wissenschaftliche Verlagsgesellschaft.

WHO [World Health Organization]. (2008). *The world health report 2008, primary health care, now more than ever*. http://www.who.int/whr/2008/whr08_en.pdf. Accessed 19 Feb 2013.

Main Characteristics of the American Healthcare System

In the following section the main features of the highly complex American healthcare system will be exhibited (see Niles 2011; Sultz and Young 2010; Davidson 2010; Greenwald 2010; Shi and Singh 2013; Jonas et al. 2007; Katz 2006; Kovner et al. 2005; Haase 2005; Anderson et al. 2003; Hsiao 2002; Huber and Orosz 2003; Dranove 2000; Katz 2006). The section will focus on the multiple payers for healthcare services existing in the United States.

The American healthcare system differs substantially from European systems in terms of the service providers as well as payers. Even if the general discussion may provide this impression, it must be acknowledged that "the one" American healthcare system does not exist. Effectively, healthcare in the United States is made up of a multitude of sub-systems, existing in parallel and partially overlapping. The healthcare systems in California and New York differ as much as that of Germany and the Netherlands at the very least. There are, however, some market segments in the United States that are uniform. This includes the Medicare programme, through which healthcare for the elderly is financed, and Veteran Affairs, the healthcare system for active and former soldiers, for example.

Considerable variation in financing and the delivery of care exists at the state level. For example, in some individual states hospitals are not allowed to hire their own physicians and must instead work with private attending physicians. In other areas, such as in the Medicaid programmes, there are also considerable differences between states. Furthermore, individual states particularly differ in terms of the penetration of managed care. Thus, there are still states that to a large extent do not have managed care, and others in which managed care now finds itself in a phase of consolidation after a phase of massive growth. The reason why managed care did not develop uniformly throughout the United States is due to the attractiveness of the markets as well as the respective legal conditions which strongly differ from state to state. The graphic (Fig. 2.1) depicts these complex structures in a simplified manner.

First, we will consider the payers for healthcare services. The programmes Medicare and Medicaid, both initiated in 1965 (Bodenheimer and Grumbach

V.E. Amelung, *Healthcare Management*, Springer Texts in Business and Economics, DOI 10.1007/978-3-642-38712-8_2, © Springer-Verlag Berlin Heidelberg 2013

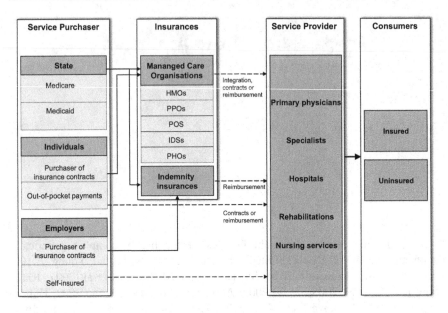

Fig. 2.1 Main features of the American healthcare system

2002, p. 5ff.; Tilson et al. 1995, p. 102ff.), account for approximately half of the healthcare expenses in America (47 % in 2008; California Healthcare Foundation 2010). In addition, there are far-reaching tax concessions, through which the government supports private healthcare, tied to the employer. When these are also included in the calculation, the percentage of public financing amounts to more than 50 % (Cacace 2010, p. 140ff.). Therefore, one can speak of a "private economy financed system" only to a limited extent.

Medicare is the system responsible for the care of Americans over 65 years old and other selected eligible people, such as dialysis patients or the handicapped. It is financed by income-based contributions from both the employers and employees. The Medicare programme is essentially comprised of three parts. Part A includes the obligatory health insurance of all retired citizens and covers inpatient treatment. Part B, on the other hand, is an optional insurance for outpatient medical care, financed through lump sum payments. Ninety percent of the insured under Medicare take out additional private insurance, nine million of them purchase Medigap (KFF 2011) for supplementary services, better hospital service and in order to avoid co-payments. The Bush administration implemented considerable changes to Medicare in 2003. With Part D, additional insurance coverage, optional for medicines administered in outpatient contexts, was introduced. However, this reform has failed to solve the essential problem areas and specifically the "frequent users" continue to have difficulties financing their medications.

Medicaid finances the medical care of the poorest Americans (medical services and nursing care). The percentage of the individual income in relation to the federal poverty line defines the general eligibility for Medicaid. Eligibility thresholds vary between the states. In contrast to Medicare, the Medicaid programme is jointly financed by the federal government as well as by individual states. The share paid by the federal government is determined by the income per person in the respective state and currently amounts to between 50 % and 77 %. While Medicare is directly managed by the CMS (Centers for Medicare & Medicaid Services), formerly HCFA (Health Care Financing Administration) in the case of Medicaid, the CMS define only the basic requirements the states have to comply with in order to receive federal matching funds. Both programmes were introduced in order to combat the lack of care for those in need and therefore are responsible for the fact that the uninsured (currently 48.6 million Americans) are not primarily the poorest Americans or the elderly, but rather many young people between the age of 18 and 35 as well as the so-called "working poor" (DeNavas-Walt et al. 2012, p. 22). The working poor are employed, but their employers do not finance their health insurance. Through the shifting of the age pyramid of America's population, the Medicare programme will be faced with great financial problems (Cleverley et al. 2010, p. 174). Thus, there are concentrated efforts to move away from traditional fee-for-service compensation and case fees to more affordable lump sum compensation forms such as capitation fees. Medicare as well as Medicaid have considerably contributed to the development of managed care. About 33 million Medicaid beneficiaries are registered in managed care plans. In addition, approximately 7.5 million covered under the Medicare programme subscribed to managed care. Medicaid's managed care clearly focuses on reduction of costs and enabling access to healthcare services. The Medicare programme, by contrast, emphasises the improvement in the delivery of services through managed care (Hurley and Sheldon 2006).

Along with public systems, private employers are the most important payers for healthcare services in the United States (Shi and Singh 2013). Two types can be differentiated here. First, there are the employers who assume the insurance function for their employees, so-called self-insurers. These are first and foremost large companies or companies who join together in order to avoid the intermediary health insurance, as their pool of insured is large enough to bear the risk on their own. Companies who offer their employees health insurance by contracting with a private health insurer are considered the second group. Depending on the size of the company, either a single health plan is offered, or the employees can choose between different alternatives.

The significance of the employer in financing healthcare has a historical as well as a tax law-related background. During World War II in the United States, the government mandated a wage freeze. However, benefits provided by the employers on a voluntary basis, so-called fringe benefits, were not affected by the aforementioned freeze and companies saw the possibility of an indirect pay increase (Knight 1998, p. 138). Additionally, premiums for health insurances are tax-exempt thus providing an incentive to offer employees such social benefits.

In the late 1980s, health insurance premiums grew by 15–20 % annually (Zelman and Berenson 1998, p. 1). In order to contain rising healthcare costs, employers were the main drivers supporting the spread of managed care. On the

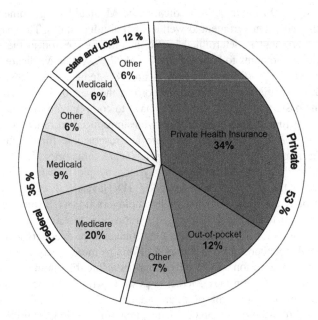

Fig. 2.2 Sources of financing in the American healthcare system (California Healthcare Foundation 2010)

other hand, they also played a crucial role in the "managed care backlash" at the beginning of the twenty-first century. The reaction of employers regarding health insurance relies heavily on the current situation in the job market. If the labour market is very tight, i.e. there is a shortage of qualified employees, then costs are not the primary deciding factor on health insurance but rather the attractiveness of healthcare products to current and potential employees.

The rapid rise of so-called consumer-driven health plans (→ CDHP) is considered to be the most significant trend in the last years (Commonwealth Fund 2006; Katz 2006). This term particularly refers to health savings accounts (HSA) and health reimbursement accounts (HRA). CDHP characteristically pairs these savings accounts with insurance with a high deductible (Lee and Zappert 2005).

Individuals, finally, are the last group of players to be considered. Characteristically, these have little influence on the way in which care is delivered. Their percentage of the health expenses essentially comprises deductibles and co-payments as well as payments for services that are not covered (out-of-pocket). As will be discussed in detail in the following chapter, co-payments can take on very different forms and essentially work as a barrier of access to healthcare services. The different financing sides are represented in Fig. 2.2.

As in most healthcare systems, there is no proportionality between sources of financing and sources of insurance coverage. The following graphic portrays the sources of insurance protection (respective to the percentage of uninsured) (Fig. 2.3).

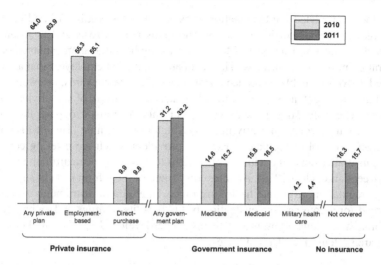

Fig. 2.3 Sources of insurance coverage in % (following DeNavas-Walt et al. 2012)

Thus, the financing of insurance as well as purchasing of services through a third party is also characteristic of the American healthcare system. These can be either public institutions or employers (Brown 1994). It should be emphasised that due to the antitrust provisions and strategic orientation, each payer has its own compensation scheme. As a consequence, providers may receive different amounts of compensation for the same service, while at the same time the reimbursement method (fee-for-service, daily rate or capitation) may vary. The insured person only plays an indirect role and also has – still – only very little influence on the design of the healthcare system. In precisely the same way as the German system, large parts of the American system are also not fully funded and are, thus, not ready for demographic change (Amelung et al. 2003). In particular, Medicare will not be able to be financed in the intermediate term and urgently requires comprehensive reforms for capital coverage.

On the provider side one must differentiate between insurances, traditional providers of healthcare services such as hospitals and nursing homes as well as Managed Care Organisations (MCOs) as a combined form. Traditional insurances refer to indemnity insurances or fee-for-service systems that compensate the service provider based on individual services. The market share of indemnity insurances has continually decreased from 73 % of all insured employees in 1988 to less than 1% (KFF/HRET 2013). Today classical indemnity insurances are quite rare. Correspondingly, the percentage of MCOs has risen in the same time frame from 27 % to 85 %. After a rapid increase in 2008/2009, CDHPs are now represented in the market with 13 %.

The American healthcare system underwent a significant change as a consequence of the healthcare reform enacted by the Obama administration in 2010 (Cacace 2010, p. 66ff.). While individual elements of the reform are already in effect, their completed implementation is expected to last until 2018 and beyond. The target of the reform is to stop the enormous rise in costs and to insure an additional 32 million Americans. Moreover, making health insurance mandatory is a central point of this reform law. This mandate is aimed at employers that are now required to offer health insurance from a certain size onwards, as well as at individuals who are now also required to acquire a form of health insurance coverage. The political opponents of the current government oppose this point with particular fervour. Currently individual states are forming "Health Insurance Exchanges", a pool of regulated insurance providers which are offering comprehensive insurance coverage with fair conditions to people who are difficult to insure on the free market (Jost 2010). Another component of the reform is dedicated to the stronger regulation of private health insurance. In addition, instruments are being reinforced for a comparative evaluation of the benefits of drugs and technologies. This branch of regulation is drastically underdeveloped in the market-based healthcare system in the United States.

Literature

Amelung, V. E., Glied, S., & Topan, A. (2003, August). Health care and the labor market: Learning from German experience. *Journal of Health Politics, Policy and Law, 28*(4), 693–714.

Anderson, G. F., Reinhardt, U. E., Hussey, P. S., et al. (2003). It's the prices, stupid: Why the United States is so different from other countries. *Health Affairs, 22*(3), 89–105.

Bodenheimer, T., & Grumbach, K. (2002). *Understanding health policy – A clinical approach* (3rd ed.). New York: McGraw Hill.

Brown, L. D. (1994, Spring). Who shall pay? Politics, money, and health care reform. *Health Affairs* (II), 175–184.

Cacace, M. (2010). *Das Gesundheitssystem der USA: Governance-Strukturen staatlicher und privater Akteure.* Frankfurt am Main: Campus.

California Healthcare Foundation. (2010). *Health care costs 101* (Annual report). Oakland.

Cleverley, W., Song, P., & Cleverley, J. (2010). *Essentials of health care finance* (7th ed.). Sudbury.

Davidson, S. (2010). *Still broken understanding the U.S. health care system.* Stanford: Stanford Business Books.

DeNavas-Walt, C., Proctor, B., & Smith, J. (2012). Current population reports, P60–243, Income, poverty and health insurance coverage in the United States: 2011 – Current population reports. US Government Printing Office, issued September 2012.

Dranove, D. (2002). *The economic evolution of American health care: From Marcus Welby to managed care.* Princeton: Princeton University Press.

Greenwald, H. (2010). *Health care in the United States: Organization, management and policy.* San Francisco: Jossey-Bass.

Haase, W. L. (2005). *A new deal for health – How to cover everyone and get medical costs under control.* New York: The Century Foundation Press.

Hsiao, W. C. (2002). Erfahrungen mit staatlicher und privater Regulierung im US-amerikanischen Gesundheitssystem. *Managed Care, 8,* 13–15.

Huber, M., & Orosz, E. (2003, Fall). Health expenditure trends in OECD countries, 1990–2001. *Health Care Financing Review, 25*(1), 1–22.

Hurley, R., & Sheldon, R. (2006). Medicare and Medicaid managed care: A tale of two trajectories. *The American Journal of Managed Care, 12*(1), 40–44.

Jonas, S., Goldsteen, R., & Goldsteen, K. (2007). *An introduction to the U.S. health care system* (6th ed.). New York: Springer.

Jost, T. S. (2010). *Health insurance exchanges and the affordable care act: Key policy issues.* New York: The Commonwealth Fund.

Katz, M. (2006). *Health care for less.* New York: Hatherleigh.

KFF [Kaiser Family Foundation]. (2011). *Medigap reform: Setting the context.* http://www.kff.org/medicare/upload/8235-2.pdf. Accessed 20 Feb 2013.

KFF [Kaiser Family Foundation]/The Henry J. Kaiser Family Foundation & HRET [Health Research and Education Trust]. (2013). *Employer health benefits 201.* Annual survey. Menlo Park/Chicago: Kaiser Foundation & HRET. http://ehbs.kff.org/pdf/2012/8345.pdf. Accessed 21 Jan 2013.

Knight, W. (1998). *Managed care – What it is and how it works.* Gaithersburg: Aspen Publishers.

Kovner, A. R., & Knickman, J. R. (2005). *Health care delivery in the United States* (8th ed.). New York: Springer.

Lee, T., & Zappert, K. (2005). Do high-deductible health plans threaten quality of care? *The New England Journal of Medicine, 353*(12), 1202–1204.

Niles, N. (2011). *Basics of the U.S. health care system.* Sudbury: Jones and Bartlett.

Shi, L., & Singh, D. (2013). *Essentials of the U.S. health care system* (3rd ed.). Sudbury: Jones and Bartlett.

Sultz, H., & Young, K. (2010). *Health care, U.S.A.: Understanding its organization and delivery* (7th ed.). Sudbury: Jones and Bartlett.

Tilson, H. H., Ross, M., & Calkins, D. (1995). Medicare and Medicaid. In D. Calkins, R. J. Fernandopulle, & B. S. Marino (Eds.), *Health care policy.* Cambridge: Blackwell Science.

Zelman, W. A., & Berenson, R. A. (1998). *The managed care blues – And how to cure them.* Washington, DC: Georgetown University Press.

Theoretical Concepts for the Assessment of Managed Care

3

The following section is particularly directed at readers who are interested in theory. Using the two main approaches of the new institutional economics (Schauenberg et al. 2005; Coase 1988, 1993; Demsetz 1967, 1968, 1988; North 1991; Jensen and Meckling 1976; Hart and Moore 1990; Furubotn and Pejovich 1974; Alchian and Demsetz 1972; Sloan 1988), certain fundamental ideas will be introduced about the design of institutions as well as incentive and monitoring systems. The transaction cost theory (Williamson 1975, 1985, 1986, 1993; Windsperger 1996) offers a method for analysing the assessment of vertical integration along the value chain and, thus, for evaluating integrated care systems, among other things. The principal-agent theory (Pratt and Zeckhauser 1985; Pauly 1968; Mooney 1993; Akerlof 1970; Arrow 1963) is concentrated on delegation relations and their inherent information asymmetries. There is hardly another field in which the considerable information asymmetries are so clear between those who delegate tasks (e.g. the patient) and those who carry out the tasks (e.g. a physician). The principal-agent theory investigates how contracts can best be designed in such a configuration.

3.1 Transaction Cost Theory

Fundamental Ideas

In his ground-breaking article "The Nature of the Firm" the founder of transaction theory, Coase, posed the question of why there are firms at all in an economic system in which the market price is the coordination mechanism. The central point of his analysis poses the questions: Why are not all transactions carried out in the market, and on the other hand, why is there not only one single giant firm? Coase assumed that the costs of transactions determine whether a transaction is carried out over the market or via the company. A state of equilibrium results at the point where the marginal costs of both organisational forms are identical (Fontaniri 1996, p. 96).

V.E. Amelung, *Healthcare Management*, Springer Texts in Business and Economics, DOI 10.1007/978-3-642-38712-8_3, © Springer-Verlag Berlin Heidelberg 2013

At the beginning of the 1970s, Williamson (1975) embraced Coase's idea again and developed it much further. In doing so, he mainly dealt with the question of which factors determined the level of transaction costs, and thus attempted to make empirical studies possible.

What was significant about Coase's as well as Williamson's considerations is that there are alternative forms of organisations which vary in their efficiency – from the market to the company and a variety of hybrid forms. The goal of transaction cost theory is to establish the determining factors and to specify the most suitable institutional arrangement for optimal transaction costs. Thus transaction cost theory deals with one of the most-discussed questions in health management: What is the optimal design of interfaces between service providers (e.g. between the outpatient sector and inpatient sector, or the inpatient sector and rehabilitation)? The fragmentation of the provision of services and poorly coordinated transition between interfaces have been seen as a considerable weak point in many healthcare systems for years, not only for reasons of cost, but also due to quality concerns.

According to the etymology of the word, transactions are "transfers" or "arrangements" (Fontaniri 1996, p. 97). Accordingly, transactions are costs accrued when a transfer is made. Williamson refers to an "...economic equivalent of friction in physical systems" (1985, p. 19). Arrow expresses it even more precisely, by referring to the operating costs of an economic system (Arrow, in: Williamson 1985, p. 9), thus emphasising that these are coordination costs. The counterpart to transaction costs are the organisational costs that accrue in an institution, or, more simply put, the costs of bureaucracy.

The goal of transaction cost theory is to determine which institutional arrangements minimise transaction costs. In doing so, it is obvious that the production costs resulting from an institutional arrangement should not be overlooked.

Transaction Costs

Transaction costs are divided into two phases and five types of costs (according to Picot et al. 1997, Fig. 3.1).

Search and information costs accrue before contract negotiation. Among these are communication costs, consultation costs, certain overhead costs from procurement, sales and marketing and preparation of the contract (Picot et al. 1997, p. 66). These are essentially the costs necessary for participating in market activities. Simply put they are costs for finding, contacting and evaluating the terms of potential market partners. For example, these costs accrue when a patient looks for a suitable hospital for their elective operations (e.g. a TEP). It also becomes apparent here that the ban on advertising as well as the scale of fees maximise transaction costs, since they impede on the gathering and evaluation of information. The systematic processing of performance data in public reporting is therefore a concept for reducing initiation costs.

Fig. 3.1 Transaction costs

Bargaining and decision costs are primarily the costs for negotiation and the signing of contracts. The transaction partners have already found one another and proceed to conclude contracts. The level of transaction costs depends on the complexity of the contract (contents of the contract must be specified) and the frequency of the transaction. The particular significance of transaction frequency is dealt with in more detail later, in what is known as the "organisational failure framework". Basically these are personnel costs which are composed of direct negotiation and decision costs. The level of the agreement costs is directly dependent on the necessary degree of specification. Case rates and additional fees ($\rightarrow$ compensation systems) further minimise transaction costs.

The third type of transaction costs is **executing costs.** These refer to the steering of the exchange process as well as general management costs. Among other things, hiring and dismissal of employees belongs to the steering of the exchange process. The costs for company management are also included among general management costs. In hospitals, these include the costs for central services (human resources, controlling, accounting – to name only a few) and the board of directors. Generally these are determined by the degree to which a hospital's overhead costs correlate with the "make-or-buy" decision.

Further transaction costs include the **policing costs.** These consist of quality and deadline monitoring as well as the development of standard purchasing values. Thus, control costs include not only the costs for determining breaches of contract, but also the costs of assessing the general advantages of a contract. Correspondingly, control costs can be divided into the inspection of assets and monitoring costs. The introduction of $\rightarrow$ guidelines and $\rightarrow$ disease management should also have a quality control function, since they restrict the freedom to manoeuvre and therefore reduce transaction costs.

The last category of transaction costs is so-called **enforcement costs.** These include additional costs that accrue due to subsequent changes (to quality, quantity, price and deadlines). These changes are caused by insufficiently specified contracts, or contracts which cannot be specified sufficiently. Contract cancellation charges should be considered a factor in the adjustment phase or as an independent phase.

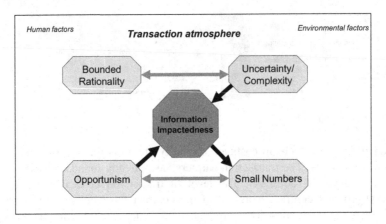

Fig. 3.2 The organisational failure framework (Modelled after Williamson 1975, p. 40)

3.2   Reasons for Market Failure: Williamson's Organisational Failure Framework (1975)

Williamson developed a model to identify the determinants of market failure on the basis of the transaction cost theory. The Organisational Failure Framework is the basis for determining optimal coordination patterns. Underlying this is the assumption that the level of transaction costs is dependent on the circumstances as well as certain design activities (Picot et al. 1997, p. 67). The following graphic depicts this model (Fig. 3.2).

One of the central assumptions is that both the key human and environmental factors must be compared in pairs. Statements about bounded rationality are only relevant in combination with statements about uncertainty and complexity. First, we will examine the four dimensions.

We understand **bounded rationality** in the sense that human behaviour is intended to be rational, but only to a certain extent (Simon 1997, preface). Complete rationality is impossible for three reasons. First of all, particular bits of information are unavailable as a matter of fact and complete information is far too costly to attain. Furthermore, human capacities (linguistic and neurophysical) are simply limited. Robinson (1997) clearly emphasises this significance for healthcare: "Bounded rationality … places severe strains on contractual relationships in health care, given a wide variety of possible diagnosis and treatments for any sets of presenting symptoms and the diversity of views on appropriate and inappropriate care."

The aforementioned quote becomes problematic when combined with **uncertainty and complexity**. Uncertainty is defined as the standard for unpredictability and the amount of necessary changes (Picot et al. 1997, p. 68). Complexity measures the amount of differing conditions that a system can attain. Both uncertainty and complexity are central in healthcare. Bounded rationality, which manifests itself in intense discussions on evidence-based medicine (→ evaluation) as well as the high level of uncertainty in diagnoses, which is particularly high in the cases of multimorbid patients, complicates the standardisation process. Likewise, the environmental uncertainty, which is characterised by rapid technological changes, can result in swiftly changing treatment methods.

Regarding individual behaviour, it is assumed that individuals restrictively maximise their own benefits and hence utilise **opportunism**: "A condition of self-interest seeking with guile" (Williamson 1993, p. 92). Thus, the manager or physician no longer primarily pursues the goals of the company, but rather their own goals which can be compatible or identical to the aims of the company but do not have to be. This is, in turn, only a problem when combined with specificity. We see **specificity** as the mutual dependence between exchange partners, i.e. to what extent further utilisation is possible. Contracts are highly specific when there is a very high level of dependency, i.e. if a service is unable to be provided when a partner drops out. Services are nonspecific when it is possible to change contract partners without accruing further costs. One example of highly specific contracts in healthcare are the maintenance contracts for customised computer programmes which manage the provision of services. The more specific the services are, the greater the risk is of being oppressed ($\rightarrow$ principal-agent theory). Unspecific contracts include, for example, the purchase of pens or laundry detergent. To put it simply, specificity measures whether a product can also be offered to other customers without difficulty, or whether one is "at the mercy" of said contract partners.

This analysis is completed with the examination of the atmosphere and frequency of the transaction. Opportunism, for example, is not a fixed parameter, but is rather dependent on external factors of technological, economic and legal nature. For example, the degree of opportunistic behaviour correlates with the risk of losing one's licence. The frequency of transaction plays a central role in determining the optimal institutional arrangement, but it is not a relevant criterion for the decision.

Market, Hierarchy or Cooperations

The core of transaction cost theory is to determine the optimal institutional arrangements. Simply put: should additional services be purchased, should joint ventures or other cooperations be aspired to, or should they be completely integrated into a company? Williamson reduced the criteria of analysis to the dimension of specificity and frequency illustrates this decision model (Fig. 3.3).

At this point, it should be mentioned that there are no substantiated statements about when a transaction is seldom and when it occurs often, and there is also a large range of freedom in the assessment of specificity. For that reason, it lends itself to not only argue for the four categories suggested by Williamson, but to assume a continuum (Fig. 3.4).

The graphic clearly shows that there are a number of intermediate phases. With the help of the terminology of transaction cost theory, there are arguments for

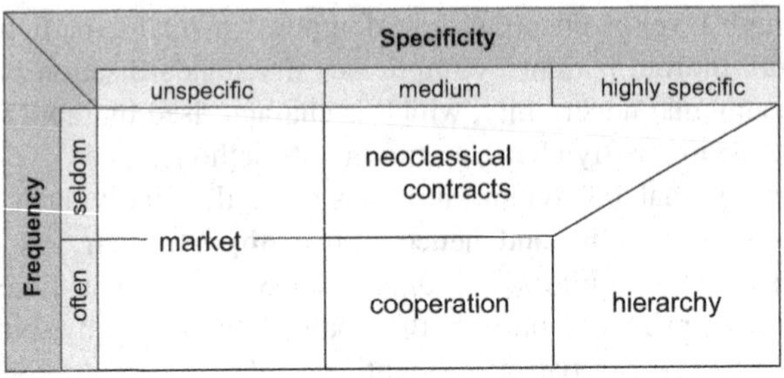

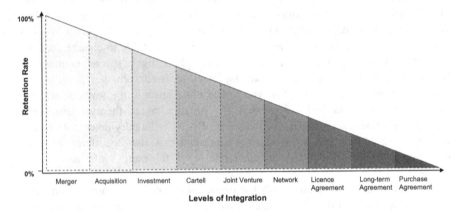

Fig. 3.3 Criteria for analysis (Williamson 1975)

Fig. 3.4 Forms of vertical integration (Williamson 1975)

individual variations, even when the theory cannot yet make quantitative statements due to the fact that the measurement of transaction costs is largely impossible.

The Suitability of Transaction Cost Theory in Healthcare

A major problem of transaction cost theory in healthcare is the pronounced complexity and variety of the value chain (Janus and Amelung 2005). The classic model of the outpatient sector, hospital and rehabilitation as vertical integration is not necessarily the rule, if it is the case at all. If the production of paper is clearly an upstream stage of production and the newspaper stand is a downstream stage, the relationship between the outpatient sector and rehabilitation to a hospital often functions differently. The private specialist physician represents an upstream production stage when referring a patient to the hospital. However, when the patient has a stroke, for example, he is brought directly to the hospital, and within the framework of rehabilitation the specialist represents the downstream stage of production. Likewise, if the patient is completely treated by the specialist and is not referred to a hospital, the specialist renders a complete added value. Two conclusions can be drawn from this: First, the order is extremely varied in healthcare, i.e. one cannot generalise upstream and downstream production stages. Sometimes the value chain even runs in a loop-shaped manner, so that a production stage is involved multiple times. Particularly in the case of multimorbid or chronically ill patients, a classic value chain is unidentifiable. Secondly, many cases that initially appear to be vertical integration are in fact cases of diversification. Upstream and downstream production stages are not integrated, but rather other service providers, in order to offer a more comprehensive range of services. However, the transaction cost theory is not suitable for this particular analysis, but rather Porter's competitive strategy should be used (1998).

The transaction cost theory still provides important stimuli, particularly in healthcare, since a temporal focus is placed on so-called "hybrid organisations" (Cacace 2010). This model of organisation is always relevant when neither the one organisational model (market) nor the other (integration) is suitable.

3.3 Principal-Agent Theory

The second theoretical approach appropriate for analysing managed care institutions and instruments is the principal-agent theory. The basic idea of the theory is quite trivial. The principal engages an agent who is meant to perform tasks for him. These tasks include a certain decision-making authority (Jensen and Meckling 1976). A realistic basic assumption is that the agent must not necessarily have the same goals as the principal who engages him. And this is precisely where the theory comes in. The principal-agent theory assumes that the agent also pursues his own interests, which can be in opposition to those of the principal. Thus, many managers consider a company car, preferably as large as possible, as a status symbol. However, the possession of the largest company car does not necessarily fall into the interests of the company owners (principal) who delegate the management to an employed manager (agent). The same is true for healthcare. The patient (principal) delegates the treatment to the physician (agent). There are also valid doubts about whether the physician only has the patient's interest in mind or whether he also pursues his own interests which are not compatible with those of the patient. For this reason the physician might consider some medical tests as being useful even though they might not help the patient. This is especially true for costly tests. In addition to divergent goals, risk profiles are also different. The principal-agent theory essentially assumes that the principal acts in a risk-neutral way, while the agent behaves risk-aversely.

However, the entire problem only arises when uncertainty is present and discrepancies in the information available to the principal and the agent exist (Arrow 1985, p. 37). Different access to information and information processing is a core element to this theory. Arrow emphasizes that "the physician-patient relation is a notorious case. Here the physician is the agent who chooses actions affecting the welfare of the principal (the patient). The very basis of the relation is the superior knowledge of the physician. Hence, the patient cannot check to see if actions of the physician are as diligent as they could be." (Arrow 1984, p. 3). The assumption that the agent to whom tasks are delegated has an informational edge – in the context of information asymmetries – over the delegating principal is a basic assumption of the principal-agent theory. The removal of this informational advantage in conjunction with monitoring is not possible, or at least not free of costs. The patient could study medicine in order to reduce the information asymmetries and to monitor the physician. This is, however, not a realistic approach and would be extremely time-consuming and costly. Furthermore, the specialist will still possess more specialised information about the patient's disease.

The principal-agent theory is now concerned with the question of how contracts should be designed. Due to differing interests and information asymmetries, there is theoretically only one optimal solution (first best). The aim of the principal-agent theory is to minimise the discrepancy between what is achieved (second best) and the theoretical solution. The agency costs result from this discrepancy, which should be minimised when possible.

The agency costs are composed of three types of costs (Jensen and Meckling 1976, p. 318):

1. Signalling costs of the agent who wants to document his commitment and ability to perform in the principal's interest. Among these are certifications.
2. Monitoring costs, i.e. money that the principal spends in order to minimise information asymmetry.
3. Residual losses, the agency costs that remain despite signalling and monitoring.

How high the agency costs are depends on the following factors (Richter and Furubotn 1996):

1. Approach/preferences of the agent,
2. The ease at which the agent can assert his preferences over those of the principal,
3. The degree of risk inclination,
4. Supervision costs and
5. Risk of losing the guarantee.

The task of the principal-agent theory is – under these conditions – to determine contract arrangements and review pre-existing arrangements. In practice, this is impeded by the fact that the principal-agent relationship is not central, but rather a network of those who could be in competition with one another. Thus, a hospital physician is not only the agent of the patient, but also of the hospital management. Each economic entity is integrated in a nearly endless number of interdependent principal-agent relationships.

In the following section, we will first discuss the most significant information asymmetries and the resulting behavioural uncertainties, in order to subsequently discuss suitable coordination patterns.

3.4 Information Asymmetries and Behavioural Uncertainties

The typology of information asymmetries and the analysis of the resulting behavioural uncertainties are integral parts of the principal-agent theory. Three types of information asymmetries are distinguished from one another (following Spremann 1990, p. 566f.):

1. Hidden characteristics: ex-ante fixed characteristics (e.g. talent, ability or qualification),
2. Hidden action/information: ex-ante variable characteristics (effort, diligence, fairness or goodwill) which are unidentifiable in retrospect, and
3. Hidden intention: ex-ante variable characteristics (effort, diligence, fairness or goodwill) which are identifiable in retrospect.

First, we will discuss quality uncertainty or hidden characteristics. The agent's behaviour is determined by external factors and cannot be influenced by the principal. It is crucial to point out that the principal is not aware of these characteristics. Adverse selection results from this situation. In the second case, we discuss hidden action and moral hazard resulting from it. It remains hidden from the principal when the agent does not comply with the goals of the principal, even ex-post. Variables include his commitment, diligence and care. The third case differs in the sense that the goals of the agent become clear to the principal ex-post. Behavioural characteristics include cooperation, goodwill and fairness. This is called hidden intention. In the following section, these three information asymmetries and behavioural uncertainties will be examined more closely and their relevance for healthcare will be highlighted. **Hidden characteristics** and **adverse selection** refer to the phase before the conclusion of a contract. Essentially, these deal with the selection of suitable contract partners. Hidden characteristics are qualities of the agent which first become apparent after the conclusion of the contract and which cannot be changed even after the fact, such as quality uncertainty (Spremann 1990, p. 567f.), i.e. there is uncertainty about services or the agent's performance potential ex-ante. That may sound very abstract, but it will become clearer when one considers concrete examples. A typical principal-agent relationship exists between an insurance company and someone who is seeking insurance coverage.

The asymmetrical distribution of information as well as the informational edge of the agent seeking insurance coverage can be demonstrated using the example of a young woman. The young woman has an informational advantage over the insurance company because only she knows if costs for a pregnancy and birth might accrue. Milgrom and Roberts (1992, p. 149) express it aptly: "Childbearing plans are a privately known, unobserved characteristic of the insurance buyer that has huge effect on insurance costs." Due to her informational advantage, if she does indeed plan to become pregnant in the near future, she will choose the insurance policy with the most comprehensive services concerning childbirth. All women planning on a pregnancy would then want to have a contract with this insurance company. This argumentation may sound absurd, but it is not. Negative risk selection is considered to be so significant in the United States that the costs are no longer covered by private individual insurance companies (Milgrom and Roberts

1992, p. 149). An adverse selection results from this information asymmetry. This means that certain offers, i.e. insurance, are more attractive to those who benefit over-proportionally. Contentious people feel a particular appeal towards legal expense insurance, less diligent physicians are particularly attracted by a fixed salary, and those who know they only have a short time to live, find life insurance especially attractive when the insurance company is unaware and unable assess their short life expectancy.

Hidden action/information and **moral hazard** arise due to the room to manoeuvre after the conclusion of a contract, i.e. ex-post opportunism. The principal is not able to completely monitor the behaviour of the agent and he must therefore assume that the agent fully utilises and can utilise this room to manoeuvre to his advantage (differing utility functions). However, it is crucial that the agent's behaviour is subject to his free decision making process, which means he decides how he wants to behave himself.

If the principal cannot gauge the efforts of the agent or monitoring is too costly and thus he cannot tell the difference between the agent's efforts and coincidence, the hidden information problem is somewhat different. Arrow (1985, p. 35) refers to this as a "lack of assessment despite observability". The agent lacks so much professional expertise that he cannot make a judgement despite his observations. This could play a major role in the field of healthcare. The relationship between patient (principal) and physician (agent) is a classic one. Due to his superior knowledge and language which is unfamiliar to the patient, it is possible for the physician to carry out moral hazard in front of the patient, who does not possess the possibility to notice such exuberant language. In this situation it is important that the physician gives the patient selective information, i.e. withholding information (hidden information). This is also a classic phenomenon when considering the physician's duty of disclosure before an operation. In this case the doctor is in a position to select or, as is rather the case, encode information so that it becomes useless to the principal. Therefore, it is argued that one must differentiate between "information" and "knowledge". A lot of information can be given, but what is critical is whether or not it is transformed into knowledge, i.e. personal information, and can thus place patients in a position to make knowledge-based decisions.

Moral hazard can be seen as a change in behaviour after the conclusion of the contract at the expense of the principal's interests. This can be illustrated using the example of insurance companies. Taking out a health insurance policy can mislead someone to neglect preventive measures (for example brushing ones teeth regularly) or to take risks which one would avoid without insurance (for example injuries in high-risk sports). However, moral hazard also plays a key role in the relationship between the insurance company and the service provider. An insurance company delegates the production of goods and services to a hospital, for example the renewal of a TEP. After the conclusion of the contract, two moral hazard problems emerge from the perspective of the insurance. First, the question arises of whether the scope of the service invoiced is justified or whether the services were rendered at the expense of the insurance company. Maybe there was a longer hospital stay than absolutely necessary. The patient is admitted into the hospital a day before the operation, although admittance on the same day would have been just as sufficient. Second, a quality problem also arises. It is very difficult for the insurance company to determine whether the quality of the service performed is appropriate. This is often due to the fact that monitoring is impossible or too costly.

Hidden intention and the resulting **hold up** become apparent to both contractual parties after the conclusion of the contract. This is essentially due to the creation of contractual gaps that should be regulated after the conclusion of contract. This can be done either with goodwill or in a self-serving manner. However, how it is decided does not remain hidden, it becomes apparent. "It is judged by A [the principal – *author's note*] as more or less 'unfair'. Yet A can neither legally nor physically force his partner B [the agent – *author's note*] to provide a service in return which he wishes and considers to be 'fair'." (Spremann 1990, p. 69). The danger of being in a position to be oppressed is particularly a crucial problem in the case of specific investments ($\rightarrow$ transaction cost theory). For example, a long-term service contract could be concluded between a hospital and an independent laboratory. Such contracts must be designed in such a way to be relatively open, particularly in fields where medical technology plays an important role. The open structure of the contract creates discretionary leeway to take advantage of the principal. Say a hospital invests in a heart transplant centre because they have an excellent specialist. These investments will become largely sunk costs when the specialist leaves the hospital. After the centre is built, the specialist quits.

Coordination Patterns

After the information asymmetries and the possible behavioural uncertainties have been demonstrated, the question of suitable coordination patterns is inevitable. Figure 3.5 (following Picot et al. 2003) provides an overview.

The following coordination patterns are strategies that are used to counteract behavioural uncertainty. In turn, we will first consider the **adverse selection** resulting from hidden characteristics. The starting premise for quality uncertainty and the danger of adverse selection is that the quality control results in high costs and at the same time the decision-theoretic value of information is very high (Spremann 1990, p. 578). Two fundamental approaches to quality control are possible. First is the disclosure which is also comprised of two variations: Screening, which is the systematic examination of the market (e.g. rankings) carried out by the principal; or signalling, which is initiated by agents. Here signals are "transmitted" to document the quality of the agent. It is crucial which party takes the initiative: The one with an informational edge or the one with an informational deficit. This is especially relevant in healthcare when contracts can be concluded selectively. In this case, classical communication instruments known from marketing can be implemented.

Second, there is the self-selection scheme, in which incentives for individual self-assessment are placed in such a way that the problem is no longer relevant. The starting point here is the assumption that the insured person is aware of their risk

Information Asymmetries					
	Hidden Characteristics			Hidden Action/ Hidden Information		Hidden Intention
Information problem of the principal	Quality characteristics unknown			Efforts neither observable nor able to be evaluated		Intentions unknown
Cause of the problem	Quality characteristics' ability to be hidden			Plasticity of resources Monitoring costs		Resource dependence, one-time resource, ability to be revoked
Agent's room to manoeuvre	Before conclusion of contract			After conclusion of contract		After conclusion of contract
Example	Taking out an additional insurance policy Private insurance			Doctor-patient relationship		Hospital-laboratory
Problem	Adverse selection			Moral hazard		Hold up
Design of cooperation	Signaling/ Screening	Self-selection	Alignment of interests	Alignment of interests	Monitoring	Alignment of interests
Examples from healthcare	Certification Rankings	Deductibles	Reputation	Gatekeeping	Utilization review	Joint venture Guarantee services

Fig. 3.5 Coordination patterns

structure and incentives for disclosure must be correspondingly placed. In the scope of managed care, → co-payments and → deductibles play a particularly important role. What they all have in common is that erroneous decisions – from the perspective of the principal – are prevented and that it is assumed that investment in information is worthwhile.

Adverse selection and the strategy of cream skimming of principals play a central role in healthcare because the costs are unequally distributed (Grobe et al. 2003). Few insured persons are in a position to get a relatively large insurance company into trouble. The same is true for patients. There are indeed several cases of hospitals that were simply unable to afford to admit patients with very expensive treatments and patients were relocated to other hospitals based on that very reasoning.

For the moral hazard problem, it is crucial that after the conclusion of the contract the principal is still not in the position to assess the behaviour of the agent. First and foremost, the principal is unable to differentiate between external risks and the behaviour of the agent (Spremann 1990, p. 571). Two strategies are suited to deal with moral hazard: Either information asymmetries are broken down, thus increasing the ability to evaluate the agent's actions, or incentives are provided which make acting in the principal's interest beneficial to the agent as well. In other words, we are aiming for harmonisation of interests. Figure 3.6 illustrates possible forms in the three relevant constellations.

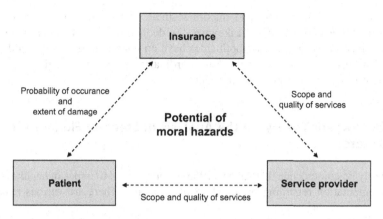

Fig. 3.6 Variations of moral hazards

The Fig. 3.6 shows that moral hazard and the corresponding strategies are relevant on all three levels. First, we will examine monitoring. The goal of monitoring is to narrow the discretionary room to manoeuvre. The tools that are used to accomplish this include classical management instruments such as accounting, management information systems, reporting or planning systems, institutions such as the supervisory board, board of trustees or other monitoring bodies, and particularly the market. The market, whether a fictional, internal market or an external market, can be considered the most effective marketing instrument, as it incurs nearly no costs, but is very instructive. Various companies and company departments submit bids for a contract. In principle, it is not possible to use discretionary room to manoeuvre since the rival companies or departments would immediately expose something of that nature. The market thus has a "cleansing" effect.

Now, we shall consider the concrete instruments in healthcare. For example, the reimbursement of costs and fee-for-services are useful as monitoring instruments between patients and the service providers. Cost reimbursement ($\rightarrow$ forms of payment), should on one hand reduce the inclination of being deceived by the physician (no moral hazard problem) and on the other hand serve to provide more transparency among services. Monitoring instruments are most important in the relationship between service providers and the insurance company. The room to manoeuvre should be restricted as much as possible using instruments such as $\rightarrow$ utilisation review and $\rightarrow$ guidelines. Instead of case-by-case evaluation, standardised forms of treatment are predetermined and steps of action require approval. However, monitoring instruments also play a role between the insurance and patients. The introduction of protocols tracking continuous prevention is nothing other than an instrument for preventing moral hazard.

Along with the development of a monitoring system, there is the possibility of preventing moral hazard by structuring systems of incentive. The utility functions should be made as compatible as possible for the players involved. A typical example in healthcare is the hiring of physicians by health insurances ($\rightarrow$ HMO) and the subsequent pay-for-performance of said physicians. The physicians partake in the success of the system and maximize their own interests by pursuing the interests of the entire system. Likewise, → deductibles are an instrument for aligning incentives. In this case both sides have an interest in reducing healthcare costs. The use of a → gatekeeper that coordinates and supervises the stages of treatment is also a widespread instrument.

Principal-Agent Theory for the Analysis of Steering Elements in Healthcare

It is surely no coincidence that Arrow (1963) often referred to issues in healthcare in his argumentation regarding principal-agent problems. There are various reasons for this.

The significance of adverse selection as well as (vice versa) the attractiveness of cream skimming is particularly high in healthcare. Few patients (10 %) make up for 90 % of the total expenditures of health insurances (Grobe et al. 2003). Thus, from a statistical point of view, a public health insurance with 100,000 insured persons has three to four haemophilia patients on long-term medication. In those cases, costs accrue which amount to between 40,000 and 120,000 Euro per patient annually, whereas a serious case can result in costs up to 3.5 million Euro per year (Ballesteros 2010). All healthcare strategies aimed at a competitive management must begin to place their main focus on risk selection. The success of an HMO is largely determined by the mix of its insured persons. The principal-agent theory lends itself to manage this problem systematically and make proposals for solutions.

There are few areas in which information asymmetries are as obvious as they are in healthcare. In turn, this is reinforced by the fact that patients' rights cement the information asymmetries, even legally. The service provider's discretionary freedom to manoeuvre is enormous. This is reinforced by the possibility of self-induced demand. In other words: the physicians work outside the view of the service payer and can largely influence the volume of orders themselves. Under these conditions, the principal-agent theory offers many methods to efficiently shape contractual relationships.

Without going into further detail, it should be noted that the principal-agent theory, with its emphasis on information asymmetry and behavioural uncertainties, can make a significant contribution to creating structures and solving problems in healthcare. In addition, it is a foundation for nearly all methods in the managed care concept. Managed care strives to reduce information asymmetries and to create positive incentive systems.

Literature

Akerlof, G. (1970). The market for "lemons": Quality uncertainty and the markets. *Quarterly Journal of Economics, 84,* 488–500.

Alchian, A., & Demsetz, H. (1972, December). Production, information costs, and economic organization. *American Economic Review, 62,* 777–795

Arrow, K. (1963, December). Uncertainty and the welfare economics of medical care. *American Economic Review, 53*(5), 941–973.

Arrow, K. (1984). *The economics of agency* (Technical Report No. 451). A report of the Center for Research on Organizational Efficiency, Stanford University.

Arrow, K. (1985). The economics of agency. In J. W. Pratt & R. Zeckhauser (Eds.), *Principals and agents* (pp. 1–38). Boston: Harvard Business School Press.

Ballesteros, P. (2010). Haemophilia in the German risk adjustment scheme. *Hämostaseologie, 30* (Suppl 1), S65–S69.

Cacace, M. (2010). *Das Gesundheitssystem der USA*. Governance-Strukturen staatlicher und privater Akteure, Frankfurt am Main.

Coase, R. (1937). The nature of the firm, *Economia, Bd. 4*. Encyclopaedia of political economy, pp. 386–405.

Coase, R. (1988). *The firm, the market and the law*. Chicago: University of Chicago Press.

Coase, R. (1993). The nature of the firm. In O. Williamson & S. G. Winter (Eds.), *The nature of the firm – Origins, evolution, and development* (pp. 18–47). New York: Oxford University Press.

Demsetz, H. (1967). Toward a theory of property rights. *American Economic Review, 58*, 347–360.

Demsetz, H. (1968). The cost of transacting. *Quarterly Journal of Economics, 82*, 33–53.

Demsetz, H. (1988). *Ownership, control and the firm* (The Organization of Economic Activity series, Vol. I). Oxford: Basil Blackwell.

Fontaniri, M. (1996). *Kooperationsgestaltungsprozesse in Theorie und Praxis*. Berlin: Duncker & Humblot.

Furubotn, E., & Pejovich, S. (1974). *The economics of property rights*. Cambridge: Ballinger Publishing Company.

Grobe, T. H., Dörning, H., & Schwartz, F. W. (2003). *GEK-Gesundheitsreport 2003*. St. Augustine: Asgard.

Hart, O., & Moore, J. (1990, December). Property rights and the nature of the firm. *Journal of Political Economy, 98*(6), 1119–1158

Janus, K., & Amelung, V. (2005). Integrated health care delivery based on transaction cost economics – Experiences from California and cross-national implications. *Advances in Health Care Management, 5*, 117.

Jensen, M., & Meckling, W. (1976). Theory of the firm: Managerial behavior, agency costs and ownership structure. *The Journal of Financial Economics, 3*(1997), 305–360.

Milgrom, P. R., & Roberts, J. (1992). *Economics, organization and management*. Englewood Cliffs: Prentice Hall.

Mooney, G. (1993). Agency in health care: Getting beyond first principles. *Journal of Health Economics, 12*, 125–135.

North, D. (1991). *Institutions, institutional change and economic performance*. Cambridge: Cambridge University Press.

Pauly, M. (1968). The economics of moral hazard: Comment. *American Economic Review, 58*, 531–537.

Picot, A., Dietl, H., & Franck, E. (1997). *Organisation*. Stuttgart: Schäffer-Poeschel.

Picot, A., Reichwald, R., & Wiegand, R. (2003). *Die grenzenlose Unternehmung* (5th ed.). Wiesbaden: Gabler.

Porter, M. E. (1998). *Competitive advantage: Creating and sustaining superior performance* (New Edition). New York: Free Press.

Pratt, J. W., & Zeckhauser, R. J. (1985). *Principals and agents: The structure of business*. Boston: Harvard Business Press.

Richter, R., & Furubotn, E. (1996). *Neue Institutionenökonomik. Eine Einführung und kritische Würdigung*. Tübingen: Mohr (Siebeck).

Robinson, J. C. (1997). Physician-hospital integration and the economic theory of the firm. *Medical Care Research and Review, 54*, 3–24.

Schauenberg, B., Schreyögg, G., & Sydow, J. (2005). *Institutionenökonomik als Managementlehre?* Wiesbaden: Gabler.

Simon, H. A. (1997). *Administrative behavior* (4th ed.). New York: Simon & Schuster.

Sloan, F. (1988). Property rights in the hospital industry. In H. E. Frech (Ed.), *Health care in America* (pp. 103–127). San Francisco: Pacific Research Institute.

Spremann, K. (1990). Asymmetrische Informationen. *ZfB, Heft 5/6*, 561–568.

Williamson, O. (1975). *Markets and hierarchies*. New York: Free Press.

Williamson, O. (1985). *The economic institutions of capitalism*. New York: Free Press.

Williamson, O. (1986). *Economic organization*. Brighton: Wheatsheaf Books.

Williamson, O. (1993). The logic of economic organization. In O. Williamson & S. G. Winter (Eds.), *The nature of the firm – Origins, evolution, and development*. New York: Oxford University Press.

Windsperger, J. (1996). *Transaktionskostenansatz der Entstehung der Unternehmensorganisation*. Heidelberg: Physica-Verlag.

Part II

Managed Care Organisations and Products

Preliminary Remarks

4

Institutions which implement management instruments and integrate the functions of insurance and the provision of services at least to a certain extent are counted among the managed care organisations (MCOs). Along with these MCOs, there are additional institutions that are active in the managed care context. These include specialised consultancy companies that aid in the development and implementation of managed care instruments and provide corresponding consultation services in dealing with managed care instruments. As previously mentioned in the introduction on the American healthcare system, this does not only include new forms of organisation, as their roots go back to the 1920s and 1930s.

The differentiation of organisational forms and products is considered to be characteristic of a competitive environment. The stronger the competition, the more pronounced these tendencies are. In the American healthcare system, managed care found itself in this stage of development in the late 1990s. New organisational forms and products continually pushed themselves onto the market and replaced old organisational forms, or developed alongside them. This is due to the fact that the traditional representations of MCOs with a simple division into three or four insurance-based types of organisation are no longer sufficient (Zelman 1996, p. xi; Wagner and Kongstvedt 2013).

After the massive growth of managed care until the end of the 1990s, the last years have been marked by a considerable consolidation (Janus 2003). Many reasons for the "managed care backlash" have been discussed in order to further explore why managed care organisations have been unable to fulfil many expectations and why some of the instruments implemented – particularly those which delegate nearly the entire financial risk to the service providers – have disappeared once again (see Peterson 1999; Reinhardt 1999; Friedman and Goes 2001; Sullivan 2000; Havighurst 2001; Draper et al. 2002). In recent years, however, the percentage of insured in managed care models has continued to increase, particularly in the public programmes Medicare and Medicaid. In the following chapters these developments will be explored in more detail.

The traditional equation of organisations and products is no longer consistent with the market conditions (Landon et al. 1997; Gold and Hurley 1997) and

V.E. Amelung, *Healthcare Management*, Springer Texts in Business and Economics, 41
DOI 10.1007/978-3-642-38712-8_4, © Springer-Verlag Berlin Heidelberg 2013

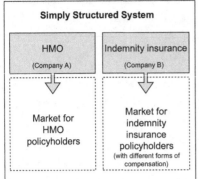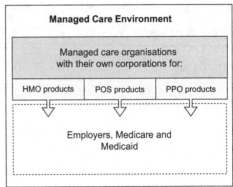

Fig. 4.1 Development from one- to multi-product companies

multiple-product companies (health plans) have developed since there are hardly any one-product companies these days. In the United States, large health insurance companies offer hundreds of different insurance products and variations of them at the same time.

These operate with different products in the same markets (providing alternatives) as well as with different products in different markets (e.g. specialised products only for Medicare's insured). It is characteristic that the different market segments (employer, Medicare, Medicaid) are processed with completely different strategies (Robinson 1999, p. 7). This can mean that the treating physician has to implement different instruments and strategies depending on the particular status of the patient.

Figure 4.1 depicts the development from a simply structured market environment to today's system of so-called "mature" managed care markets.

In doing so, there is the possibility that the represented MCO was originally a hospital or an insurance company. Systematisation can be differentiated according to the source of the services offered and not according to the initiator, i.e. the owner. Thus, the source does not refer to an institution but rather the point of departure in regard to contents. Regardless of whether it is provided by a hospital or insurance, an HMO product is originally an insurance product. An analogue example are management service organisations with consultation-based products which are separate from the owner. In this form of systematising there are also things which overlap, but they are less problematic than in other divisions. Figure 4.2 shows an overview of the essential forms.

The pure forms can rarely be found in a competitive environment, as previously mentioned. For this reason and in keeping with the goals of this book, the main ideas and management aspects will be discussed in the following section.

Even though the "managed care backlash" led to certain shifts within the segment, the trend away from classic indemnity insurance continues without interruption in the United States. From 1988 to 1998 their market share declined from 73 % to 14 %, and from 1999 to 2010 it further declined to 1 %. Despite the

Managed Care Field

Insurance-based products	Provider-based products
- Staff, group, IPA and network model HMOs - Point of service products - Consumer-driven health plans	- Preferred provider organisations - Provider networks - Integrated delivery systems - Physician hospital organisations

Institutions in the managed care field
-Management service organisations -Physician practice organisations

Fig. 4.2 Typology of MCOs and institutions in the managed care environment

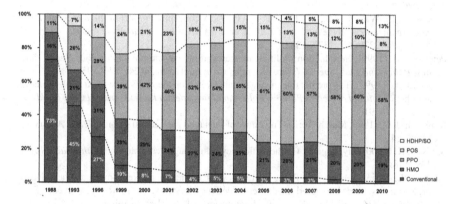

Fig. 4.3 Distribution of enrolled insured employees among the different "health plans" (KFF 2010)

current criticism of managed care and slight market downswings, one can surely speak of a market collapse and a complete market upheaval. Of course this does not mean that companies have necessarily vanished from the market on this scale, but rather that companies have changed their products (Fig. 4.3).

Along with a consideration of the developments of all market shares, in the United States one must strongly differentiate according to market segments. Thus, among employees of large companies the percentage of people insured with HMOs has drastically decreased, whereas this number has significantly increased among smaller companies (Cooper et al. 2006, p. 10).

In the following sections the individual organisational forms will be explored in more detail.

Literature

Cooper, P., Simon, K., & Vistnes, J. (2006). A closer look at the managed care backlash. *Medical Care, 44*(5), I-4–I-11.

Draper, D., Herley, R., Lesser, C., et al. (2002, January–February). The changing face of managed care. *Health Affairs, 21*(1), 11–23.

Friedman, L., & Goes, J. (2001). Why integrated health networks have failed. *Frontiers of Health Service Management 17*(4), Summery, 3–28.

Gold, M., & Hurley, R. (1997). The role of managed care "products" in the managed care "plans". *Inquiry, 34*, 29–37.

Havighurst, C. (2001, July–August). Consumers versus managed care: The new class actions. *Health Affairs, 20*(4), 8–27.

Janus, K. (2003). *Managing health care in private organizations transaction costs cooperation and modes of organization in the value chain*. Frankfurt am Main: Peter Lang.

KFF [Kaiser Family Foundation], & HRET [The Henry J. Kaiser Family Foundation & Health Research and Education Trust]. (2010). *Employer health benefits 2010, annual survey*. Menlo Park/Chicago: Kaiser Foundation & HRET. http://ehbs.kff.org/pdf/2010/8085.pdf. Accessed 5 Oct 2012.

Landon, B. E., Wilson, I. B., & Cleary, P. D. (1997). A conceptual model of the effects of health care organizations on the quality of medical care. *JAMA: The Journal of the American Medical Association, 279*(17), 1377–1382.

Peterson, M. (1999). Introduction: Politics, misperceptions, or apropos? *Journal of Health Politics, Policy and Law, Special Issue: Managed Care Backlash, 24*(24), 873–895.

Reinhardt, U. (1999). The predictable managed care kvetch on the rocky road from adolescence to adulthood. *Journal of Health Politics, Policy and Law, Special Issue: Managed Care Backlash, 24*(24), 898–910.

Robinson, J. C. (1999, March/April). The future of managed care organizations. *Health Affairs, 18* (2), 7–24.

Sullivan, K. (2000, July/August). On the 'efficiency' of managed care plans. *Health Affairs, 19*(4), 139–148.

Wagner, E. R., & Kongstvedt, P. R. (2013). Types of health insurers, managed health care organizations, and integrated health care delivery systems. In P. R. Kongstvedt (Ed.), *Essentials of managed health care*. Burlington: Jones & Bartlett Learning.

Zelman, W. A. (1996). *Changing health care marketplace*. San Francisco: Jossey-Bass.

Insurance-Based Managed Care Organisations and Products

5

Insurance companies are often considered the origin of MCOs. Even though this is true regarding the revival of managed care since the mid-1970s, MCOs in the United States originated in the form of prepaid group practices (PGP) connected to the assumption of risks by service providers in the 1920s. In rural areas physician group practices offered to let residents use the services of the group practice without restrictions in return for monthly or annual payments. Services outside of the group practice were not covered (Brown 1998; Erdmann 1995, p. 11ff.).

The term health maintenance organisation (HMO) was coined by the physician Paul Ellwood at the beginning of the 1970s (Knight 1998, p. 6ff.) in order to replace the negatively connotated term prepaid group practice. However, HMOs did not achieve their breakthrough with market successes, but rather through state regulations. The HMO law introduced by Nixon in 1973 prescribed that employers with 25 or more employees who provided their staff with healthcare as a social benefit had to offer at least one HMO product (Barrett 1997, p. 49f.). HMOs could only become established thanks to this state stimulus, which opened doors to potential customers.

In addition, all types of HMOs characteristically use managed care instruments to manage their provision of services. They consider themselves to be not only the point of purchase; they also actively intervene in the process of the provision of services.

5.1 Staff, Group, IPA and Network Model HMOs

Basic Idea

Managed care is often still equated with HMOs, although the classical form, i.e. the complete fusion of insurance and the provision of services, has become extremely rare in practise. Furthermore, there is not merely one kind of HMO, but rather HMOs have developed with very different structures and widely differing market success.

V.E. Amelung, *Healthcare Management*, Springer Texts in Business and Economics,   45
DOI 10.1007/978-3-642-38712-8_5, © Springer-Verlag Berlin Heidelberg 2013

However, all HMOs have one thing in common: They remove the strict separation between the purchase and provision of services at least partially. In their most narrow and original form, HMOs render all of the services themselves or contract the provision of certain services to a defined group of people (members). Even in the case of services that they do not directly render themselves, the process of providing services is indirectly influenced by the structure of the contract. The HMO receives a monthly or annual payment that is determined ex-ante and carries the full financial risk of the provision of services. What is decisive is that in this form the HMO only has to pay for the services it performed itself and those it contracted out. In these originally closed-panel HMOs, services outside of the system were not financed, i.e. the insurance coverage was limited to its own provider. These restrictions have been progressively loosened in recent years for marketing reasons, since it is nearly impossible to sell an insurance product that limits the freedom of choice so drastically, at least in densely populated areas. For this reason, models have been developed in which external service providers are only compensated with the same amount that the service would have cost in ones own system (open panel). The insured then have the power to decide themselves whether they want to be treated in the system without a co-payment or outside of the system and assume extra costs. But not only the marketing aspects are crucial in this: By opening this up, the HMOs create internal competitive pressure and can offer a more complete range of services. This is particularly true of tertiary care with high-performance medicine which could not be offered without this option. In recent years the trend of withdrawing restrictive managed care elements has become more widespread (Draper et al. 2002, p. 13) and this can also be seen as the decisive shift which the managed care backlash brought about. It should not be overlooked that this trend limits the ability to manage and, thus, the potential of managed care as a concept could be significantly weakened.

A critical characteristic is also the reversal of the incentives. Due to the compensation form, an HMO does not profit from the illness of its members, but rather from their health. What the service providers earn from the illnesses, hence their low financial interest in health, is one of the major weaknesses of the fee-for-service compensation system ($\rightarrow$ compensation systems). Profiting from health gives the prevention of illnesses a greater significance, or at least this should be a result. Thus, HMOs theoretically have a great interest in all forms of preventive measures (fitness programmes, programmes to quit smoking etc.), since these investments have a high return on investment (Fox and Kongstvedt 2013). Every Euro spent on immunisations can prevent subsequent costs that can accrue due to insufficient immunisation, which are considerably higher than the immunisations themselves. These arguments are used again and again by supporters of the HMO method, but they are only feasible when the system is predominantly a closed system. An investment in the health of members becomes very questionable when 25 % of the population annually changes their permanent address or employer – such as in the United States – and, thus, their insurance company as well. This advantage functions more or less only in a static environment, but not in a society as mobile as the American society. The average time that an American stays with their health

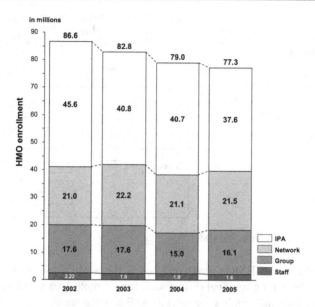

Fig. 5.1   Number of members in HMOs (Sanofi 2002, p. 8, 2006, p. 6)

insurance is 30 months, which does not allow prevention to become a true business case for the health insurances.

The plurality of different HMO models is no coincidence, but rather the result of competition between forms of organisations. No MCO has an interest in offering HMO products that are identical to the products of their direct competitors in the eyes of the customers. In the same way, the features of a Mercedes and a BMW may be similar, but product differentiations are deliberately made. It is similar with American MCOs. These rather positive and competition-based perspectives are not shared by all. That is why Weiner and Lissovey (1993) refer to an "unintelligible alphabet soup of three-letter health plans".

Due to changing marketing strategies, new terms are created again and again which differ only marginally. For this analysis the combination of single elements within an organisation is particularly problematic. It is indeed common that some of the physicians are employees (staff model), whereby others are a group practice (group model) and yet others belong to an IPA (Independent Practice Association). This is also a result of market conditions and historical developments.

In recent years, after major growth among HMO members a considerable market downturn and a shift between market segments took place, as is apparent in Fig. 5.1. In total, the number of members of HMOs declined from 99.3 million insured to 79.5 million between 2000 and 2011 (Sanofi 2012). After a dramatic increase from 16 % to 31 % between 1988 and 1996, the number of members has continuously decreased since 1996. It is critical to note that the decrease was primarily influenced by the choices of the insured. HMOs have a considerable image problem and for many insured people they pose limitations to the freedom of choice they are used to and to the range of services covered (Cooper et al. 2006, p. 10).

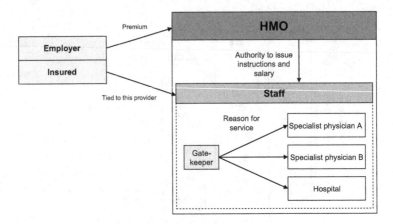

Fig. 5.2 Structure of a staff model HMO

The importance of HMOs, however, is not the same throughout the United States. There are strong regional differences, for example East Coast versus West Coast, between the metropolitan regions as well as rural areas.

In the following section, we will primarily explore the contractual relationship between HMOs and physicians, although essential statements hold true for all relevant career groups.

Staff Model HMOs

Staff model HMOs are the purest form of HMOs. The physicians and other service providers are hired by an HMO and receive a regular salary. The provision and purchase of services is managed completely by one source and the service providers are required to follow instructions. Since staff physicians usually have a performance-related component in their salaries, their prime function is largely identical to that of the service purchasers (Wagner and Kongstvedt 2013). The problem of the supply-induced demand falls away, as there is no incentive for an increase of supply in this system. However, there are considerable incentives for the denial of services, which results in a significant need for internal and external controls (Fig. 5.2).

Staff models may reveal considerable advantages through their direct influence on the provision of services, but they are rather unpopular and difficult to market for various reasons. In the United States it is quite unpopular and even forbidden in some states to be on staff (although this can be circumvented with exclusive contracts). Thus, the system of private attending doctors was established for legal and historical reasons in the hospital sector – i.e. when doctors are not staff members they invoice insurance companies and are able to remain the owners of their practices. Accordingly, in the 1990s only 10 % of American doctors were permanently employed and 90 % worked completely or predominantly in outpatient medical care (Erdmann 1995, p. 58). Likewise, today a mere 19 % of all American physicians in hospitals are on staff (Bureau of Labor Statistics 2011). The incentives for giving up the freelancer status, which is familiar and respected, must be considerable. In addition, staff models are associated with high investments, as the resources not only have to be managed but also procured. The high risk of a bad investment is also inherent in this particular model.

Staff model HMOs are also unpopular among the insured, as the level of trust with a staff physician is less than with a freelance doctor, who is supposedly more neutral. For example, physicians who are on staff at a hospital have the reputation that they mainly aim for a higher strain on the beds the hospital has available than individual patient interests. In practise, the staff model HMOs were, to a large extent, unable to convince the insured to limit their freedom of choice (Robinson 1999, p. 19).

A staff model is generally limited to classical medical areas. For example, a smaller staff model HMO does not have sufficient demand to provide a heart transplant team, but rather to purchase these services on the market.

In turn, the significance of staff model HMOs is not only very restricted, it is also on the decline. Out of 36 staff model HMOs in 1997, only 13 were still active in 2009 (Sanofi 2010, p. 15). Nevertheless, the staff model HMO represents the original version and paved the way for other staff models.

Group Model HMOs

In the case of group model HMOs the physicians are not directly employed by the HMO, but are rather organised into large group practices. In turn, these practices often transact exclusively with an HMO and are usually compensated with a capitation fee ($\rightarrow$ compensation systems). Larger groups in HMOs can deliver more physicians within one contract. However, if the contract fails, the HMO faces difficulties in delivering the service obligations (Shi and Singh 2012) (Fig. 5.3).

Internal compensation remains untouched by this and can either take the form of capitations or fee-for-service. Technically physicians in a group model HMO are either employees or freelancers. There is normally still close contact between the HMO and the group practice. Thus it is common that the HMO assists the group practice with administrative tasks and can even give the external impression that it is a staff model (Wagner and Kongstvedt 2013). This is also the reason for the misjudgement that there are so many staff model HMOs in the United States.

Staff as well as group model HMOs are classically closed panel HMOs. Both forms have the disadvantage that they can only offer very limited options.

Correspondingly, there has also been a massive decline from 94 group model HMOs in 1997 to 36 HMOs in 2009 (Sanofi 2010, p. 15), whereby these numbers cannot determine the size of individual institutions.

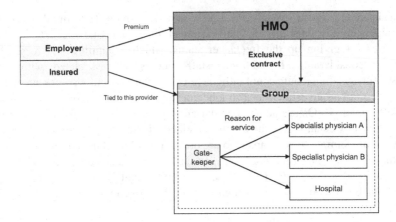

Fig. 5.3 Structure of a group model HMO

Case Study 1: Kaiser Permanente: The Classic
Kaiser Permanente can be considered one of the few models in the United States that has successfully organised and coordinated the provision of services (hospitals and networks of physicians) with the purchasing of services (in the form of an HMO) in one system over decades (Janus 2003; Crossen 2010; Liang and Berwick 2010).

Starting Point
The foundation of Kaiser Permanente goes back to the 1930s. It was originally a health insurance plan for shipyard and steelworks workers to give them access to healthcare services. It was only over the course of time that the insurance opened up to all professions and was given the name Kaiser Permanente in 1952, after its founder Henry J. Kaiser. Since the introduction of Kaiser Permanente, it has become the largest non-profit health maintenance organisation in the United States. The organisation has 8.9 million members in nine states and the District of Columbia, 37 hospitals, 611 medical offices and other outpatient facilities and 16,658 physicians. Its annual operating revenue amounts to approximately $47.9 billion (Kaiser Permanente News Center 2013). The system is characterised by the cooperation between managers and doctors, who share the responsibility for the organisation, purchase and provision of services.

Model
Kaiser Permanente consists of three separate organisations that are dependent on one another – Kaiser Foundation Health Plan, Kaiser Foundation Hospitals and Permanente Medical Groups. Each of the three organisations has specific

(continued)

Case Study 1 (continued)

tasks. Kaiser Foundation Health Plan is responsible for database maintenance, finances, as well as contracts with new members. Kaiser Foundation
Hospitals are responsible for the organisation and provision of medical and
nursing services. Thus, they guarantee the inpatient and outpatient care of
their members, as well as any home care that may be necessary. The
Permanente Medical Groups consist of a decentralised, multidisciplinary
group of physicians, who only treat members of Kaiser Permanente health
plan and are paid with capitations. At the national level, Permanente Medical
Groups are represented in a Permanente Federation (Kaiser Permanente News
Center 2013).

Change in Strategy

At the end of the 1990s Kaiser Permanente recorded losses for the first time.
More and more internal inflexibility and increasing competition in the
healthcare sector pulled the organisation into a drastic crisis. At the centre
of the change in strategy was the electronic information system called Kaiser
Permanente Health Connect. This system was supposed to create more
flexibility in terms of the healthcare market and legal regulations as well as
a better financial management (Garrido et al. 2004, p. 18). Today Kaiser
Permanente Health Connect is a perfect example of the effective use of
information technology (Liang and Berwick 2010).

The organisation took advantage of technology in order to improve administrative as well as clinical processes for decades, but the breakthrough was
not achieved until 2003, when the electronic health information system was
introduced (Chen et al. 2009, p. 324). It is based on an electronic patient file
(electronic health record, EHR) which contains data such as clinic stays,
prescriptions, lab results and x-rays, which aids physicians in making
decisions based on given guidelines (Detmer et al. 2008, p. 3). KP Health
Connect offers Kaiser Permanente members the opportunity to contact their
service providers via the Internet portal "My Health Manager", but also to
gain medical knowledge about one's own health status. In addition, it
contains instruments which help the patient to influence their state of health,
for example one can take part in a programme to change ones habits
(McCarthy et al. 2009). In the meantime 25 % of the KP members use "My
Health Manager," which shows the positive effects it has on healthcare
(Silvestre et al. 2009, p. 337).

These effects include:

1. The frequency of contact with one's family doctor decreased by 25 % and
   with specialists by 21 %
2. A higher level of patient compliance and satisfaction, as well as
3. A reduction of duplicate examinations and medication errors was achieved
   (Chen et al. 2009, p. 328).

(continued)

Case Study 1 (continued)

Along with the implementation of information technology, further care management programmes were also implemented in order to steer the focus towards prevention methods. Among these is the project "PHASE", which was introduced in Northern California in 2004. PHASE (Prevent Heart Attacks and Strokes Everyday) offers therapeutic methods that are meant to prevent the development of cardiovascular diseases, for example through motivational training to change high-risk lifestyles such as smoking and unhealthy diets. In Northern California, the prevalence of tobacco consumption was decreased from 12.2 % (2002) to 9.2 % (2005). The amount of blood pressure checks increased from 36 % (2001) to 77 % (2008) due to extensive patient education and training, which enables an essential factor in cardiovascular disease to be monitored and, thus, facilitates intervention at an earlier stage (McCarthy et al. 2009, p. 6ff.).

In addition to the introduction of information technology and care management programmes, operational processes in hospitals should also be improved. The concept "MedRite" was among the solutions. The occasion for the project was the report "To Err Is Human: Building a Safer Health System" by the Institute of Medicine, in which the main reason for medication errors is noted as continual interruptions and distractions while preparing the medications. "MedRite" was meant to foster an environment free of interruptions for nurses and to develop instruments that minimize disruptions (Blakeney et al. 2009). One example is the introduction of a wide, yellow sash that nurses wear as a signal that they should not be disturbed. By implementing this particular method, the security and reliability of the work processes increased, as well as patient and nurse satisfaction (McCreary 2010, p. 5).

Evaluation

Kaiser Permanente was a pioneer in integrated healthcare by combining the provision and purchase of healthcare services along a continuum into one system. This organisation paved the way for better, more effective healthcare with the aid of innovative methods. Through the development of KP Health Connect, by optimising processes and further developing care management, the number of emergency admissions in Northern California between 1997 and 2008 sank by approximately 33 % (McCarthy et al. 2009, p. 15). The public also took notice of the organisation's transformation. Furthermore, physicians from the Permanente Medical Group in the region of Sacramento were the only ones distinguished for their care by the HMO report card with the distinction "excellent" in March 2011 (Sacramento Business Journal 2011).

An approach such as Kaiser's should still be seen critically, as a high degree of integration also has disadvantages:

(continued)

IPA Model HMOs

It is characteristic for IPA (Independent Practice Associations) model HMOs that physicians maintain their practices and do not only treat the patients of an HMO. This form much better suits physician needs. A good deal of autonomy remains for the physicians even when it is accepted that they have to be affiliated with one or the other form of MCO (Kongstvedt 2009) (Fig. 5.4).

The IPA is in effect an umbrella organisation for freelance physicians. The physicians are able to keep their independence but are organised via the IPA. The main idea behind the founding of an IPA is simple: Individual doctors fear being defrauded by the MCOs as well as by the hospitals. The only possibility to counter this danger is to unify into a "countervailing force".

This has particularly gained importance because a new form of professionalisation took place through managed care. Instead of the classically managed health insurances, now innovative organisations dominate the market (for-profit and non-profit equally). Physicians are organising themselves in IPAs as a strategy against this commercialisation and professionalisation.

Since the HMOs represent only one source of patients for the IPAs, there are no exclusive contracts. Since all physicians who meet the selection criteria ($\rightarrow$ quality management) of an IPA are granted membership, they are referred to as "open panel" organisations (Wagner and Kongstvedt 2013).

Network Model HMOs

Network model HMOs are an extension of group model HMOs. In order for an HMO to be able to sell its products, it must have a sufficient degree of market coverage. Even large HMOs can often only cover a market to a limited extent, which leads to considerable inconveniences for the members as well as significant competitive disadvantages. Since the MCOs make contracts directly with employers, products that do not fully take the places of residence of the employees

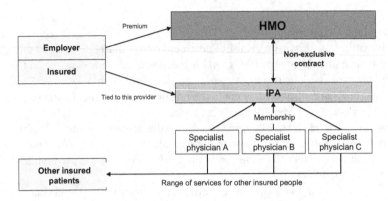

Fig. 5.4 Structure of an IPA model HMO

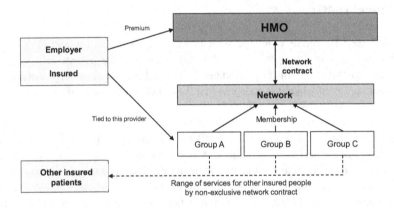

Fig. 5.5 Structure of a network model HMO

into consideration tend not to sell well. Thus, HMOs develop networks in order to attain a sufficient degree of geographical coverage. These networks can include specialised as well as general medical group practices (Fig. 5.5).

Network model HMOs represent an attempt to combine the advantages of staff, group and IPA model HMOs while reducing the disadvantages. On the one hand, the product range should be as extensive as possible – which is of essential interest for the continued existence in metropolitan regions. On the other hand, the control over the type of provision of services should be higher than with IPA model HMOs, in which the direct influence on the provision of services – as already demonstrated – is very limited.

However, it remains an unsolved conflict as it is not possible to have nearly complete control of the provision of services on the one hand – the central idea of HMOs – and to guarantee the absolute freedom of choice for the insured on the other, similar to the classical indemnity system. There is always a trade-off between control and freedom of choice. The main task of an HMO is to find out how much freedom of choice is necessary for the marketing and which type of control over the use of resources (contract solutions or property) should be implemented. No general statements can be made about the first question since healthcare is a local market. In New York, for example, the tri-state area (City of New York, New Jersey and Connecticut) of the metropolitan region with its ten million residents had to be covered as much as possible. As this is not realistic, such markets are made up almost exclusively of open panel HMOs in which external service providers can be consulted.

5.2   Consumer-Driven Health Plans (CDHPs) and Health Savings Accounts

Guidelines and Health Policy Goals

Consumer-Driven Health Plans (CDHPs) are a relatively new form of insurance for medical expenses, offered by private insurers (e.g. Schreyögg 2003; Fuchs and Potetz 2007; Fuchs and James 2005; Robinson 2005).[1] CDHPs combine a savings account for healthcare expenses with an insurance contract comprising a very high deductible, the so-called High-Deductible Health Plan (HDHP). While a number of individual and state ordinances regulate health insurance in the United States (Cacace 2010), the tax laws anchored in the Internal Revenue Code are particularly relevant for the CDHPs.

The savings accounts serve to accumulate income from employment that will then be available to the beneficiary and earmarked for purchasing healthcare services. The state subsidises these savings by exempting them from taxes. Particularly important are the savings options Health Savings Accounts (HSA) as well as Health Reimbursement Accounts (HRA) which were previously discussed in the basic principles of the → American healthcare system. The insured[2] as well as their relatives can use this balance for healthcare expenses. However, if they use them for other purposes they must retroactively pay taxes on said income and possibly even pay a penalty tax (Jost and Hall 2005, p. 396). CDHPs play an important role in private insurance – whether individual or sponsored by employers – as well as in the state Medicare programme to a certain extent. The concept of CDHPs is principally compatible with managed care (Robinson 2005). However, the high deductibles in HDHPs contradict the principle of → HMOs, which are characterised by a comprehensive range of services and low co-payments. That is why insurers have almost exclusively combined CDHPs with → PPOs. In this case, the limit for the annual deductible is lower if the insured person uses the services of a provider in the PPO network (Jost and Hall 2005, p. 405).

---

[1] The subsequent section was written by Prof. Dr. Mirella Cacace.

[2] It should be emphasised that CDHP is only a rudimentary form of insurance with limited risk pooling. However, as for example Schreyögg (2003) argues, it is still justified to call it an insurance because the savings are also a form of risk coverage.

CDHPs are debated controversially from the perspective of healthcare policy. They assume that the high costs of the American healthcare system are caused by moral hazard, and are thus based on an excess demand for services due to insurance coverage which is too comprehensive. The high deductible in HDHPs is meant to reduce the use of less effective or unnecessary services. As responsible consumers, patients should competently weigh the price and performance aspects and then carefully choose providers according to their performance. In addition, the deductible aims to heighten patients' willingness to search for information. The goal is to increase price and quality pressure on the service provider and, thus, increase efficiency, which eventually leads to the reduction of insurance premiums. According to the supporters of CDHPs, low premium costs enable more people to buy insurance. Thus, the CDHPs can positively contribute to solving the urgent problem of the already high and steadily increasing percentage of the population in the United States without insurance coverage.

Critics of this demand-based management argue that asymmetric distribution of information between patient and provider in particular will impede competition based on quality. Thus, consumers' choices will first and foremost orient themselves on the price. In addition, the insured tends to not only forgo low quality service, but possibly also services which are necessary, particularly preventive care (Dixon et al. 2008; Buntin et al. 2011). In the long term, this increases expenses in the healthcare system. Others maintain that a small percentage of chronically, severely ill patients cause the majority of expenses in the healthcare system. The steering mechanism of CDHPs, however, is only effective when the deductible is reached, which is usually exceeded by the aforementioned group of people (Fuchs and Potetz 2007, p. 5). Finally, CDHPs are also suspected of primarily attracting young and healthy people. For this reason, traditional insurance structures, which are usually much more comprehensive in scope, could be forced to raise their prices if their risk structure deteriorates. Thus, it is only the structure of expenses which shifts; their amount remains at best unchanged.

Forms and Prevalence

In the quite short span of the existence of CDHPs, a series of savings options emerged, some of which have since disappeared from the market. In 1996 Clinton's government introduced the first form, medical savings accounts (MSAs), into private health insurance (Atchinson and Fox 1997). One year later the savings package in the Balanced Budget Act also paved the way for the implementation of MSAs in the Medicare programme. MSAs had little popularity and are rarely offered today. The so-called flexible spending accounts (FSAs) are likewise declining in popularity. Unlike other savings forms, FSAs can basically only be used for services not covered by common insurance policies, such as over-the-counter medications (OTC) and optional services in hospitals. FSAs have the disadvantage that only a small portion of the amount saved can be transferred over at the end of the year to the next year. Unused savings are thus returned and are at the employer's discretion.[3]

One of the most common savings options today is the HSA, which was introduced with the Medicare Modernization Act in 2003. Employers as well as employees are entitled to deposit money into HSAs. The maximum amount of these deposits is US $3,100 annually per person, and $6,250 for a four-person family. Employees over 55 years of age are allowed to save an additional $1,000 per year. Furthermore, tax legislation sets a minimum and maximum amount for the deductible in the supplementing HDHP. In 2012, the minimum for a single person was $1,200 (families: $2,400) and the maximum annual out-of-pocket expenses were $6,050 (families: $12,100) (Department of the Treasury 2012).

The funds saved in HSA are fully transferable from one year to the next. Even when employees change jobs, they are able to transfer the savings to a new account. The regulating financial authority allows a broad utilisation of the savings by loosely defining the allocation of funds. In addition to the normally covered services, HSAs cover expenses such as transportation costs. Weight loss programmes or programmes to quit smoking can also be financed from an HSA (Fuchs and Potetz 2007, p. 22). Along with the use for illness-associated costs, HSAs also present the option to save for private insurance premiums that accrue during retirement. If the beneficiaries are over 65 years old, they are also allowed to use their available balance for private nursing care insurance payments or to finance deductibles in the Medicare programme.

In recent years, the number of HRAs, which were introduced in 2001, has sharply increased. Legislation stipulates that only employers may maintain these HRA accounts. The employer has the power to determine which amount or percentage of the savings is transferable into the next year when the contract is concluded. The remaining balance, however, must be dissolved and subsequently taxed. After the loss of employment, the employer usually closes the account. HRAs are often combined with an HDHP, but there is no legal requirement. There is, thus, no minimum or maximum deductible.

In employer sponsored insurance, which covers the majority of the insured in the United States (approx. 56 %), CDHPs have been discernibly represented since around 2006 (DeNavas-Walt et al. 2010; KFF/HRET 2010). At that point in time, CDHPs had a market share of around 4 % of all employees with health insurance coverage. The Bush government in particular facilitated the spread of CDHPs by increasing their attractiveness and advertising them with a series of campaigns. In order to protect consumers, the government, for example, stipulated that the insurer can exclude certain preventive services from the deductible, but they are not

---

[3] This prompted Uwe E. Reinhardt from Princeton University to write an amusing (though probably fictitious) anecdote in the Economix blog of the New York Times. He describes how his wife signs him up for a coloscopy shortly before Christmas in order to use up the remaining available balance in his FSA (see U. E. Reinhardt: The Trouble with (In)flexible Spending Accounts: http://economix.blogs.nytimes.com/2009/05/29/the-trouble-with-flexible-spending-accounts/).

required to do so by law (Fuchs and Potetz 2007, p. 9). Nowadays 94 % of all HRAs and 92 % of all HSAs reimburse the expenses of preventive services even when the deductible is not reached (KFF/HRET 2010, p 129). On the basis of this support CDHPs made a significant jump from 2007 to 2008 and raised their market share from 5 % to 8 %. In the following year, 2009, the percentage of CDHPs rose again sharply, so that in 2010 13 % of all employees with insurance coverage were insured this way. The reason for the increase, however, lies rather in the difficult financial situation and job market crisis of 2008/2009 (Cacace 2010). In view of the economic downswing, employers particularly expected a rapid decrease in their additional wage costs from the CDHPs. In recent years the structure within CDHPs has also changed, as HRAs grew faster than HSAs. While only 3 % of all employees were registered with HRAs in 2009, this percentage climbed to 7 % within just one year (KFF/HRET 2010: p. 128). In the case of individual insurance, the percentage of total CDHPs was even a bit higher than in the employer-sponsored insurance. Approximately 11 % of all singles and 23 % of all families take advantage of the opportunity to save tax-free income for an earmarked purpose (AHIP 2009, p. 15). In the public Medicare programme, however, CDHPs are almost non-existent.

Assessment

Based on their goals, the central question which arises regarding CDHPs concerns the overall effects they can have on the costs and quality of healthcare. It should first be noted that CDHP as a management instrument is trusted by employers. In 2010, 25 % of employers in the United States considered CDHPs to be a very effective instrument for limiting expenses in the American healthcare system, whereas the percentage in 2009 was only 16 %. In total nearly 60 % of employers considered CDHPs to be either very or somewhat effective (KFF/HRET 2010, p. 184). Are these expectations justified, and can they be empirically demonstrated? Evaluation studies first examine whether the individual expenses for healthcare services in CDHPs are indeed lower than in other forms of health insurance. On the other hand, these studies question whether the services used by the insured in CDHPs are also actually high quality services, which is suggested by the concept of the consumer as a sovereign decision maker.

From an assessment perspective, it is problematic that the evaluation studies available have yet to render a uniform profile (RWJF/HCFO 2011). A recent, wide-ranging study from the RAND Corporation examined the level of service use in CDHPs and concluded that the insured used fewer services in the first year of their membership than those in conventional insurances (Buntin et al. 2011). Longitudinal studies, however, had to revise their initial observations that those insured in CDHPs consumed less than the managed care populations which they were compared to. This points to catch-up effects, indicating that CDHPs do not reduce demand in the long run (Feldman et al. 2007). In the first year of their observations, Hibbard et al. (2008) also discovered a decline in the demand for outpatient services among those enrolled in CDHPs. In order to determine whether those insured with CDHPs in particular abstained from less effective services, they divided the available medical services into two groups. The first group was comprised of evidence-based services with higher priority; a second group was made up of services which were not evidence-based (or only to a limited extent) with lower priority. Their results showed no evidence that individuals enrolled in CDHPs had a higher demand for more effective services. Instead, those concerned went without services with both higher and lower priorities to the same extent (Hibbard et al. 2008). According to Rosenthal et al. (2005), a possible reason for this deficit in managing CDHPs is the lack of information relevant to decision-making. In particular, therefore, insurers should be obliged to record data from long-term observations about the cost efficiency of service providers and make them publicly available in order to prevent consumers from making erroneous decisions (Rosenthal et al. 2005). In addition, there is the suspicion that not all of the insured in CDHPs also understand how they truly function. The RAND study previously mentioned also showed that families insured under an HDHP required significantly less preventive care, although their insurance excluded these services from the deductible (Buntin et al. 2011). These results suggest that instruments to assess quality of services and to increase transparency should be interdependently linked with the development of CDHPs.

Literature

AHIP (America's Health Insurance Plans). (2009). *Individual health insurance 2009 – A comprehensive survey of premiums, availability, and benefits*. Washington, DC. http://www.ahipresearch.org/. Accessed 19 Feb 2013.

Atchinson, B. K., & Fox, D. M. (1997). The politics of the health insurance portability and accountability act. *Health Affairs, 16*(3), 146–150.

Barrett, D. (1997). Health maintenance organizations. In K. Miller & E. Miller (Eds.), *Making sense of managed care* (Vol. 1, pp. 47–62). San Francisco: American College of Physician Executives.

Blakeney, B., Carleton, P. F., Mc Carthy, C., et al. (2009). Unlocking the power of innovation. *The Online Journal of Issues in Nursing, 14*(2), Manuscript 1.

Brown, L. D. (1998). The evolution of managed care in the US. *PharmacoEconomics, 14*(Suppl 1), 37–43.

Buntin, M. B., Haviland, A. M., McDevitt, R., & Sood, N. (2011). Healthcare spending and preventive care in high-deductible and consumer-directed health plans. *The American Journal of Managed Care, 17*(3), 222–230.

Bureau of Labor Statistics. (2011). http://www.bls.gov/home.htm. Accessed 24 Feb 2011.

Cacace, M. (2010). *Das Gesundheitssystem der USA: Governance-Strukturen staatlicher und privater Akteure*. Frankfurt am Main: Campus.

Chen, C., Garrido, T., Chock, D., et al. (2009). The Kaiser Permanente electronic health record: Transforming and streamlining modalities of care. *Health Affairs, 28*(2), 323–333.

Cooper, P., Simon, K., & Vistnes, J. (2006). A closer look at the managed care backlash. *Medical Care, 44*(5), 4–11.

Crossen, F. J., & Tollen, L. A. (2010). *Partners in health, how physician and hospitals can be accountable together*. San Francisco: Jossey-Bass.

DeNavas-Walt, C., Proctor, B. D., & Smith, J. C. (2010). *Income, poverty, and health insurance coverage in the United States: 2009*. U.S. Census Bureau, Current Population Reports (pp. 60–238). Washington, DC: U.S. Government Printing Office.

Department of the Treasury. (2012). *2012 instructions for form 8889: Health Savings Accounts (HSAs)*, Cat No. 37971Y. http://www.irs.gov/pub/irs-pdf/i8889.pdf. Accessed 13 Mar 2013.

Detmer, D., Bloomrosen, M., Raymond, B., et al. (2008). Integrated personal health records: Transformative tools for consumer-centric care. *BMC Medical Informatics and Decision Making, 8*(45), 3.

Dixon, A., Greene, J., & Hibbard, J. (2008). Do consumer-directed health plans drive change in enrolees' health care behavior? *Health Affairs, 27*(4), 1120–1131.

Erdmann, Y. (1995). *Managed Care. Veränderungen im Gesundheitswesen der USA in den letzten 30 Jahren*. Baden-Baden: Nomos.

KFF [Kaiser Family Foundation], & HRET [The Henry J. Kaiser Family Foundation & Health Research and Education Trust]. (2010). *Employer health benefits 2010, annual survey*. Menlo Park/Chicago: Kaiser Foundation & HRET. http://ehbs.kff.org/pdf/2010/8085.pdf. Accessed 5 Oct 2012.

Feldman, R., Parente, S. T., & Christianson, J. B. (2007). Consumer-directed health plans: New evidence on spending and utilization. *Inquiry, 44*(1), 26–40.

Fox, P. D., & Kongstvedt, P. R. (2013). A history of managed care and health insurance in the United States. In P. R. Kongstvedt (Ed.), *Essentials of managed health care*. Burlington: Jones & Bartlett Learning.

Fuchs, B., & James, J. A. (2005). *Health savings accounts: The fundamentals*. Washington, DC: National Health Policy Forum (NHPF). http://www.nhpf.org/library/background-papers/BP_HSAs_04-11-05.pdf. Accessed 19 Feb 2013.

Fuchs, B., & Potetz, L. (2007). *The fundamentals of health savings accounts and high-deductible health plans*. Washington, DC: National Health Policy Forum (NHPF). http://www.nhpf.org/library/background-papers/BP_HSAs&HDHPs_Fundamentals_04-23-2007.pdf. Accessed 19 Feb 2013.

Garrido, T., Raymons, B., Jamieson, L., et al. (2004). Making the business case for hospital information systems – A Kaiser Permanente investment decision. *Journal of Health Care Finance, 31*(2), 16–25.

Hibbard, J. H., Greene, J., & Tusler, M. (2008). Does enrollment in a CDHP stimulate cost-effective utilization? *Medical Care Research and Review, 65*(4), 437–449.

Janus, K. (2003). *Managing health care in private organizations. Transaction costs, cooperation and modes of organization in the value chain*. Frankfurt am Main: Peter Lang.

Jost, T. S., & Hall, M. A. (2005). The role of state regulation in consumer-driven health care. *American Journal of Law & Medicine, 31*, 395–418.

Kaiser Permanente News Center. (2013). http://xnet.kp.org/newscenter/. Accessed 20 Mar 2013.

Knight, W. (1998). *Managed care. What it is and how it works*. Gaithersburg: Aspen.

Kongstvedt, P. R. (2009). *Managed care: What it is and how it works* (3rd ed.). Sudbury: Jones and Bartlett.

Liang, L., & Berwick, D. (2010). *Connected for health: Transforming care delivery at Kaiser Permanente*. San Francisco: Jossey-Bass.

McCarthy, D., Mueller, K., & Wrenn, J. (2009). *Kaiser Permanente: Bridging the quality divide with integrated practice, group accountability, and health information technology* (Case study organized health care delivery system). New York: Commonwealth Fund.

McCreary, L. (2010). Kaiser Permanente's innovation on the front lines. *Harvard Business Review*. www.hbr.org. Accessed Apr 2011.

Reinhardt, U. E. (2009). *The trouble with (in)flexible spending accounts*. Economics Blog of the New York Times online: http://economix.blogs.nytimes.com/2009/05/29/the-trouble-with-flexible-spending-accounts/. Accessed 7 Nov 2012.

Robinson, J. C. (1999, March/April). The future of managed care organizations. *Health Affairs, 18*(2), 7–24.

Robinson, J. C. (2005). Managed consumerism in health care. *Health Affairs, 24*(6), 1478–1489.

Rosenthal, M., Hsuan, C., & Milstein, A. (2005). A report card on the freshman class of consumer-directed health plans. *Health Affairs, 24*(6), 1592–1600.

RWJF/HCFO (The Robert Wood Johnson Foundation/Changes in Health Care Financing & Organisation). (2011). *High deductible health care coverage: Snapshot of some mixed evidence.* http://www.hcfo.org/publications/high-deductible-health-care-coverage-snapshot-some-mixed-evidence. Accessed 10 Nov 2012.

Sacramento Business Journal. (2011). HMO report card rates Kaiser "excellent", 11.03.2011

Sanofi. (2002). *HMO-PPO/Medicare-Medicaid managed care digest series*, Vol. 5; Bridgewater.

Sanofi. (2006). *Managed care digest series – HMO-PPO Digest for 2006*, Bridgewater.

Sanofi. (2010). *Managed care digest series – HMO-PPO Digest 2010–11*, Bridgewater.

Sanofi. (2012). *Managed care digest series – HMO-PPO Digest for 2012–13*, Bridgewater

Schreyögg, J. (2003). Demographic development and moral hazard: Health insurance with medical savings accounts. *The Geneva Papers on Risk and Insurance, 29*(4), 689–704.

Shi, L., & Singh, D. A. (2012). *Delivering health care in America: A systems approach* (5th ed.). Sudbury: Jones & Bartlett Learning.

Silvestre, A. L., Sue, V. M., & Allen, J. Y. (2009). If you build it, will they come? The Kaiser Permanente model of online health care. *Health Affairs, 28*(2), 334–344.

Wagner, E. R., & Kongstvedt, P. R. (2013). Types of health insurers, managed health care organizations, and integrated health care delivery systems. In P. R. Kongstvedt (Ed.), *Essentials of managed health care.* Burlington: Jones & Bartlett Learning.

Weiner, J., & De Lissovey, G. (1993). Razing a tower of Babel: A taxonomy for managed care and health insurance plans. *Journal of Health Politics, Policy and Law, 18*, 75–103.

Provider-Based Managed Care Organisations and Products

6

Managed care also led to various forms of organisations constituted by providers of healthcare services. Traditional models such as Independent Practice Associations (IPAs) defend the physicians' interests and Preferred Provider Organisations (PPOs) represent sales cooperatives. Besides these and classical network structures, two new organisational forms have developed. On the one hand, so called Accountable Care Organisations (ACOs) that are in charge of the healthcare provision for a specific population have been established. On the other hand, Patient Centered Medical Homes (PCMHs) focus on care delivery on the GP-level.

6.1 Independent Practice Associations (IPA)

In Sect. 5.1, IPA model HMOs were discussed in detail and the basic idea of an IPA was outlined. However, the establishment of an IPA must not necessarily be considered in terms of transacting with an HMO. An IPA is first and foremost an association of freelance resident physicians for the representation of common interests.

There are three central aspects: First, the establishment of market power, second, the professionalisation of management and third, the ability to manage the provision of services. IPAs bundle medical interests and, depending on their size, can even completely exclude competition. The stronger and more integrated the purchasers of healthcare services are (health insurances of all types and employers), the more important the establishment of a countervailing power is to balance it out. It has been mentioned at various points that managed care has and will continue to contribute to professionalisation of the entire healthcare system. Thus, single physicians cannot reasonably cover the additional costs which accrue for administrative tasks, as they have neither the quantities nor the qualifications at their disposal. Since they do not necessarily take on every interested applicant, IPAs have the opportunity to delegate the portfolio to participating doctors and, thus, increase their attractiveness for insurance companies. This delegation option applies to the quality and the qualification aspects, as well as the composition of the diverse specialisation groups (e.g. number of general practitioners).

6.2   Preferred Provider Organisations (PPO)

The organisational form of PPOs is based on the number of doctors or hospitals which join together or are associated with one another in order to offer a competitive range of services in comparison to employers who directly insure employees or traditional indemnity insurance companies. Thus, they can be seen as the service providers' direct answer to the increasing pressure of HMOs. Incentives should be created in order to reduce the attractiveness of HMOs. For this reason, PPOs offer their contract partners so-called "discounted fee-for-service" premiums. While the principle of fee-for-service compensation remains, there are considerable price reductions in some cases (Shi and Singh 2013). In addition, PPOs allow → utilisation reviews to a certain extent.

A service provider participating in a PPO is interested in the acquisition of patients and protection against the increasing pressure caused by growing market penetration by HMOs. For example, a hospital's motivation for participating in a PPO can be to regain lost market shares, or to prevent the loss of further market shares.

It is characteristic of a PPO that service providers outside of the system can also be principally chosen. However, higher co-payments or deductibles (→ insurance contracts) must be paid for these service providers, who are not "preferred" (Fox and Kongstvedt 2013). These co-payments can reach magnitudes of up to $10,000 and more (Robinson 1999, p. 14). This should at least steer the demand a bit.

PPOs are considered the major winners in recent years. Their market share amounts to 58 % (KFF 2010) and has significantly increased over the past years. The reasons for this are due to the supply as well as the demand side. For the most part, service providers have now accepted that their provision of services is influenced by external sources. From their point of view, PPOs are the lesser evil. Considerable concessions were also made with the prices. In the United States, the discounts are around 25–35 % of the established charges (Shi and Singh 2012). The savings potential may not reach the dimensions that the HMOs can attain, but it is still significantly higher than that of the classical indemnity products. The incentives for supply-induced demand remain, but the use of management and steering instruments (→ guidelines and → utilisation review) can reduce them. On the other hand, PPOs fulfil the main need for a more or less free choice of doctors. Even when this is made difficult due to co-payments, there is at least the theoretical possibility. It is particularly relevant when the insured have long-term relationships with the doctors, which are severed by HMOs, among others. It can be assumed that an insured person who was formerly registered with an HMO and thus subject to sometimes-strict rules does not majorly change their behaviour after transferring to a PPO.

6.3 Networks

Networks are associations of service providers with similar or different levels of service to develop strategic alliances.

Networks can be analysed from two very different perspectives (Bazzoli 1999). On one hand they serve to improve coordination and communication in the provision of services. Through the association with one another, the selection of levels of care, e.g. between acute care and rehabilitation, should be optimised in networks. Likewise, networks are formed in order to provide academic medical centres with the necessary standards of high-end medicine. This form is a precursor to integrated care systems, which will be explored in detail in the following section (van Servellen 2009).

In metropolitan areas, there is a third reason for forming networks. High-priced but prestigious, inner-city academic medical centres are continually faced with ever growing external pressure. The cross subsidising of educational training and research with patient care is accepted less and less by MCOs and there are limited opportunities to design these organisations more efficiently. Competitive strategies must be developed in order to survive. The association of networks with one another prevents MCOs from being ignored in selective contracting. In the metropolitan region of New York, for example, it is unthinkable that an MCO would provide products that do not include the most significant four or five networks, as this would mean a far-reaching limitation of the choices for the insured.

Thus, networks can also be purely a defensive strategy of the service providers. This strategy is particularly important when there are enormous overcapacities that generate incentives for supply-induced demand, such as in the hospital sector.

The goal of a network strategy plays a major role because of the inability of many systems to integrate clinical functions. This is referred to as the failure of the concept of integrated systems. However, a network solely oriented on the creation of market power through market shares can be a very successful strategy without even integrating one function.

One must be extremely careful in the evaluation of the networks (Olden et al. 2002). On the one hand, market strategy aspects can play a dominant role, on the other the reason for creating partnerships can be to "block" other potential constellations. For example that is why the number of well-known academic medical centres is so limited. It is quite practical to include these in a network in order to precede the competition. In many aspects the situation is comparable with the situation of the European airlines before the year of 1992. Strategic alliances were formed without becoming immediately active. The dominant motivation was the division of the market and the creation of powerful blocks.

Case Study 2: Swiss Physician Networks
Initial Situation
The Swiss healthcare system is characterized by its decentralised structure and relatively prominent regional autonomy.[1] Switzerland is a country where the healthcare systems in the 26 cantons differ slightly from canton to canton. Health insurance, which has been obligatory since 1996, guarantees all insured a comprehensive package of services. The insurer is not allowed to refuse insured persons with high risks, for example. The risk sharing between the insurers is currently based only on age and sex (starting in 2012 it has been supplemented with hospital or nursing home stays in the previous year), but risk selection is still a much discussed topic. Freelance doctors in private practices mainly carry out outpatient care. Patients usually have direct and unlimited access to general physicians and specialists, unless they decided on a premium discount with an alternative model of (managed care) insurance with a limited choice of doctors and treatments within a physician network or HMO (OECD 2011; Cheng 2010; Reinhardt 2004).

Model
In Switzerland, two forms of integrated organisations have developed since 1990: The physician networks and what is known as HMOs. Both forms define themselves as organisations that provide health services that are tailored to meet patients' needs. They do so by using cooperations regulated with contracts between the participating doctors, external service providers and the insured. What all of these organisations have in common is the "gatekeeping principle": the insured are obligated to always enter the healthcare system in the same way – through the same gate – when they have a medical need. A physician network, HMO or a medical call centre can function as a so-called "gate". Specialist or inpatient treatments require a referral from a "gatekeeper". In return, the insured receive a discount on their premiums. Emergency cases are excluded and there are special provisions for consultations with gynaecologists and paediatricians. There are currently 86 physician networks (see Fig. 6.1).

The Northeast Swiss regions as well as several other cantons (e.g. Geneva and Aargau) have an above-average amount of physician networks, while there are no networks in the French- and Italian-speaking regions (besides Geneva). Around 50 % of all Swiss primary care providers (general practitioners, internists, paediatricians) and over 400 specialists participate in these physician networks. 73 of the 86 networks (84 %) agreed upon joint

(continued)

---

[1] According to Berchtold, P., Peytremann-Bridevaux, J., Integrated care organizations in Schwitzerland (2011).

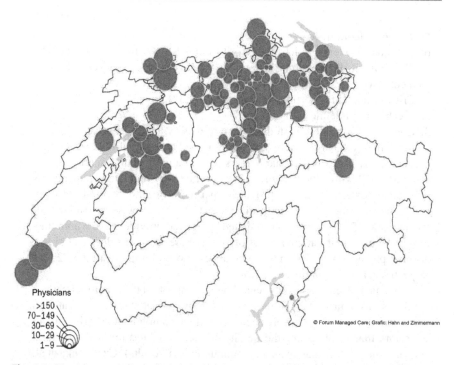

Fig. 6.1 Physician networks in Switzerland: regional distribution and participating doctors

Case Study 2 (continued)

responsibility for the budget in their contracts with the health insurances, i.e. joint responsibility to maintain an agreed-upon target cost for the group of patients affiliated with the network.

Results

The development of integrated care in Switzerland has been evaluated in an annual or biannual rhythm over the past 10 years. The data is gathered from all physician networks and HMOs in Switzerland (using online surveys and direct contact) which have concluded contracts with one or several health insurance companies (Berchtold et al. 2010).

In 2010, on average every eighth person, and in north-eastern Swiss regions every third insured person chose to receive care from a general practitioner in a physician network or in an HMO. This represents an increase of 34 % in comparison to 2008, whereby the canton of Zurich ranks at the top with an increase of 52 %.

Almost all physician networks have implemented one or more elements of quality work all throughout the network. The quality circle is the main focus

(continued)

Case Study 2 (continued)

of said quality work, which obligatorily binds 96 % of the networks. The median value of the compulsory circle is 8 per year (4–20 per year). Further elements are:

1. Critical incident reporting systems (CIRS, 53 %)
2. Treatment guidelines (41 %)
3. Contractually agreed upon disclosure of quality and/or cost data (55 %)

More than half of the networks (58 %) display the quality work using a regular report for external stakeholders (43 %) and/or with a quality certificate (40 %). 43 % of the networks have contractually regulated cooperations with other (external) service providers, particularly with hospitals (36 %), emergency services (33 %) and call centres (19 %). Likewise, around half of the networks (51 %) work with so-called "preferred providers", to whom they primarily refer their patients. Most often these are specialist doctors (45 %), hospital physicians (35 %), physiotherapists and radiology institutes (27 %, respectively) and laboratories (23 %).

There have been few results regarding the impact on the quality of care of the Swiss physician networks until now. A more recent study investigated to which extent physician networks actually fulfil a catalogue of criteria with 43 indicators that were set for the quality of care (organisation and structure, cooperation, process management, communication, results) (Czerwenka et al. 2010). In the process it was demonstrated that the 19 participating physician networks fulfilled 69 % of the 43 quality indicators on average, but with great differences among the individual networks (47.4–81.8 %).

Evaluation

At this point it should be noted that up until now no laws or policy guidelines exist for the Swiss physician networks. Physician networks, HMOs as well as the integration instruments that are implemented within these frameworks were created primarily based on physician and health insurance initiatives. The only legal basis for them to this date is the Federal Health Insurance Act of 1994 (KVG) which allows for such initiatives and developments. This fact is particularly significant because the contractual obligation of integration and budget accountability is in diametric opposition to the traditional medical concept (Edwards et al. 2002). The development of the Swiss physician networks can be thus seen as a model for how, despite the logic to the contrary, the individual players can still succeed in having service providers and purchasers collectively implement integrated care. It also shows how clinical autonomy and budget accountability can be brought together to form a functional balance (Degeling et al. 2003).

In the United States, managed care similarly leads to a consolidation in the healthcare market. It can be assumed that few large providers, consumers or both will be able to remain on the market. Today's market structures, which are fragmented and characterised by interfaces, will be a thing of the past.

6.4   Integrated Delivery Systems (IDS)

Integrated delivery systems (IDS) are described as the most highly developed form of MCO and can be considered "umbrella organisations" (Lega 2007, p. 259). An IDS is a network of organisations which provide services themselves or organise the services throughout the entire continuum of health needs. At the same time, an IDS takes on medical and financial responsibility for the care of pre-defined population groups (Shi and Singh 2013). There are numerous different concept definitions and terms. For example, organised delivery systems are often referred to.[2] No other topic in managed care is discussed as much as the advantages and disadvantages of integrated care systems and particularly the question of how such systems should be configured (Janus 2003; Braun 2003; Scott et al. 2000). However, it must first be clearly emphasised that this is truly the most complex task in designing a healthcare system.

It is characteristic for an IDS to provide the necessary services themselves or purchase them, in which case the integrated delivery system also coordinates the services. This does not only apply to a treatment period but rather a more indefinite time period; in its simplest form the span from birth until death. In this way the fragmentation of healthcare is abandoned in favour of all-encompassing, system-wide care. Along with the type of service provision, the question of responsibility is critical. The IDS takes on the complete medical and financial responsibility. This inevitably means that the integrated care systems either also take on the insurance function, i.e. by directly transacting with large employers, or they compensate with complete capitation.

This form of care is still a goal in the United States which has not been reached by a long shot. Most systems – even when they call themselves integrated care systems – are still in the process of attaining this status (Shortell 1997, p. xiv, Shortell et al. 2000). In the following section, first the essential functions to be integrated will be portrayed (in accordance with Sanofi 2006, p. 2) (Fig. 6.2).

The significance of the individual factors and the difficulties of implementation differ greatly. Usually one should begin with the integration of functions and a uniform management structure and subsequently implement an information network. Medical services can be integrated as a next step and → quality management

---

[2] Shortell prefers this term in order to leave the term "integrated care system" open for organisational forms that are not yet on the market. These would also interact in direct cooperation with public social administrations for health management – Shortell et al. see its particular strength in this (Shortell et al. 1996, p. 8).

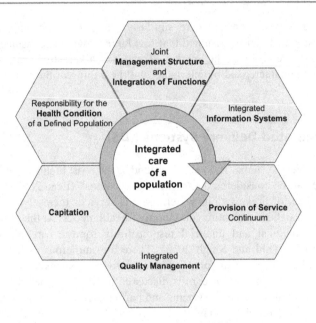

Fig. 6.2 Integrated functions of an IDS (following Sanofi 2006)

can be established. When these steps have been completed, financial and medical accountability can be assumed. As nearly all aspects have already been covered in other sections or will be explained in more detail, only the basic ideas will be further dealt with here.

The **integration of functions** refers to the integration of non-medical services such as the personnel department, financing and accounting, as well as marketing or strategic planning. However, that does not necessarily refer to their centralisation or standardisation, but primarily how they are adapted to suit one another. This type of function integration has succeeded in many IDSs as adapting or merging personnel departments proves to be much easier than integrating clinical units. This is also surely due to the readiness, understanding and the closeness to the "designers of the system", who usually come from the administration. The integrated management structure plays a central role in this (Faass 2001).

Although **integrated information systems** belong to the core functions of an IDS and are strategically relevant, problems arise in the praxis. In principle, each piece of information about a patient must be accessible at every location and the financial transactions must also be integrated into the system. There are three primary causes for difficulties with information systems: First, they deal with immense amounts of money. Investment sums of over $100 million per IDS are referred to[3] which are necessary for the development of such systems. This poses a

---

[3] Thus Montefiore, one of the most significant healthcare systems in New York, invested $200 million in the establishment and expansion of IT over the last 10 years.

nearly insolvable problem for many non-profit organisations with very little access to the capital market. Secondly, the resistance is very high. In recent years, local solutions have been developed which principally can never be integrated into a system. This means a transition to a completely new IT-system for all people involved. it raises considerable questions regarding data protection.

It is particularly important that IDS is in the position to offer a **continuum of services** beyond their system limits, although this does not necessarily include all services or their own services. In the literature, it has become established that at least three service components must be included (Sanofi 2006, p. 3). Along with the dominant components of "clinical services" and "hospital services", this primarily applies to home health agencies, retirement homes, outpatient operation centres or day clinics.

The planning of medical service provision is highly important. In a competitive system such as in the United States, it is nearly impossible to intervene in a regulatory way. This results in an enormous surplus of specialists and completely insufficient care through primary physicians. This phenomenon can be dealt with by monitoring the provision of medical services, at least within the system. This is because while IDSs are competitively oriented from the outside; internally they have a "centrally planned economy". The concrete planning of necessary services which Canada or the United Kingdom implements in their system structures is only implemented within the integrated delivery system (IDS). For example, for 270,000 employees and 30,000 pensioners, they calculated a requirement of 171 general practitioners (one physician per 2,000 working people, respectively one per 900 pensioners), 81,300 days of hospital stay and 13,020 ambulant operations (Golembesky 1997). In principle, this corresponds well to the directive on-demand planning. This precise, internal management of service requirements is one of the major strengths of integrated care systems.

This internal IDS planning pursues two goals. Firstly, overcapacity should be avoided, and precisely the right amount of care should be provided. Secondly, and more importantly, expensive treatment levels should be restructured to be more affordable. This is not necessarily related to rationing, but rather to care in optimal cost service levels (Witgert and Hess 2012). The potential main advantage of IDSs also lies here. Based on the premise that prevention is more cost-effective than treatment, corresponding incentives should be organised.[4] For example, prevention could save between $14,000 and $30,000 for a "low-weight birth". One dollar investments in prenatal care result in savings of $3.38 in later treatment costs (Office of Technology Assessment and Institute of Medicine, cited in: Shortell et al. 1996, p. 25). In the United States, however, only 13–16 % of the premium dollars were used for primary physicians, 22–26 % for specialists, 40 % for hospital

---

[4] This premise, however, is not without critics, and there are sufficient examples that prove the opposite. Also refer to the chapter on gatekeeping.

services and 17–20 % for insurance services (Zelman 1997, p. 55), although a large portion of general practitioners' requirements could be fulfilled.[5] These cost advantages, however, can only be attained when the incentive structures are reversed. An IDS must have incentives to profit from health and not sickness. This is a fundamental argument for integrated care systems which will become increasingly important with the rise in multimorbid and chronically ill patients. For this reason, the integration of public health tasks is called for again and again (Schlesinger and Gray 1998; Schlesinger et al. 1998).

Alongside the management functions, it is continually emphasised that through integrated care, economies of scale and savings can be attained through the prevention of duplicate examinations.

In comparison, the prevention of duplicate examinations is a classic example of dual goal setting in order to reduce costs as well as to improve quality from the patient's perspective. Along with the uniform standards, an infrastructure must be provided which makes the duplicate examinations unnecessary. Communication technologies also play an important role in this.

The following functions will not be explored in further detail here ($\rightarrow$ capitations, $\rightarrow$ integrated quality management and the assumption of responsibility for a population's condition of health), as they will be described in more detail in the third section of this book. In order to implement these aspects it is essential that the functions already described are integrated, at least to a certain degree.

A conclusive evaluation of IDS proves to be quite difficult (Cleverley et al. 2010; Crossen and Tollen 2010; Kongstvedt 2009; Green and Rowell 2008; Kongstvedt 2013; Amelung and Janus 2005), as it is still a theoretical model and too few empirical results are available. At least in New York there is evidence that IDSs have resulted in a shortening of ALOS (average length of stay) in hospitals (IDS = 5.9 days, other hospitals = 7.0 days) and to higher capacity utilisation (IDS = 76.5 % vs. 72.2 %) (Sanofi 2003, p. 18f.), whereby no conclusions about the costs per case can be drawn across all care levels.

Theoretically, the effects of vertical integration can be explained by using $\rightarrow$ transaction cost theory (Stiles et al. 2001; Williamson 1985; Amelung and Janus 2005). Transaction costs are generally high when the uncertainty is high, when there are few alternative providers and, thus, a high risk of opportunistic behaviour or when there is a considerable need for coordination between the service providers on different levels of services. These three criteria could be present in health products (Gaynor and Haas-Wilson 1998, p. 145). That is why IDSs have advantages in terms of transaction cost theory. Costs such as initiation costs, agreement, contract, control and adjustment costs can be saved and from this perspective vertically integrated IDSs can certainly be considered as more efficient institutional arrangements. The transaction costs between an insurance company

---

[5] Also this thesis, which is supported by Lega (2007, p. 259), for example, is debated. Some supporters see specialist treatment as the more cost-effective variation since unnecessary misdiagnoses can be thus prevented.

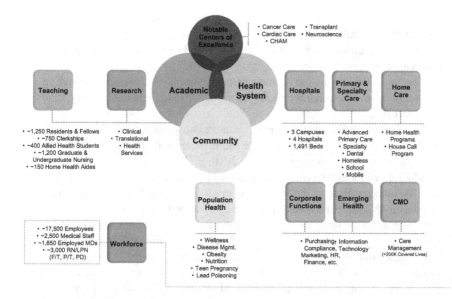

Fig. 6.3 Organisational structure of Montefiore (Source: Montefiore 2013)

and an integrated care system are thus much lower than if the insurance company were to conclude individual contracts with every single service provider. In a large empirical study (Janus 2003), vertically integrated systems in California were assessed on the basis of transaction cost theory. Janus comes to the conclusion that along with the scope of integration, the type of integration is critical. In the case of the systems examined, it was shown that particularly the hybrid organisational forms (management via contracts) are suitable for this.

However, it must be pointed out that a large part of the services covered in an integrated care system do not constitute vertical integration, but rather diversification.

Case Study 3: Montefiore: Integrated Care for Vulnerable Population Groups in New York City

Initial Situation

Montefiore is one of the oldest integrated care systems within the United States. It was founded in 1884 as a "home for chronic invalids" with an average stay of more than 350 days. Elements of an integrated care system were already adopted in the first half of the twentieth century (outpatient clinics in 1920 and home healthcare in 1947). At the end of the 1980s, the massive development of primary care networks began. Today the

(continued)

Case Study 3 (continued)

organisation focuses on the needs of people with low incomes and vulnerable population groups. It concentrates on:

1. The improvement of the management of chronic illnesses by expanding access in the community through outpatient and general primary care strategies,
2. Opening up access to high quality care and hospital services, and
3. Providing a stronger integration of the provision of specific services and stable e-health technologies (Chase 2010, p. 2) (Fig. 6.3).

Montefiore includes nearly the complete portfolio of health services. The care begins very close to the foundation in schools in the Bronx – Montefiore also has mobile facilities – and then builds upon primary care centres. These are comparable to large medical care centres. Specialist care is provided in these centres as well as in gateway and outpatient clinics. The interface of acute care and rehabilitation care should be particularly emphasised. A nursing home is directly on campus, thus facilitating the improvement of this interface which is critical because of its cost and quality aspects. The range of services is rounded out with an expanded outpatient care service and a call centre. Currently, Montefiore is establishing → patient-centred medical homes (PCMH) in two of its primary care centres – Family Health Center and Bronx East. However, it must be stressed that not all system elements must be in ownership, but that such a system can also be managed with binding contracts. With these structures, Montefiore is not only active as a classic service provider; it also takes over the complete risk for over 500,000 residents of the Bronx. Montefiore is compensated with capitations for former Medicaid and Medicare patients who switch to Montefiore.

Disease management programmes can also be reasonably implemented with these types of structures. Montefiore's disease management programmes focuses on the care of the chronically ill. Programmes for coronary heart disease (CHD), diabetes, depression, high blood pressure and liver failure – i.e. the indicators known as widespread diseases – have been developed and implemented accordingly. The concepts are characterised by a strong focus on primary care and interdisciplinary concepts as well as considerable telemedical support. Thus, for example, with the diabetes programme the haemoglobin HbA1c value could be reduced to under the 9 % level. Only 14 % of the Montefiore patients show a higher value, whereas the percentage in Medicaid plans is over 45 % and in the commercial plans it is 28 % of the patients.

Along with these indicator-based methods, Montefiore began to develop programmes tailored to target groups in 2007. That is how the challenges of senior care are specifically being addressed in a programme (here, for example, fall prevention in domestic environments is a large challenge). In another

(continued)

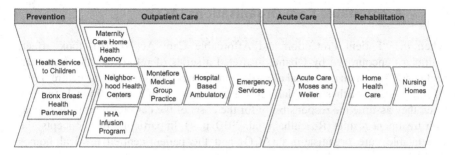

Fig. 6.4 Montefiore's value chain

Case Study 3 (continued)
initiative Montefiore is operating directly with schools in the Bronx. They developed a campaign to encourage schools to offer only milk with a lower percentage of fat in order to decrease the calories consumed. It is estimated that more than 40 % of the kids in the Bronx suffer from obesity.

Evaluation
In the evaluation of Montefiore, one must remember that the system in the Bronx is operating in one of the most complicated and difficult social environments in the United States. With its 1.4 million residents, the Bronx belongs to the ten largest American metropolises and is one of the poorest city districts in the nation. Since 75 % of the population is entitled to Medicare or Medicaid and one third of the population has a yearly income of less than US $10,000; along with a population of ¾ non-whites and a child mortality rate of 13.3 %, there is no doubt that it represents one of the most disadvantaged social milieus.

The services of Montefiore are all the more impressive against this background. Montefiore demonstrates that integrated care concepts involving large parts of the value chain are also – or perhaps are particularly – able to be implemented in such an environment. In another form, Fig. 6.4 depicts how the complete value chain is included.

All of the "fruits" of this type of comprehensive integration can perhaps only be realised in an environment characterised by very little fluctuation.

Despite a population structure that is very clearly more difficult to supply care to, – the prevalence of asthma, for example, is 42 % – in New York State Montefiore attains better results in all of the quality indicators than the average. This high quality of care can only be attained because Montefiore has consistently invested in the improvement of care. Between 1995 and 2005, a total of $950 million were invested in the healthcare system, $200 million of which in information technology.

Further information about Montefiore: www.montefiore.org.

6.5   Accountable Care Organisations (ACO)

When the "Patient Protection and Affordable Care Act" (2010) took effect, politicians encouraged by Obama instituted a series of reforms in the American healthcare system on a national as well as individual state level. At the centre of the reforms are approaches in which service providers receive an additional stimulus when they assume the responsibility for the costs of the care for their patients and their treatment results (Rosenthal et al. 2010, p. 7). In particular two concepts, the accountable care organisations (ACO) and the patient-centred medical homes (PCMH), are discussed in this section.

The Center for Medicare and Medicaid Services (CMS) defines an ACO as a legally recognised unit authorised in accordance with the applicable state legislation. It is comprised of different service providers such as general practitioners, specialists and hospitals (Crossen and Tollen 2010; Merlis 2010). Together they are committed to ensuring the best care for the regional population, to reduce costs and to reorganise management structures (Shortell et al. 2010, p. 1293). Unlike in previously discussed concepts, there is no obligatory enrolment in an ACO for patients. The free choice of doctors remains. However, the commission of the Commonwealth Fund recommends that patients be informed about ACO membership and its potential benefits (Zessa and Guterman 2011, p. 2).

The financial incentives for the service providers are decisive in this model. When an ACO fulfils the prescribed standards, it can then receive additional payments from the state Medicare programme. Communication and organisational structures, which can be helpful in preventing repeated and erroneous examinations, can be developed and expanded through an ACO merger. In doing so, treatment costs can be reduced while at the same time quality of services is improved (Davis and Schoenbaum 2010, p. 1). The service provider is compensated with the desired savings as additional income.

The concept of the ACO is based on structures that were already introduced in the United States in the last years. The integrated delivery system (IDS), the multi-specialty group practice (MSGP), the physician hospital organisation and the independent practice association (IPA) have the largest potential to transform into an ACO (Crossen and Tollen 2010, p. 53). Despite the different structuring possibilities, each model is based on the same principles. On one hand, primary care is the basis of the concept, and on the other hand the compensation of service providers is connected to the quality of treatment (McClellan et al. 2010, p. 983).

Each organisation that wants to be registered as an ACO must possess the formal legal structures allowing accrued savings to be distributed among the service providers. In addition, the service providers have to supply care to at least 5,000 patients from the Medicare programme. An adequate risk adjustment can only be carried out with this number of patients in order to quantitatively demonstrate the reduction of costs and the improvement in quality (Dove et al. 2009, p. 2). Along with these conditions, participation for a minimum of 3 years is also obligatory (CMS 2011, p. 6).

	Level 1	Level 2	Level 3
Requirements for the organisations	Legal organisations with information technology and the ability to carry out performance reporting	Established infrastructure with expanded IT and the use of employees for better coordination	Highly developed infrastructure, entire service spectrum
Key figures for performance	Assessment of quality, efficiency and patient satisfaction as well as preparations for the measurement of further factors such as outcomes, functional status and risk reduction		Further performance goals and heightened requirements for reporting
Compensation model	Fee-for-service, small bonus payments and "shared savings" when set goals are reached	Fee-for-service, sometimes capitation and larger "shared savings" with compensation for additional costs which accrue	Risk-adjusted capitation with bonuses for quality

Fig. 6.5 Characteristics of an ACO in the different levels (Following McClellan et al. 2010)

CMS developed a three-step system in order to qualify as an ACO. The three levels make it easier for the service providers to attain ACO status (see Fig. 6.5).

An evaluation of the ACOs is not yet possible. Based on their fundamental principle, they are comparable with population-related integration contracts.

6.6 Patient-Centred Medical Homes (PCMH)

The concept of patient-centred medical homes (PCMH) is central for the realisation of the foundation necessary for primary care. The success of an ACO can be increased with a strong basis of primary medical care such as PCMH.

The model has been tested for more than 40 years in the United States (Fields et al. 2010, p. 819). Initially, this model was only concerned with the care of chronically ill children, until it was further developed into an integrated, patient-centred medical home by four medical associations[6] (Sia et al. 2004, p. 1473ff.). The creation of an integrated care system in which the physician and the care team assume the coordination of the comprehensive, continuous, acute, preventive and chronic care of patients is central to the PCMH. The general practitioner acts as the contact point in this process and aids the patients by providing them with information when they need to make a decision ($\rightarrow$ gatekeeping). The consideration of the patient's individual needs in different settings results in diverse manifestations of the concept (Stange 2010, p. 601f.) (Fig. 6.6).

In order to be considered a PCMH, the following seven principles essentially apply: (1) Each patient has a continuous relationship with a personal physician.

---

[6] The American Academy of Family Physicians, the American Academy of Pediatrics, the American College of Physicians and the American Osteopathic Association.

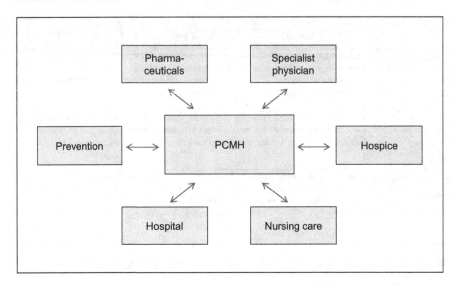

Fig. 6.6 Concept of the ACO on the primary care basis of the PCMH (own representation)

(2) This physician must be in a position to lead the care team and thus take responsibility for on-going supervision. (3) The treatment is aimed holistically at the needs of the patient and (4) care is coordinated and integrated across the whole spectrum in all areas of the healthcare system. (5) Quality and safety are facilitated by the use of evidence-based medicine and decision aids. (6) Access to healthcare services is made easier with open scheduling, additional opening times and the use of modern communication tools, such as e-mail consultations. (7) In addition, service providers who use this model must be compensated for the additional work accordingly (Kaye and Takach 2009, p. 7; Rakel and Rakel 2011).

In 2008 the American National Committee for Quality Assurance (NCQA) drafted standards for recognition as a PCMH. At the end of 2010 more than 1,500 groups fulfilled this norm (NCQA 2011).

Unlike with the new model of ACO, there are studies regarding the benefits of a PCMH. In Pennsylvania, the Geisinger Health System is implementing the structures of a PCMH. Through the introduction of electronic patient records and the integration of monetary incentives, hospital referrals were reduced by 20 % and treatment costs by 7 %. Similar results were found in Community Care in North Carolina. Among asthmatics, more than 40 % of hospital stays were prevented through patient-centred care (Schilling 2009).

A study by the Commonwealth Fund found that PCMH reduce disparities in the access to care services. Independent of origin and ethnic background, patients receive significantly better care in a medical home than patients receiving regular care (Beal et al. 2007, p. 3ff). Rosenthal concluded that the quality of treatment in a medical home is higher due to the low rate of error and the higher level of patient satisfaction (Rosenthal 2008, p. 427).

The combination of accountable care organisations and patient-centred medical homes is meant to lead to more efficient and effective care structures. These concepts demonstrate a rethinking of the healthcare system and the compensation of healthcare services.

Literature

Amelung, V. E., & Janus, K. (2005). Erfolgsfaktoren für die integrierte Versorgung unter Einbeziehung von Erfahrungen aus den USA. In W. Hellmann (Ed.), *Handbuch integrierte Versorgung*, 3. Erg. Lfg. 4/05, Economica Bonn, pp. 1–26

Bazzoli, G. J., Shortell, S. M., Dubbs, N., et al. (1999, February). A taxonomy of health networks and systems: Bringing order out of chaos. *HSR: Health Service Research 33*(6), 1683–1725.

Beal, A. C., Doty, M. M., Hernandez, S. E., et al. (2007). *Closing the divide: How medical homes promote equity in health care: Results from the commonwealth fund 2006 health care quality survey*. New York: Commonwealth Fund.

Berchtold, P., Peytremann-Bridevaux, J. (2011). Integrated care organizations in Schwitzerland, Vol 11, Special 10th Anniversary Edition, International Journal of Integrated Care, 1–8.

Braun, G. E. (2003). *Management vernetzter Versorgungsstrukturen im Gesundheitswesen IBG* (Diskussionspapier Nr. 13). Neubiberg : IBG.

Chase, D. (2010). *Montefiore Medical Center: Integrated care delivery for vulnerable populations*. The Commonwealth Fund. http://www.commonwealthfund.org/~/media/Files/Publications/Case%20Study/2010/Oct/1448_Chase_Montefiore_Med_Ctr_case_study_v2.pdf. Accessed 23 Feb 2013.

Cleverley, W. O., Cleverley, J. O., & Song, P. H. (2010). *Essentials of health care finance* (7th ed.). Sudbury: Jones & Bartlett Learning.

CMS (Centers for Medicare and Medicaid Services). (2011). *Proposed rules for accountable care organizations participating in the Medicare shared savings program*. www.cms.gov. Accessed 19 Feb 2013.

Crossen, F. J., & Tollen, L. A. (2010). *Partners in health, how physician and hospitals can be accountable together*. San Francisco: Jossey-Bass.

Czerwenka, W., Metzger, K., & Fritschi, J. (2010). Hoher Qualitätsstand in Schweizer Ärztenetzen. *Schweiz Ärztezeitung, 91*, 1856–1858.

Davis, K., & Schoenbaum, S. C. (2010). Toward High-Performance Accountable Care: Promise and Pitfalls, In *The Commonwealth Fund Blog*, pp. 1–5.

Degeling, P., Maxwell, S., Kennedy, J., & Coyle, B. (2003). Medicine, management, and modernisation: a "danse macabre"? *BMJ: British Medical Journal, 326*, 649–652.

Dove, J. T., Weaver, D., Lewin, J., et al. (2009). Delivery system reform, accountable care organizations. *Journal of the American College of Cardiology, 54*(11), 1–4.

Edwards, N., Kornacki, M. J., & Silversin, J. (2002). Unhappy doctors: What are the causes and what can be done? *BMJ: British Medical Journal, 324*, 835–838.

Faass, N. (2001). *Integrating complementary medicine into health systems*. Gaithersburg: Aspen Publication.

Fields, D., Leshen, E., & Patel, K. (2010). Driving quality gains and cost savings through adoption of medical homes. *Health Affairs, 29*(5), 819–826.

Gaynor, M., & Haas-Wilson, D. (1998). Vertical relations in health care markets. In M. Morrisey (Ed.), *Managed care & changing health care markets* (pp. 140–163). Washington, DC: AEI Press.

Golembesky, H. E. (1997). A structured perspective of market evolution, San Francisco. In R. C. Coile (Ed.), *The five stages of managed care*. Chicago: Health Administration Press.

Green, M., & Rowell, J. H. (2008). *Understanding health insurance: A guide to billing and reimbursement* (9th ed.). Clifton Park: Thomson Delmar Learning.

Janus, K. (2003). *Managing health care in private organizations. Transaction costs, cooperation and modes of organization in the value chain.* Frankfurt am Main: P. Lang.

Kaye, N., & Takach, M. (2009). *Building medical homes in state Medicaid and CHIP programs.* www.commonwealthfund.org. Accessed 20 Oct 2012.

KFF (Kaiser Family Foundation), & HRET (The Henry J. Kaiser Family Foundation & Health Research and Education Trust). (2010). *Employer health benefits 2010, annual survey.* Menlo Park/Chicago: Kaiser Foundation & HRET. http://ehbs.kff.org/pdf/2010/8085.pdf. Accessed 5 Oct 2012.

Kongstvedt, P. R. (2009). *Managed care: What it is and how it works* (3rd ed.). Sudbury: Jones and Bartlett.

Kongstvedt, P. R. (2013). *Essentials of managed health care* (6th ed.). Burlington: Jones & Bartlett Learning.

Lega, F. (2007). Organisational design for health integrated delivery systems. *Theory and Practice Health Policy, 81*(2–3), 258–279.

Merlis, M. (2010). *Accountable care organizations. Health affairs.* Princeton: Robert Wood Johnson Foundation.

McClellan, M., McKethan, A. N., Lewis, J. L., et al. (2010). A national strategy to put accountable care into practice. *Health Affairs, 29*(5), 982–990.

Montefiore. (2013), "Introduction to Montefiore", Presentation.

NCQA (National Committee for Quality Assurance). (2011). http://www.ncqa.org/tabid/631/Default.aspx. Accessed 5 Nov 2012.

OECD (Organisation for Economic Cooperation and Development). (2011). *OECD Reviews of Health Systems: Switzerland,* Paris.

Olden, P. C., Roggenkamp, S. D., & Luke, R. D. (2002). A post-1990s assessment of strategic hospital alliances and their marketplace orientations: Time to refocus. *Health Care Management Review, 27*(2), 33–49.

Rakel, R. E., & Rakel, D. P. (2011). *Textbook of family medicine* (8th ed.). Philadelphia: Elsevier Saunders.

Reinhardt, U. E. (2004). The Swiss health system: Regulated competition without managed care. *JAMA: The Journal of the American Medical Association, 292,* 1227–1231.

Robinson, J. C. (1999, March/April). The future of managed care organizations. *Health Affairs, 18* (2), 7–24.

Rosenthal, T. C. (2008). The medical home: Growing evidence to support a new approach to primary care. *Journal of the American Board of Family Medicine, 21,* 427–440.

Rosenthal, M., Abrams, M. K., & Bitton, A. (2010). Evaluation and the patient-centered medical home. *Medical Home News, 2*(9), 4–7.

Sanofi. (2003). *Integrated health system managed care digest series,* Vol. 6, Bridgewater.

Sanofi. (2006). *Managed care digest series – HMO-PPO Digest for 2006,* Bridgewater.

Sanofi. (2012). *Managed care digest series – HMO-PPO Digest for 2012–2013,* Bridgewater.

Schilling, B. (2009). *Purchasing high performance, what is the patient-centered medical home?* www.commonwealthfund.org. Accessed 9 Nov 2012.

Schlesinger, M., Gray, B., Carrino, G., et al. (1998, September/October). A broader vision for managed care. Part II: A typology of community benefits. *Health Affairs 17*(5), 26–49

Schlesinger, M., & Gray, B. (1998, May/June). A broader vision for managed care. Part I: Measuring the benefit to communities. *Health Affairs 17*(3), 152–168.

Scott, W. R., Ruef, M., Mendel, P. J., & Caronna, C. A. (2000). *Institutional change and healthcare organizations.* Chicago: University of Chicago Press.

Shi, L., & Singh, D. A. (2012). *Delivering health care in America: A systems approach* (5th ed.). Sudbury: Jones & Bartlett Learning.

Shi, L., & Singh, D. A. (2013). *Essentials of the U.S. health care system* (3rd ed.). Sudbury: Jones & Bartlett Publishers.

Shortell, S. M., Gillies, R. R., Anderson, D. A., Erickson, K. M., & Mitchell, J. B. (1996). *Remarking health care in America.* San Francisco: Jossey-Bass.

Shortell, S. M. (1997). Managed care: Achieving the benefits, negating the harm. *Health Services Research, 32*(5), 557–560.

Shortell, S. M., Gillies, R. R., & Anderson, D. A. (2000). *Remaking health care in America. The evolution of organized delivery systems* (2nd ed.). San Francisco: Jossey-Bass.

Shortell, S. M., Casalino, L. P., & Fisher, E. S. (2010). How the Center for Medicare and Medicaid Innovation should test accountable care organizations. *Health Affairs, 29*(7), 1293–1298.

Sia, C., Tonniges, T. F., Osterhus, E., et al. (2004). History of the medical home concept. *Pediatrics, 113*(5), 1473–1478.

Stange, K. C. (2010). Defining and measuring the patient-centered medical home. *Journal of General Internal Medicine, 25*(6), 601–612.

Stiles, R. A., et al. (2001). The logic of transaction cost economic in health care organization theory. *Health Care Management Review, 26*(2), 85–92.

Van Servellen, G. (2009). *Communication skills for the health care professionals: Concepts, practice, and evidence.* Sudbury: Jones & Batlett Publishers.

Williamson, O. E. (1985). *The economic institutions of capitalism – Firms, markets, relational contracting.* New York: Free Press.

Witgert, K., & Hess, C. (2012). Including safety-net providers in integrated delivery systems: Issues and options for policymakers. *Issue Brief Commonwealth Fund publication 1617, 20,* 1–18.

Zelman, W. A. (1997). Consumer protection in managed care: Finding the balance. *Health Affairs, 16*(1), 158–166.

Zessa, M. A., & Guterman, S. (2011). *Achieving accountable care: Are we on the right path?* www.commonwealthfund.org. Accessed 28 May 2011.

Institutions in the Managed Care Environment

7

Since "Wall Street discovered healthcare", not only is the age of peaceful coexistence between service providers and payers is over, but an entirely new consulting market has developed. However, the types of products differ widely. The products can be broken down into three categories. First, there are consultation products that are meant to increase the efficiency of the provision of services. Among these, the following are particularly relevant: Management service organisations (MSO), physician practice management companies (PPMC) and pharmacy benefit management organisations (PBM). The second type of consultation products concentrates on the individual managed care instruments. Therefore, consulting services have partially specialised in conducting → utilisation reviews or developing → guidelines. These forms of consultation will not be explained in more detail here because individual instruments will be extensively discussed.

7.1 Management Service Organisations (MSO)

Even though Management Service Organisations are often depicted as such, they are not a new type of organisation, since their roots go back to the beginning of the last century in the United States (Kongstvedt 2009, p. 39).

MSOs include the complete management sector of the provision of services and are involved in capital interests. This capital interest can apply to premises, equipment, furnishing or the inventory. At the same time, physicians receive shares of the MSO, although they often realise that the net asset value of their practice is very low, since most of them are either rented or leased. Along with the capital interest of the MSO, it is also characteristic that the non-medical personnel of a practice are often provided by the MSO (Wagner/Kongstvedt 2013). It is crucial that the MSO is never a service provider in the medical sense and also never assumes the responsibility for patients, but rather always has a merely supporting function. As the name implies, it offers services to ensure the efficient provision of services (Fig. 7.1).

V.E. Amelung, *Healthcare Management*, Springer Texts in Business and Economics, DOI 10.1007/978-3-642-38712-8_7, © Springer-Verlag Berlin Heidelberg 2013

Management Service Organization **(MSO)**		
Management Services	**Services in Combination with Managed Care Organizations**	**Financial Management**
- Personnel management - Personnel (non-medical) - Scheduling - Utilization review - Quality management - Personnel recruitment - Personnel development - Founding of practices - Network management - Patient administration system - Information technologies	- Negotiations - Designing contracts - Complaint management - Marketing - Member service - Development of fee systems	- Acquisition of capital - Financing and accounting - Central purchasing - Budgeting - Guarantees

Fig. 7.1 Scope of services in an MSO (following Hoffman 1997, p. 93)

This list demonstrates that MSOs offer an extensive scope of services. But along with the management services, which can certainly be seen as essential, MSOs play an important role in raising capital. Hospitals as well as physician practices are notoriously undercapitalised. While for hospitals this is often due to their non-profit status and resulting limited access to the capital market, physician practices are typical personnel service providers. MSOs also provide an ideal introduction to the healthcare market for investors. Instead of buying a hospital, it can be much more practical to indirectly invest through an MSO, which can take on every legal form. Therefore, it is useful to examine the initiators more closely (Nauert and Weissman 1999, p. 38) (Fig. 7.2).

Hospitals are the prime initiators of MSOs. The MSO can either be directly integrated in the structure of the hospital or have an independent legal personality (Terry 2006). Often the fact that the internal departments have grown so much makes it attractive to outsource them as independent business segments. This is particularly relevant when non-profit hospitals are worried about their tax-exempt status (DeMuro 1997, p. 377).

The advantages and disadvantages are difficult to discuss because they largely depend upon who the initiator of the MSO is. However, in all forms MSOs are a suitable instrument to provide urgently needed capital and management expertise in the provision of medical services. From the perspective of the physicians who are affiliated with an MSO (and not founders), it should be particularly emphasised that when one side "upgrades itself" (namely the MCOs) and develops the necessary know-how, this then leaves the physicians with no other choice than to cooperate. The "nice, little practice at the corner, in which the married physician couple does the bookkeeping and arranges their schedule on the weekend" is a model that certainly has no chance of survival in a managed care environment. Physicians must have access to professional management, otherwise they will be "overrun" and completely lose their independence. Thus, participation in an MSO can also be seen as a defence strategy on the part of the service provider.

Fig. 7.2 Initiators of an MSO

The initial growth of MSOs was very realistic because a new market for professional management and consultation in general was created through the emergence of new organisational forms. However, the amount of MSOs on the healthcare market reached its climax in 1996 and has been declining since then (Cebul et al. 2008). In 1996 more than 22 % of hospitals belonged to an MSO, while it was only 9 % in 2009 (AHA 2010).

7.2   Physician Practice Management Companies (PPMC)

The essential characteristics of physician practice management companies (PPMCs) are identical with those of MSOs, but the two do differ in that PPMCs are solely medical associations and accordingly have no cross-institutional access (Kongstvedt 2013). In a certain sense these are physician networks (→ networks) among provider-based MCOs, although in the following section the management roles will be focused on.

This does not necessarily mean that only physicians practising independently should be brought together; physician groups should likewise be coordinated beyond local markets (Todd 2011, p. 5). The fact that PPMCs include groups of physicians does not mean that the physicians have to be the owners.

In 1998 there were 140 PPMCS in the United States, and the market manifested oligopolistic structures. The three market leaders (PhyCor, PhyMatrix and Heritage) had a market share of 37 % of the 108,000 physicians organised in PPMCs (Hoechst Marion Roussel 1999, p. 31). After the considerable surge in growth at the end of the twentieth century, the number of PPMCs decreased rapidly. This was due to disputes regarding payment and increased dissatisfaction among physicians with the organisations. Consequently, the organisations either shrank in size or dissolved (Greenwald 2010, p. 134). Through the collapse of two of the three major PPMCs in 1998 (FPA and MedPartners), the market is currently viewed critically (Haas-Wilson 2003, p. 30).

Despite its failure in the United States, the concept offers interesting approaches. Here the basic ideas should be outlined which contributed to its advancement.

PPMCs were developed on one hand to meet the need to bundle market power and on the other hand to significantly improve the management of medical services. Medical services caused costs amounting to US $506 billion in the United States in

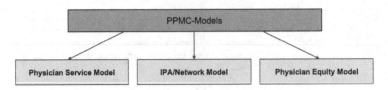

Fig. 7.3 PPMC organisational models

2009. That was 20 % of the entire healthcare expenses, which amounted to US $2,486 trillion (California Healthcare Foundation 2011). On the basis of data from 1995, Burns and Robinson (1998) calculated that for every dollar of expenses caused by doctors, an additional $2.24 in healthcare services accrues. It is therefore only logical to pay particular attention to the enormous direct as well as indirect potential of PPMCs. There are three significant organisational models (Burns/Robinson 1998, p. 7) (Fig. 7.3).

PPMCs aim to directly generate economies of scale which can very easily be classified into four areas (Robinson 1998, p. 65ff. and Zuckerman et al. 1998, p. 13f.). Firstly, they have advantages in the acquisition of capital (Conrad et al. 1999, p. 324). Not only is it much simpler for supra-regional PPMCs to acquire capital, they also have access to better conditions as well as more appropriate financial instruments (e.g. bonds) due to their size. In addition, PPMCs have a legal form that better suits the acquisition of capital than that of most physician groups. Secondly, PPMCs can generate clear economies of scale in the procurement of material. Large PPMCs can, for example, purchase pharmaceuticals directly from the producer. Thirdly, they are in the position to utilise rebates in negotiations with insurance companies (Guest and Collins 2010). A fourth aspect has become more and more significant: Resident physicians also see themselves faced with ever increasing demands for information technology, which is often associated with high investment costs. In the development and introduction of such systems PPMCs were able to implement considerable economies of scale. Economies of scope, however, also play an important role. These deal with the potential of benchmarking, which requires access to comparison data, and addresses the structuring of organisational development ($\rightarrow$ quality management).

Like other MCOs, PPMCs aim to precisely consolidate the fragmented healthcare market. Alongside quite positive goals such as raising efficiency in the provision of services through economies of scale and scope (Burns and Robinson 1998, p. 24), it is often simply a question of market power. Exactly as is the case with networks and IDSs, a decisive goal of PPMCs is to attain a market position that makes it virtually impossible not to take PPMCs into account in selective contracting. For example, a PPMC with a market share of 25 %, which in the extremely local form of healthcare markets does not have to include many doctors at all, leads to a situation in which managed care products which do not include the PPMC are nearly impossible to sell. Although this is not often the case in cross-field PPMCs, among specialised PPMCs, such as those who specialise in cancer therapy, a local monopoly develops almost automatically. In this way "antitrust" considerations play a very decisive role in the American discussion regarding PPMCs.

7.3 Pharmacy Benefit Management (PBM)

In contrast to inpatient and outpatient services, pharmaceuticals were not part of the service spectrum of health insurances for a long time. It was only in the 1960s that American employers implemented the reimbursement of medication costs, i.e. "pharmaceutical benefits", in the insurance programme (Grabowski and Mullins 1997). It soon became clear that insurance companies as well as self-insured employers were unable to cope with the countless claims for the reimbursement of medication costs. At first, relatively small companies emerged as "Pharmacy Benefit Managers" (PBM), who initially offered to take on the administrative processing and invoicing of cost reimbursement claims for health insurance companies.

These companies further developed their range of services in pharmaceutical information and invoicing systems. Particularly with these invoicing systems – today complex, electronic invoicing systems – the PBM companies became indispensable. At the same time, they strategically positioned themselves at the information interface between insurer and the pharmaceutical industry (Fig. 7.4).

According to this positioning and the IT-expertise they developed, the PBM companies increasingly offered management services for the integrated control of the entire supply of pharmaceuticals in addition to their administrative services. When President Nixon made the service of an HMO compulsory for all employers with the "HMO Act" in 1973, the PBM companies took advantage of this nationwide introduction of managed care organisations (MCO) to expand their management services (Navarro 2009). With the introduction of HMOs and the range of complex payment and supply options, the PBM companies' management knowhow became crucial. The numerous newly formed MCOs went on to become the main customers of the PBMs (Fig. 7.5).

PBM companies currently offer a broad scope of services for the supply of pharmaceuticals. According to PWC (2007), they supply 71 % of the entire population of the United States.[1] Green (2008) further estimates that in merely 5 % of the insured who have an insurance policy with reimbursement for pharmaceuticals no PBM company is involved.[2]

There are around 60 PBM companies serving 210 million Americans. Between 2012 and 2021 they will lead to savings of 35 %, around US $2 trillion, compared to the situation without PBM (PCMA 2010; Visante 2011).

---

[1] The portion of the population registered with a health plan that has an external PBM.

[2] The medicinal needs of the approx. 65 % working per cent of the American population are nearly always covered. Since 2006, Medicare policyholders also receive pharmaceutical coverage.

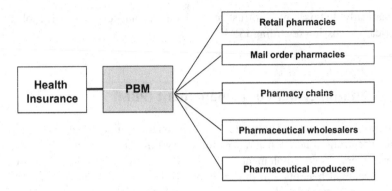

Fig. 7.4 PBM as interface between insurance company, pharmacies and industry

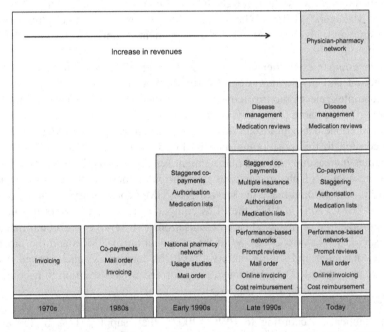

Fig. 7.5 The development of PBM companies' range of services in the United States (Following Cap Gemini, E&Y 2003)

Elements of Pharmacy Benefit Management

In the scope of the contract with a health plan, the entire management of the pharmaceutical supply is often transferred to the PBM company. The main objective is to offer a suitable selection of medications as well as an affordable, smooth transfer of these services. As indispensable information interfaces, PBM companies are in contact with all parties concerned in the supply (Fig. 7.6).

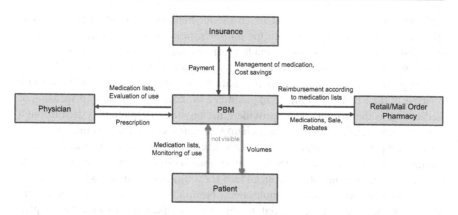

Fig. 7.6 Partner and business model from PBM companies (Source following: Cap Gemini, E&Y 2003)

The core aspect of every PBM programme is the creation and continual mainte-nance of the drug benefit plan (Navarro 2009). It defines all services and together with the incentives for insured persons and physicians in consultation with the health plan. Medication lists (positive lists, "formularies") are created and maintained according to their therapeutic category, effectiveness, side effects, costs and co-payments. In the case of a low-cost insurance rate/premium from an MCO, these medication lists can be extremely restrictive and compulsory for insured persons as well as doctors ("closed formularies"). In order to combat higher premiums, the medication lists include a large selection of drugs and also allow non-listed pharmaceuticals to be prescribed ("open formularies") (KFF 2005).

The PBM companies generally communicate via internet portals, brochures, telephone hotlines, directed telephone consultations and specialist consultations with the physician and the insured persons. They are involved in disease manage-ment programmes particularly for chronic, medication-intensive illnesses such as asthma (Santerre and Neun 2010). They also develop medicine programmes as necessary as well as guidelines for each stage of the illness. Particularly for chronic illnesses, improved compliance often has the advantage that co-payments are discontinued. Likewise, consultants from PBM companies contact physicians who prescribe medications which are not on the medication list and whose active ingredients cannot be substituted. The prescription that follows is discussed with the physician on the basis of clinical studies and, if necessary, a "switch" to a comparable medication on the medication list is arranged. The prescription activities of the physicians are actively influenced by the medication list. Using computer-operated algorithms, such prompt reviews ("drug utilisation reviews") record potential side effects, drug interactions, allergy complications and tolerance warnings due to age, pregnancy, dosage etc. during the dispensing of medication (Smith et al. 2005). The prescription activities of physicians and the insured persons' use of medication are evaluated and commented on using retrospective analysis of the invoicing data. In addition, a list with particularly expensive, controversial, lifestyle-dependent or cosmetic medications is maintained. These drugs can only be prescribed with the *authorisation* of the insurance company or physician. The insured person is made aware of their use of medication through further specific co-payment programmes and incentives for using generic drugs.

Along with the implementation and maintenance of a medication list, the main business of the PBM companies is to guarantee the consumer-friendly dispensing of medication to the insured. They provide a nationwide distribution system through contracts with retail, mail order and chain pharmacies. The PBM companies offer the insured persons incentives to use their low-cost distribution channels, such as the mail order pharmacies. Depending on the number of insured persons in care, the PBM companies can negotiate reduced fees for selling medication and considerable rebates with the industry and wholesalers. Normally, there is an agreement that approx. 70–80 % of the negotiated savings must be passed on to the health plan (Kopenski 2008).

Assessment

In light of the increasing relevance of chronic diseases and multimorbidity, pharmaceutical management programmes are becoming increasingly important. With the elements of PBM already explained, a reduction of costs is attained in comparison to self-paying patients without controlled drug provision.

It should be particularly noted that PBM could both increase quality as well as simultaneously cutting spending. Moreover, the potential for an improvement in quality is enormous. Through targeted drug control, medication errors can be detected and prevented. In addition, compliance is increased, through individual packaging for instance, and simultaneously results in a significant cost reduction. Thus, in order for the concept of PBM to function, it is critical that PBM companies are independent. The experience of American firms has shown that the inclusion of PBM companies within pharmaceutical companies is incompatible. The concept of PBM firms can only be realised when these businesses remain as an independent broker as well as service provider. In the future, personalized medicine will promote the individual design of drug supply and demand.

Literature

Burns, L. R., & Robinson, J. C. (1998). Physician practice management companies: Implications for hospital-based integrated delivery systems. *Frontiers of Health Service Management, 14* (2), 3–35.

California Healthcare Foundation. (2011). *Health care costs 101* (Annual report), Oakland.

Cap Gemini, Ernst & Young. (2003). *Versandhandel mit Arzneimitteln in den USA – Ein Konzept für Deutschland?* Internationale Studie, ausführliche Fassung. http://www.phagro.de/_phagro/upload/standpunkte/ff42e485-b275-4f4e-b2f6-aa1b7ee334cb.pdf. Accessed 19 Feb 2013.

Cebul, R. D., Rebitzer, J. B., Taylor, L. J., et al. (2008). *Organizational fragmentation and care quality in the U.S. health care system* (NBER Working Paper Series), Cambridge, MA.

Conrad, D. A., Koos, S., Harney, A., et al. (1999). Physician practice management organizations: Their prospects and performance. *Medical Care Research and Review, 56*(3), 307–339.

Demuro, P. R. (1997). Evolution of management service organizations. In R. B. Conners (Ed.), *Integrating the practice of medicine* (pp. 375–389). Chicago: Jossey-Bass.

Grabowski, H., & Mullins, C. D. (1997). Pharmacy benefit management, cost-effectiveness analysis and drug formulary decisions. *Social Science & Medicine, 45*(4), 545–554.

Green, K. (2008). *Regulation of pharmacy benefit managers: An economic analysis of regulation and litigation as agents of health care change* (Working Paper). http://works.bepress.com/context/kevin_green/article/1000/type/native/viewcontent/. Accessed 15 Dec 2012.

Greenwald, H. P. (2010). *Health care in the United States: Organization, management, and policy.* San Francisco: Jossey-Bass.

Guest, B. C., & Collins, M. E. (2010). Is it time to resurrect physician practice management organizations? *Health Leaders Media.* http://www.healthleadersmedia.com/page-1/PHY-247842/Is-it-Time-to-Resurrect-Physician-Practice-Management-Organizations. Accessed 25 Feb 2013.

Haas-Wilson, D. (2003). *Managed care and monopoly power: The antitrust challenge.* Cambridge, MA: Harvard University Press.

Hoechst Marion Roussel. (1999). *Medical group practice digest* (Managed care digest series). Kansas City: Hoechst Marion Roussel.

Hoffman, J. R. (1997). Management service organizations. In K. Miller & E. Miller (Eds.), *Making sense of managed care* (pp. 91–99). San Francisco: American College of Physician Executives.

KFF [Kaiser Family Foundation]. (2005). *The effect of formularies and other cost management tools on access to medications: An analysis of the MMA and the final rule.* Menlo Park: Kaiser Family Foundation.

Kongstvedt, P. R. (2009). *Managed care: What it is and how it works* (3rd ed.). Sudbury: Jones & Bartlett.

Kongstvedt, P. R. (2013). *Essentials of managed health care* (6th ed.). Burlington: Jones & Bartlett Learning.

Kopenski, F. (2008). Prescription drug benefit design – The building blocks and their impact on costs. *Benefits Quarterly, Fourth Quarter, 24*(4), 7–11.

Nauert, R. C., & Weissman, D. C. (1999). MSO development: Progress versus pitfalls. *Journal of HealthCare Finance, 25*(3), 37–43.

Navarro, R. P. (2009). *Managed care pharmacy practice* (2nd ed.). Sudbury: Jones and Bartlett Publishers.

PCMA [Pharmaceutical Care Management Association]. (2010). *Pharmacy benefit manager (PBM) 101.* http://www.pcmanet.org/images/stories/uploads/PBM%20101.pdf. Accessed 26 Feb 2013.

PWC [PriceWaterhouseCoopers]. (2007). *Pharmacy benefit management savings in Medicare and the commercial marketplace & the cost of proposed PBM legislation, 2008–2017.* http://www.pwc.com/en_US/us/national-economic-statistics/assets/pharma_savings_medicare_pbm_leg.pdf. Accessed 23 Feb 2013.

Robinson, J. C. (1996, Summer). The dynamics and limits of corporate growth in health care. *Health Affairs, 15*(2), 155–169.

Robinson, J. C. (1998, July/August). Financial capital and intellectual capital in physician practice management. *Health Affairs, 17,* 53–74.

Santerre, R. E., & Neun, S. P. (2010). *Health economics: Theory, insights, and industry studies* (5th ed.). Mason: South-West Cengage Learning.

Shi, L., & Singh, D. A. (2013). *Essentials of the U.S. health care system* (3rd ed.). Sudbury: Jones & Bartlett Publishers.

Smith, M. I., Wertheimer, A. I., & Fincham, J. E. (2005). *Pharmacy and the U.S. health care system* (3rd ed.). Binghamton: Haworth Press.

Terry, K. (2006). *Can an MSO help you?* https://www.med3000.com/cms/program/adminlinks/docs/Can%20an%20MSO%20help%20you.pdf. Accessed 6 June 2011.

Todd, M. K. (2011). *The physician employment contract handbook: A guide to structuring equitable arrangements* (2nd ed.). New York: Productivity Press.

Visante. (2011). *Pharmacy benefit managers (PBMs): Generating savings for plan sponsors and consumers.* http://www.pcmanet.org/images/stories/uploads/2011/Sept2011/pbms%20savings%20study%202011%20final.pdf. Accessed 26 Feb 2013.

Zuckerman, H. S., Hilberman, D. W., Andersen, R. M., et al. (1998). Physicians and organizations: Strange bedfellows or a marriage made in heaven? *Frontiers of Health Service Management, 14*(3), 3–34.

Conclusion

8

Managed care leads to a considerable increase in the number of different institutional arrangements. The former "cottage industry" of healthcare has transformed into a differentiated service industry with diverse providers. There are several reasons for the development from the simple division of the delivery and purchasing of services to this variety of different organisational forms. In the following section the most important objectives will be outlined and explained with concrete examples:

- Lowering of transaction costs,
- Utilisation of economies of scale,
- Development of market power as a defence strategy,
- Diversification in an emergent consultancy market,
- Creation of investment markets and
- Creation of greater choice.

Usually it is not just a single aspect which plays a decisive role, but the combination of several aspects at the same time. The decrease of → transaction costs is a common argument for the emergence of new organisational forms. Transaction costs are always particularly high when the uncertainty and risk of opportunistic behaviour is high and when there is a considerable need for coordination between service levels. This is certainly the case in healthcare services and there is good reason for an increased level of vertical integration (Shi and Singh 2013). MCOs are doubtlessly able to reduce transaction costs on various levels of the system. Thus, the need for coordination between the inpatient and outpatient sector is very immediate and there is considerable potential to save costs as well as to improve quality at the same time. In the case of a shift to chronic illnesses, the optimal coordination of interfaces becomes increasingly significant.

The realisation of economies of scale is also an important objective (Robinson 1996). This can be applied to the purchasing (advantageous access to capital markets) as well as to the concrete provision of services. Due to high fixed costs, hospitals in particular depend on a high capacity utilisation. This can be more easily attained through strategic alliances. However, considerable economies of scale can

V.E. Amelung, *Healthcare Management*, Springer Texts in Business and Economics, DOI 10.1007/978-3-642-38712-8_8, © Springer-Verlag Berlin Heidelberg 2013

also be realised by using cutting edge technology or material procurement (particularly pharmaceuticals) (Geisler et al. 2003).

The realisation of economies of scale still does not sufficiently explain the merger and acquisition fever in the American healthcare market, since its potential is rather low, particularly in cross-market mergers (Robinson 1999, p. 21). This is also heightened by the fact that the administrative costs of MCOs are nearly 40 % higher than those of traditional indemnity insurances (Herzlinger 1998, p. 22).

The third objective is the creation of market power. One of the significant characteristics of managed care is the service purchasers' attempt to contract selectively. Instead of concluding contracts with all service providers, only certain selected providers are meant to become contract partners, and the purchasers will exercise concrete influence over their delivery of services. This strategy is always particularly significant when there are considerable overcapacities in a market. This is also true in many market segments of healthcare. MCOs attempt to distance overcapacities from their areas of responsibility and develop precise internal requirement planning. For this reason it is crucial for service providers to develop market power on multiple levels. Networks are established and integrated care systems are developed with the sole purpose of assuming such a critical role on the market that an MCO cannot transact selectively because the sale of products would be too difficult. Many of the organisations described here can be seen as a response to the strategies of market players, i.e. "structure follows strategy".

A fourth objective is to satisfy the high demand for consultancy in the managed care context. What has once been a very stable field has become a turbulent, competitive environment, in which all market participants have a high demand for consultancy. When one side is "equipped" with management techniques, then the other side must answer with corresponding strategies in order to prevent becoming a mere adapter. The compensation via capitations from the service purchaser requires consultancy services from the service providers. Due to the immense demand, different products and organisation forms were developed which compete with one another for the large market of consultation services in healthcare.

In addition, the emergence of investment markets must be discussed. Some MCOs are merely the result of Wall Street's insight that a large sum of money can be earned in the healthcare sector. However, this money cannot be earned via already existing organisational forms, such as hospitals established as non-profit organisations, but rather via new organisational forms, such as MSOs and PPMOs. The former do not struggle with problems of legal forms or a long-standing history of benefactors. It is easier for an MSO to behave in a profit-orientated manner than a hospital that served the local community for hundreds of years.

Lastly, the creation of greater choice should also be discussed. It is often assumed that there is *one* optimal organisational form, *one* optimal service package, *one* evidence-based set of → guidelines and *one* type of market management. However, Robinson (1999, p. 9) rightly emphasises that this is a fundamentally false assumption and that options should be available. This is equally true for the supply and demand side, as it is simply impossible to completely satisfy all requirements with a single organisational form.

Literature

Geisler, E., Krabbendam, K., & Schuring, R. (2003). *Technology, health care, and management in the hospital of the future.* Westport: Praeger Publishers.

Herzlinger, R. (1998). *Market driven health care.* Reading: Addison-Wesley.

Robinson, J. C. (1999, March/April). The future of managed care organizations. *Health Affairs, 18* (2), 7–24.

Part III

Managed Care Instruments

Contract Design

9

9.1 Selective Contracting

Introductory Remarks

One of the most important preconditions for high-quality and economically effective treatment results is a selection of suitable service providers with whom an MCO concludes supply contracts (selective contracting). The conclusion of selective contracts is so significant for managed care and healthcare management that it is considered crucial to the definition of managed care by not only the authors of this book, but the literature supports this claim as well.

Selective contracting means that a service purchaser is not required to cover the costs for the use of any doctor, hospital or nursing facility. On the contrary, only the services of those providers who have concluded a supply contract with the MCO are compensated. Thus, on the one hand the insured's freedom of choice is restricted when selecting service providers. On the other hand, the restriction of the freedom of choice of the service provider depends on the design of the contract. The service provider can conclude an exclusive contract, according to which they can only treat the insured from a certain MCO (closed panel). The contract, however, can also enable patients from other insurance companies and MCOs to be treated (open panel).

The following goals are associated with selective contracting:

1. Cost control,
2. Assurance of quality in respect to influencing the provision of services (definition of goals) and
3. Planning certainty.

An MCO can use its power of negotiation for cost control in order to negotiate more affordable prices (rebates). The threat of not concluding a contract is particularly effective in those regions in which there is a surplus of hospital beds and doctors, especially in urban areas. In some areas, however, there can be so few providers that exclusion, particularly of well-respected providers, is virtually

V.E. Amelung, *Healthcare Management*, Springer Texts in Business and Economics,
DOI 10.1007/978-3-642-38712-8_9, © Springer-Verlag Berlin Heidelberg 2013

impossible. An MCO's power of negotiation is limited regarding the implementation of more favourable conditions in this case.

At the same time, a provider can influence the level of quality of a contract partner through selective contracting by choosing them based on their abilities and reputation. Concentrating on only a few service providers promotes the learning effect. Thus, it is generally accepted that the process quality of operations increases with the number of operations carried out. In turn, Waldman et al. (2003) found considerable evidence for learning curve effects: "a strong positive volume-outcome relationship has been shown for various procedures and conditions, including neonatal intensive care, cancer surgery, cardiac transplantations and abdominal and trauma surgery" (2003, p. 47). At the same time, case costs sink considerably (Porter and Guth 2012), whereby opinions differ on this point. The potential of MCOs to direct patients into such facilities in which a number of operations are carried out via selective contracting is a decisive strategy to decrease costs and raise the quality of care (Porter and Teisberg 2006).

Finally, the selective contract design enables better capacity planning by the MCO because it only has to purchase as many services as are necessary for the supply model and the desired quality of care. Selective contracting has become a significant strategic option in nearly all healthcare systems. This is particularly due to the fact that a comprehensive discussion about quality and differences of quality in healthcare services slowly began. Particularly the esteemed publications of the Institute of Medicine ("To Err is Human" 1999 and "Crossing the Quality Chasm" 2001) have provided significant impulses in this area. In the United States it is assumed that only 55 % of Americans receive services that are in line with the guidelines (McGlynn et al. 2003). Selective contracting can play a decisive role in this. In addition, the consequences of selective contracting and the danger of insufficient care are becoming less important.

In the following section the procedure and problems of selective contracting in the managed care system will be demonstrated. We have limited our discussion to contracts with physicians and hospitals. Selective contracts are also available for annex services such as laboratory, radiology or physiotherapy services (Knight 1998).

Selective Contracts with Physicians

The selection of physicians through MCOs takes place through **credentialing.** In a narrower sense, this refers to a process that assesses a physician's competence to practise their career. The basis for this is first and foremost the medical licence, certifications, any malpractice cases as well as vocational training (Kongstvedt 2013). In a broader sense, the term "credentialing" includes the examination of all characteristics of a physician and their practice which comprise the necessary quality and efficiency of care in the managed care context (Hajen et al. 2011).

Many MCOs orient themselves on the criteria issued by accreditation organisations such as the Joint Commission on Accreditation of Healthcare

Organisations (JCAHO)[1] or the National Committee for Quality Assurance (NCQA).[2] The information system the NCQA developed, $\rightarrow$ HEDIS (Health Plan Employer Data and Information Set), contains the indicators for evaluating the quality of MCOs. The NCQA evaluation process is divided into two phases: The initial evaluation and the recredentialing phase (Matzka 2008).

In the initial evaluation phase it is crucial that the applicants have a good reputation in the hospital in which they primarily work. This is particularly true for hospitals belonging to the MCO network. Other criteria include the applicants' training, the health status of their patients and enquiries with the Peer Review Organisation (PRO)[3] as well as the national database of practising physicians to see if any problems with credentialing or malpractice were recorded in the past. Additional criteria for credentialing could be foreign language skills or particular areas of interest. The NCQA also requires an on-site visit in order to observe the structure of the practice and the accounting.

The **recredentialing** procedure developed by the NCQA includes a routine examination of certain data (opening hours for consultation, number of transfers, dispensing medications or liability issues), periodic visits to primary physicians and gynaecologists as well as specialists who have above-average revenue. The procedure also requires the investigation of complaints, surveying satisfaction, the existence of quality control measures and an evaluation of the data from the $\rightarrow$ utilisation review (Kongstvedt 2013).

Whether credentialing should also consider economic criteria (economic credentialing) is disputed. However, since the physicians will work in a managed care system, the service providers whose profiles do not promise cost-effective care, are less attractive. Particularly in Physician Hospital Organisations the necessity to evaluate the style of care in respect to economic aspects is shared by the administration as well as the physicians (Shi 2007, p. 181). For example, a good basis for economic credentialing is the billing data of physicians to which the MCO itself has access, such as from contract hospitals, or data received from the service purchaser (Kazmir 2008; Crossen and Tollen 2010).

The task of credentialing can be delegated to special organisations (CVOs - Credentials Verification Organisations). Therefore, multiple credentialing is unnecessary for individual doctors when switching to another MCO. The MCO itself receives data faster and more completely. The CVOs can be certified through the NCQA (Peden 2012). Public reporting is also closely connected to credentialing.

---

[1] The JCAHO (www.jointcommission.org) is the oldest and largest standard-setting and accredited organisation in the US healthcare system. Along with MCOs it monitors a wide spectrum of facilities for outpatient care, nursing and laboratory facilities.

[2] The NCQA (www.ncqa.org) is an independent, non-profit organization, which was established in 1979 to promote quality and certification, particularly of HMOs, in order to aid employers in selecting insurance providers.

[3] The PRO is an organisation run by physicians, which evaluates the quality and use of healthcare services in the Medicare programme.

One problem with credentialing is the weighing of benefits between a strict selection process, which results in a rather small network of efficiently working physicians, and a rather lenient procedure, which allows for the inclusion of more physicians in the network and hence a higher likelihood that less qualified physicians are included. However, lenient credentialing gives a larger number of insured access to the customary doctor-patient-relationship and improves the distribution of risk.

Independent of the methods implemented – which have become more and more precise through information technology and corresponding concepts – the selection of service providers is the key for the success of a care system.

There are also options for the patients to assess the qualifications of individual physicians. For example, the Castle Connolly (www.castleconnolly.com) or DrScore (www.drscore.com) websites are suitable for this purpose.

Selective Contracts with Hospitals

When transacting with hospitals there is also a conflict in determining the number of hospitals contracts are to be concluded with. The lower the number of hospitals, the greater the negotiating power is when determining the conditions of compensation and control measures. On the other hand, a larger number of contract hospitals can improve the competitive position of the MCO because the service purchasers often base their selection on these criteria.

Until recently, only few studies were available which provided information about the criteria upon which the selection of hospitals is based. It is plausible that quantifiable data such as the occupancy rate, the costs and the range of services as well as qualitative characteristics such as the reputation of the hospital in public and among physicians plays a role (Kongstvedt 2013). Somewhat older studies by Feldman et al. (1990) and Zwanziger and Meirowitz (1998) provided more detailed results.

Feldman et al. (1990) proved that the hospitals investigated were first and foremost selected on the basis of their quality, which was assessed using certain aspects of a hospital (public or private hospital, existence of a training programme, scope of the service programme). Private hospitals with training programmes were particularly favoured. In contrast, the prices of hospitals played a minor role in their selection. The prices were indeed relevant for controlling the patient flows within contract hospitals.

Zwanziger and Meirowitz's (1998) empirical study confirmed the relatively low significance of the price factor for concluding contracts; however, it also showed that among the hospitals they surveyed, the level of prices was apparently interpreted by the MCOs as a quality indicator. Hospitals with very low costs had a lower chance to receive a supply contract than hospitals with average costs. On the other hand, hospitals with very high costs also had a lower chance. In this case, the quality objective was obviously dominated by the goal of economic effectiveness.

The study also showed – somewhat surprisingly – that MCOs did not favour for-profit hospitals. This result allows multiple interpretations. One can consequently conclude that for-profit hospitals may be less willing to offer price concessions. The cause of this, however, could also be the comparatively low number of physicians in these hospitals which restricts the freedom of choice of the insured or this type of hospital is associated with a lower level of quality (Zwanziger and Meirowitz 1998). In decisions today, the cost criteria most likely gained increased significance.

Assessment of Selective Contracting

Physicians as well as the insured are rather sceptical about selective contracting. The insured miss their freedom of choice and are afraid that providers are chosen not based on their quality, but rather on their willingness to offer rebates (Zelman and Berenson 1998). However, a change is taking place. This is primarily driven by the discussion of quality.

Physicians complain that they are forced to accept less compensation or they are excluded from networks. The government responded to this criticism and now regulates access so that physicians cannot be fundamentally excluded from a contract if they accept the conditions of the HMO (any willing provider law, Blum 1997). Some physicians also criticise that they have to integrate themselves into networks with unknown doctors or with physicians whom they know are less qualified (Zelman and Berenson 1998).

However, some of the criticism of selective contracting should be taken seriously. In many cases it is utilised as a crude instrument, particularly to select doctors with a "low-risk" pool of insured and to negotiate discounts instead of using it as an instrument to coordinate and further develop a high quality network. In recent years, some MCOs have improved this instrument in their selection by developing more precise practice profiles and comparing indicators based on their success with one another. However, the affected physicians criticise that the health status of their patients and the quality of care are not considered enough in these indicators (Bindman et al. 1998).

It should once again be emphasised that selective contracting is the most significant instrument in managed care. As unspectacular as it may seem at first, it is critical for the design of healthcare systems. Selective contracting largely means that healthcare policy becomes healthcare management. Thus, selective contracting influences key aspects of the healthcare system's structure (Amelung 2007).

In a healthcare system based on competition, selective contracting is the deciding factor for efficient competition. Assuming that service providers are "distributed normally", the desired partners should be chosen. Whoever wants to be competitive must accept selective contracting as a core instrument. New information technology facilitates selective contracting that is more finely tuned to goals. The main driving force behind selective contracting will be the differing quality of results, which is increasingly gaining interest in health policy discussions. Service providers' lobbies successfully thwarted these types of discussions for many decades. It is only a question of time until more comprehensive information about healthcare services understandable for the general public is made available in more countries,

However, it must be clearly emphasised that selective contracting increases the demands on healthcare policy, as questions regarding the guaranteeing of quality and accessibility will take on central significance.

9.2   Structuring the Insurance Contracts

Basic Concepts

While managed care is largely associated with the management of the service provider, influencing the behaviour of the insured is also a significant aspect. Many methods that are by no means new play a role in this. The risks prior and subsequent to concluding the contract can be distinguished. Before concluding the contract there is the risk that negative selection will be used. The insured is more aware of their own individual risks (hidden characteristics) than the MCO and will look for the most affordable offer. Subsequent to the conclusion of the contract, there is the risk of excessive use of services (moral hazard). In order to prevent this, incentives and monitoring instruments must be used ($\rightarrow$ introduction) (Fig. 9.1).

This graphic demonstrates that there are diverse possibilities for structuring contracts and influencing behaviour.

Options for Managing Pre-contract Risks

The primary instrument for managing pre-contract risks are optional tariffs and risk exclusion through an MCO. Optional tariffs mean the exclusion of entire service areas or portions of them. One assumes here that the insured can best evaluate their own risk. Therefore it is a so-called self-selection. In this model the insurance service is basically presented as a modular system in which the insured can choose according to their individual benefits and risks (self selection). What is particularly problematic from the perspective of the insured is the divergence between the purchasing of services and the average time when the services are carried out – i.e. insuring benefits today for future use. Young insured persons tend to exclude many services, since the present benefit of lower premiums is more highly valued than the future purchasing of services (Zweifel et al. 2009; Henderson 2011, p. 197ff.). However, optional tariffs only work when one is also willing to accept the consequences for earlier decisions. In concrete terms, this means for example that a smoker who buys an insurance policy that does not cover the consequences of their addiction would not be treated in the case of a causal disease – at least not at the expense of the health insurance – even when said person could be treated.

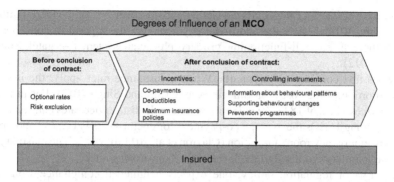

Fig. 9.1 Degree of influence of MCO before and after the conclusion of contract

Less dramatic but of a similar nature is the exclusion of tooth replacement or the consequences of extreme sports (paragliding, skiing or even soccer). Both can be very strongly influenced by individual behaviour. However, this presupposes mono-causalities which play a rather minor role in the case of really serious illnesses. As already demonstrated, over half of the expenses accrue due to patients with three or more chronic illnesses. Correspondingly, mono-causal methods are not effective here.

Even more problematic is the exclusion of performance packages, which is a common occurrence in American MCOs, through the insurer rather than the decisions of the insured. This describes a case of risk exclusion. In this way some HMOs completely exclude services for mental illnesses. In general, company decisions to remove certain services from the benefits catalogue (so-called carve-outs) can be critical, as well as the case-by-case exclusion due to pre-existing conditions or heightened probability of risks. These indicate a restriction of services on the individual level.

Options for Managing Post-contract Risks

There are many more possibilities for managing risks after the conclusion of a contract. These can be divided into two types of instruments based on their goals. On one hand, those which are meant to limit demand by creating incentives for the insured when they do not use any services. These incentives are primarily based on a form of risk sharing which takes place between the insured and the MCO. The second type of instrument is meant to reduce the probability of the occurrence of health hazards (e.g. prevention programmes). They deal with monitoring and the use of control instruments.

MCOs pay particular attention to instruments for financial contribution of the insured towards healthcare costs. These take the form of co-payments (i.e. a certain percentage as payment), deductibles (a fixed co-payment) or maximum insurances. When compared internationally, the amount of a co-payment for the insured ranged from just over 0.6 % of the GDP (the Netherlands) to over 2 % of the GDP (United States) in 2010, whereby the additional payments are the highest in countries in which there is no well-functioning primary physician system (→ gatekeeping) (OECD 2012).

Let us first consider **co-payments**. When coinsurance rates apply, the insured pays a portion of the costs determined ex ante (Shi and Singh 2012). For primary care services, rates of 18 % are common, whereas dentist service rates can run up to 50 %. Among HMOs the average co-payment for doctor visits is US $22 and up to $107 for emergency room admission (Claxton et al. 2011, p. 1945). The elasticity of demand is influenced through the level of the coinsurance rate.

In terms of regulation policy, one expects heightened compliance from co-payments. Compliance means the active participation of patients in the healing process, and non-compliance correspondingly refers to deviant behaviour. Studies from the United States presume that at least 10 % of hospital admissions are a result of non-compliance (Koenig et al. 2012).

Further studies from the United States particularly show the impact this form of regulation has on medications. Depending on the indications, a doubling of the co-payments leads to savings between 26 % and 45 % (Goldman et al. 2004), whereby it should not be ignored that this can also result in higher costs in other areas, i.e. emergency room admissions.

The second instrument are so-called **deductibles.** Deductibles establish a minimum amount above which insurance coverage begins. For example, an insured person must first pay a minimum of $200 before the insurance begins to cover further costs. Furthermore, it does not make a difference if the further costs amount to $10 or $10,000. Accordingly, the insured must pay invoices amounting to over $195 on their own. In practise, deductibles vary from health plan to health plan between $600 and $1,900; on average an insured person in an HMO pays the least, with $691, in comparison to members of a POS, who pay $1,014 (KFF 2012). From the perspective of incentive theory, two theories must be differentiated: The phase below the deductible and the phase above it. Until the deductible is reached the insured behaves just as someone without any insurance protection. Once the limit has been reached, the insured acts as if he or she had complete insurance coverage without any deductibles. The problem of unreasonably high demand becomes even larger now because the insured has already paid the complete deductible, and now wishes to "distribute" this among the highest possible total amount of expenses. For healthcare costs of only $250 per year and a deductible of $200, the relation of covered and uncovered services is 1:5. Through the increase of healthcare demand, the insured can "improve" this relation. In practise there are many examples of mixed forms. Deductibles and coinsurances are often implemented simultaneously. In doing so, there is a possibility to combine co-payments and deductibles. This is how the instruments are used in tandem in Switzerland. In this way the negative incentives are limited.

In Europe, Switzerland is considered the country that utilises these instruments most consistently. In doing so, both of the aforementioned methods are applied at once. Depending on their options, the Swiss pay a deductible ranging from 300

Swiss francs annually in the ordinary basic health insurance up to 2,500 Swiss francs. Additionally, a coinsurance of 10 % for medical goods and services beyond the deductible exists. However, there is a ceiling for the co-insurance of 700 Swiss francs. (OECD 2011)

The third variation is **maximum payment limits**. Similar to the limitation of liability in car insurances, this variation only finances a pre-determined maximum. This can either be a number of hospital days, an annual maximum payment limit or a lifetime maximum. The impact is just the opposite of that of deductibles. While the insured is virtually without insurance up to a certain amount with deductibles, in this case they are virtually uninsured above a certain amount (Feldstein 1993, p. 109; Jensen et al. 1997, p. 133). This form of insurance was relatively popular for a long time in the United States because it offers much cheaper rates. However, today the trend is rather that a maximum amount is fixed for out-of-pocket services. From a European perspective, this kind of insurance contract is contradictory to basic volumes of the healthcare system design.

The establishment of maximum payment limits is quite common for mental illnesses. An older study from 1989 showed that back then 58 % of the MCOs had established a maximum payment limit throughout an insured person's entire life for inpatient psychiatric care (Sorkin 1992, p. 183).

The second area, the so-called **monitoring** and **control instruments,** refers to the obligation of the insured to limit the probability of occurrence. In this case the behaviour of the insured is influenced. This method is largely based on the fact that the patient can considerably influence whether a need for services arises through their behaviour, and if so, to what extent. A classic example is tooth replacement. It is assumed that regular dental care and dentist visits can lower the risk to nearly zero. For this reason health insurances have coupled the purchasing of services and the amount of the partial payments with regular dentist visits. As a result a portion of the responsibility for limiting benefits is transferred to the insured. Instead of an "all-inclusive insurance" mentality, now there is the jointly responsible patient, who is aware of their role as the "co-producer" of health and is forced to assume this role.

Three methods can be distinguished among the monitoring and control instruments: **information about consequences of certain behaviour, support of changes in behaviour** and **classic prevention.** The weakest form of behavioural influence is mere information about the impact of behaviour. These are usually informational campaigns to raise awareness about modes of behaviour, and can take the form of TV spots, informational material, mailings or other communication instruments. It is critical that the insured are not directly influenced, but that the materials are appealing. The insured is urged to give up behaviour which harms ones health, however without incentives or the threat of sanctions.

The second method aims to facilitate behavioural changes. The MCO assumes the much more active role in this method (Solberg 1998, p. 37). The following graphic demonstrates the significance of these instruments using the example of smoking cessation programmes (Fig. 9.2).

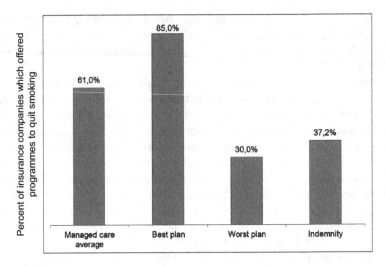

Fig. 9.2 Prevention programmes in MCOs (following Zelman and Berenson 1998)

On average, programmes to help people quit smoking play a much larger role for MCOs than they do for classical indemnity insurances, although it must be stated that the spectrum is extremely broad.

The third approach is the traditional prevention programme. This programme is distinguished into three stages (Bodenheimer and Grumbach 1995, p. 134):

1. Primary prevention: Measures to prevent the occurrence of illnesses (e.g. immunisations).
2. Secondary prevention: Measures intended to identify illnesses as early as possible. A typical example is cancer prevention screenings.
3. Tertiary prevention: Measures meant to limit effects of illnesses, such as physiotherapy for rheumatoid arthritis.

Strictly speaking, secondary and tertiary preventions are medical interventions and not prevention in a narrower sense, as the illness itself is not prevented. However, at least in the United States, breast cancer screenings play an important role in MCO prevention programmes. Although illnesses cannot be prevented through screenings, the chances of healing are increased through early detection.

The facilitation of behavioural change as well as preventive measures are often implemented in combination with financial steering mechanisms. For example, it is possible that the insured consistently demonstrate that they are not overweight. Obesity, which is often already diagnosed at an early age, usually does not lead to healthcare expenses until much later (e.g. cardiovascular diseases). Most integrated forms of healthcare (→ MCOs) emphasise the role of the insured as a co-producer of their health status. "Maintenance" takes the place of "cure", which can be considered a general trend in the healthcare sector (→ disease management).

Case Study 4: The "Leapfrog Group": Informing Choices, Rewarding Excellence, Getting Healthcare Right

"The problem is not carelessness, but that highly qualified people are working under stress in a setting with many complex processes. Those processes could be improved to reduce avoidable errors." (The Leapfrog Group 2003)

Initial Situation

In 1999, a group of employers came together and discussed ways to improve patient safety (Janus 2003). The report "To Err is Human" from the United States' Institute of Medicine provided the impetus for this dialogue. They found that up to 98,000 of Americans died from preventable medical errors each year (IOM 1999). The Leapfrog Group, which arose from this initiative, was founded by The Business Roundtable, The Robert Wood Johnson Foundation and more than 100 other public and private agencies in November of 2000 and is supported up to this day. The aim of the Leapfrog Group is to create impulses to improve the safety, quality and financial viability of healthcare in the United States. The Leapfrog Group works on the basis of a voluntary reporting programme which aims to mobilise the buying power of the employers in order to make the American healthcare industry aware that great "leaps" in patient safety and value demonstration are recognised and rewarded. In order to do this the organisation works with medical experts; together they work to identify security gaps and provide solutions to avoid preventable errors.

In recent years the organisation received increased attention for its efforts to encourage hospitals to implement evidence-based procedures and, thus, promote patient safety. The Leapfrog Group developed assessment criteria which help in assessing and evaluating their hospitals. The results of the hospitals which participated voluntarily have been published and can thus be used by purchasers of healthcare services to inform themselves about service providers. The Leapfrog Group implemented four indicators as evaluation standards (Leapfrog Group 2013):

1. Computer Physician Order Entry (CPOE) : Physicians enter medication orders in computers that possess error-prevention software.
2. Evidence-Based Hospital Referral (EHR) : Transfer of patients who require complex medical procedures to hospitals that have demonstrated the best survival rates.
3. ICU Physician Staffing (IPS): ICUs (intensive care units) are staffed with physicians who have credentials in critical care medicine.
4. Leapfrog Safe Practices Score: National quality forum which includes 34 methods to reduce hazards in certain processes.

The selection of indicators is based on scientific evidence, feasibility, value demonstration and accessibility. It is expected that the published data

(continued)

Case Study 4 (continued)

refers patients to the hospitals with the highest safety standards. At the same time, pressure is put on the other hospitals to attain similar standards.

Evaluation

Leapfrog Group's approach is taken very seriously by a large number of participants. It has considerably improved cooperations in the healthcare market and has had a significant influence on organisational structures. Today the Leapfrog Group represents around 37 million Americans in all 50 states (Feldman et al. 2012).

It is assumed that the introduction of CPOE has reduced serious prescription errors by 50 %. A 40 % reduction in the mortality rate is attributed to evidence-based hospital referrals and ICU physician staffing. Multiple studies have shown that the safety and quality of hospitals in the United States can be improved by the "leaps" of the Leapfrog Group (Brooke et al. 2008; Pronovost et al. 2006). In total, it is assumed that the initiatives of the Leapfrog Group have the potential to save up to 58,300 lives and prevent 522,000 medication errors annually.

Even when the figures are only approximate, the potential for improvement of patient safety by lowering the amount of medical errors is certainly of great importance. In addition, the Leapfrog method creates "signalling" potential in medicine, which increases transparency and reduces the unequal distribution of information. This development can be furthered by the Leapfrog Group's buying power as well as by the public and political interest in medical outcomes and standardisation.

For further information about Leapfrog: Janus 2003 and www. leapfroggroup.org.

Assessment

All of the measures to reduce the probability of the onset of a disease are mainly unproblematic. It can be assumed that this sector will gain considerable significance because there is more and more knowledge that different illnesses which manifest in old age originate much earlier (→ disease management).

It is also reasonable to combat the "comprehensive insurance" mentality and to require more initiative from the insured. This should not only take the form of financial services but also fundamental "health maintenance". Sophisticated bonus/ malus systems can make a major contribution to this. However, there is also the danger that the system can become counterproductive. Those who have already left the positively sanctioned area because they did not go to the dentist every year, for example, have considerable incentives to behave in a particularly destructive manner, or at least they have no further positive incentives. Therefore, it is crucial that possibilities for "re-entry" are created instead of a long-term punishment.

In the case of instruments which are implemented without financial consequences, such as informational brochures or seminars, the problem always arises that on one hand their effectiveness can barely be evaluated, and on the other hand, from the perspective of the MCOs it only makes sense when there is a high probability that the insured will not switch insurances and reap the "fruits" themselves. This is the fundamental problem: Future investments are only profitable in a static model, i.e. in one in which the insured does not change MCOs.

However, the methods that are particularly convincing at first glance must be carefully assessed for effectiveness. Among these are definitely preventive measures (the return on investment for vaccinations in the United States has been calculated to be between 12 % and 18 % (Andre et al. 2008)). In addition, it must be strongly emphasised that prevention does not necessarily lead to a positive return on investments (ROI). Bodenheimer and Grumbach (1995, p. 149) carried out studies that found clearly negative results regarding the monitoring of high blood pressure and measures to lower cholesterol level.

A critical evaluation of financial management models is particularly difficult. One should always remember that healthcare expenses are not equally distributed, but rather a very small percentage of the population creates considerable expenses while only negligible healthcare expenses arise from the majority of the insured. There are impressive empirical studies in this area. In the United States, 30 % of the entire healthcare expenses can be attributed to 1 % of the insured, 5 % are responsible for 58 % of expenses and the 50 % "healthiest people" create a mere 3 % of expenses (Kühn 1997, p. 4). These figures demonstrate that the role of the insured in creating total expenses is less significant for insurance companies than the risk selection is. Figures from the GEK Gesundheitsreport (GEK healthcare report) show comparable results for Germany (Grobe et al. 2003).

Here it must be emphasised that the management of care for the chronically ill is particularly important for the efficiency of any healthcare system. In this way the enormous potential of disease and case management becomes quite apparent, and at the same time the imminent threat of risk selection and hence the boundaries of competition.

When assuming that out-of-pocket payments should be limited, it becomes apparent that the potential for financial contributions is relatively low. Those who create the majority of the expenses cannot be reached through such steering mechanisms since they have already reached the co-payment limits by the end of January.

Newhouse (1993) examined the effects of co-payments and deductibles in a comprehensive study. The study by the RAND Corporation, which was presented as a health insurance experiment, was meant to primarily examine the effects of HMOs ($\rightarrow$ MCOs), but at the same time it also analyses the effects of deductibles. Newhouse (1993, p. 338) also reaches the hardly surprising conclusion that the higher the out-of-pocket expenses were, the lower the demand was. This is true without exception for all medical service sectors. However, the decisive result is that this apparently did not lead to a degradation of the health status (Newhouse 1993, p. 339).

The exclusion of service sectors through the MCOs is particularly problematic. Even though it is considered a good thing when patients articulate their preferences and conclude individualised contracts based on their individual benefit, there is a considerable risk that insurance companies would filter out more interesting risks (insured persons) and address them separately. The exclusion of service sectors is a suitable management instrument when there is a catalogue of defined services that cannot be excluded. This especially applies to mental illnesses which insurance companies like to exclude because they are relatively easy diagnosed due to medications. From the perspective of the community of insured persons, it is valid that services justified only through individual preferences be excluded (i.e. extreme sports and the healthcare costs which result from them).

In addition, it should not be overlooked that all rates which are based on financial incentives – particularly rates with premium refunds – lead to resources being withdrawn from the system and correspondingly to an overproportional rise in healthcare expenses for the ill, since they do not profit from this due to their situation.

Literature

Amelung, V. E. (2007). Integrierte Versorgung – von Pilotprojekten zur "wirklichen" Regelversorgung. *Gesundheits- und Sozialpolitik, 1*(2), 10–13.

Andre, F. E., Booy, R., Bock, H. L., et al. (2008). Vaccination greatly reduces disease, disability, death and inequity worldwide. *Bulletin of the World Health Organization, 86*(2), 140–146.

Bindman, A. B., Grumbach, K., Vranizan, K., et al. (1998). Selection and exclusion of primary care physicians by managed care organizations. *JAMA: The Journal of the American Medical Association, 279*, 675–679.

Blum, J. D. (1997). Economic credentialing moves from the hospital to managed care. In P. R. Kongstvedt (Ed.), *Readings in managed health care* (pp. 108–115). Gaithersburg: Aspen.

Bodenheimer, T. S., & Grumbach, K. (1995). *Understanding health policy – A clinical approach*. Norwalk: Appleton & Lange.

Brooke, S., Perler, A., Dmonici, F., et al. (2008). Reduction of in-hospital mortality among California hospitals meeting Leapfrog evidence-based standards for abdominal aortic aneurysm repair. *Journal of Vascular Surgery, 47*(6), 1155–1164.

Claxton, G., DiJulio, B., Whitmore, H., et al. (2011). Health benefits in 2010: Premium rise modestly, workers pay more toward coverage. *Health Affairs, 29*(10), 1942–1950.

Crossen, F. J., & Tollen, L. A. (2010). *Partners in health, how physician and hospitals can be accountable together*. San Francisco: Jossey-Bass.

Feldman, R., Chan, H., Kralewsky, J., et al. (1990). Effects of HMOs on the creation of competitive markets for hospital services. *Journal of Health Economics, 9*, 207–222.

Feldman, H. R., Alexander, R., Greenberg, M. J., Jaffee-Ruiz, M., McBride, A., McClure, M., & Smith, T. D. (2012). *Nursing leadership: A concise encyclopaedia* (2nd ed.). New York: Springer.

Feldstein, P. J. (1993). *Health care economics* (4th ed.). Albany: Delmar Publishers.

Goldman, D. P., Joyce, G. F., Escarce, J. J., et al. (2004). Pharmacy benefits and the use of drugs by chronically ill. *JAMA: The Journal of the American Medical Association, 291*(19), 2344–2350.

Hajen, L., Paetow, H., & Schuhmacher, H. (2011). *Gesundheitsökonomie: Strukturen – Methoden – Praxis* (6th ed.). Stuttgart: Kohlhammer.

Henderson, J. W. (2011). *Health economics and policy* (5th ed.). South Western: Educational Publishing.

IOM [Institute of Medicine]. (1999). *To err is human: Building a safer health system*. Washington, DC: Institute of Medicine.

IOM [Institute of Medicine]. (2001). *Crossing the quality chasm: A new health system for the 21st century*. Washington, DC: Institute of Medicine.

Janus, K. (2003). *Managing health care in private organizations. Transaction costs, cooperation and modes of organization in the value chain*. Frankfurt am Main: P. Lang.

Jensen, G. A., Morrisey, M. A., & Gaffney, S., et al. (1997, January/February). The new dominance of managed care: Insurance trends in the 1990s. *Health Affairs, 16*(1), 125–136.

Kazmir, J. L. (2008). *Health care law*. New York: Delmar Publications.

KFF [Kaiser Family Foundation]. (2012). *Employer health benefits 201, annual survey*. Menlo Park/Chicago: Kaiser Foundation & HRET. http://ehbs.kff.org/pdf/2012/8345.pdf. Accessed 21 Jan 2013.

Knight, W. (1998). *Managed care – What is it and how it works*. Gaithersburg: Aspen.

Koenig, H. G., King, D. E., & Carson, V. B. (2012). *Handbook of religion and health* (2nd ed.). New York: Oxford University Press.

Kongstvedt, P. R. (2013). *Essentials of managed health care* (6th ed.). Burlington: Jones & Bartlett Learning.

Kühn, H. (1997). *Managed care – Medizin zwischen kommerzieller Bürokratie und Integrierter Versorgung* (WZB-Paper), Berlin.

Leapfrog Group. (2013). *What does Leapfrog ask hospitals?* http://www.leapfroggroup.org/patients/hospitals_asked_what. Accessed 15 Feb 2013.

McGlynn, E. A., Asch, S. M., Adams, J., et al. (2003). The quality of health care delivered to adults in the United States. *The New England Journal of Medicine, 348*(26), 2635–2645.

Newhouse, J. P. (1993). *Free for all? Lessons from the RAND health insurance experiment* (2nd ed.). Boston: Harvard University Press.

OECD [Organisation for Economic Cooperation and Development]. (2011). *OECD reviews of health systems: Switzerland*. Paris: OECD.

OECD [Organisation for Economic Cooperation and Development]. (2012). *OECD statistics on health*. http://stats.oecd.org/index.aspx?DataSetCode=HEALTH_STAT. Accessed 23 Feb 2012.

Peden, A. H. (2012). *Comparative health information management* (3rd ed.). Delmar: Cengage Learning.

Porter, M. E., & Guth, C. (2012). *Chancen für das deutsche Gesundheitssystem: Von Partikular-interesse zu mehr Patientennutzen*. Berlin/Heidelberg: Springer/Gabler.

Porter, M., & Teisberg, E. (2006). *Redefining health care – Creating value-based competition on results*. Boston: Harvard Business School Press.

Pronovost, P., Thompson, D. A., Holzmueller, C. G., et al. (2006). Impact of the Leapfrog Group's intensive care unit physician staffing standard. *Journal of Critical Care, 22*, 89–96.

Shi, L. (2007). *Managing human resources in health care organizations*. Sudbury: Jones and Bartlett.

Shi, L., & Singh, D. A. (2012). *Delivering healthcare in America: A systems approach* (5th ed.). Sudbury: Jones and Bartlett.

Solberg, L. I. (1998). Prevention in managed care. In P. R. Kongstvedt & D. W. Plocher (Eds.), *Best practice in medical management*. Gaithersburg: Aspen.

Sorkin, A. L. (1992). *Health economics* (3rd ed.). New York: Lexington Books.

Waldman, J. D., Yourstone, S. A., & Smith, H. L. (2003). Learning curves in health care. *Health Care Management Review, 28*(1), 41–54.

Zelman, W., & Berenson, R. A. (1998). *The managed care blues & how to cure them*. Washington, DC: Georgetown University Press.

Zwanziger, J., & Meirowitz, A. (1998). Strategic factors in hospitals for HMO and PPO networks. In M. A. Morsey (Ed.), *Managed care and changing health care markets* (pp. 77–94). Washington, DC: AEI Press.

Zweifel, P., Breyer, F., & Kifmann, M. (2009). *Health economics* (2nd ed.). Berlin/Heidelberg: Springer.

Compensation Systems

10

10.1 Foundation

The design of compensation systems for service providers is an essential control instrument in managed care. In order to better understand this instrument and its effects, the basic principles of compensation systems will first be generally described (see Fig. 10.1) so that the managed care compensation systems can be outlined in more detail.

A compensation system for health services should primarily fulfil the following **goals** and **functions**:

1. The control and incentive function of a compensation system should motivate the provider to offer services economically and according to demand. Compensation systems should thus be developed in such a way that they include incentives which reward efforts to lower costs and improve the quality of services. In addition, they should counteract the provision of services that are not required (risk sharing). This is based on the behavioural hypothesis that a physician's actions are not only based on the interest of the patient, but are also significantly influenced by financial motives.
2. The distribution role of a compensation system is meant to guarantee health service providers' income based on performance, while at the same time preventing too high a financial burden for service purchasers (payers of premiums, fees or taxes). Among other things, that requires compensation regulations in which the financing risks are fairly divided between the service providers and the service purchasers.
3. The innovation function of a compensation system should foster the implementation of new methods of diagnosis and therapy that improve the quality of care and the cost-effectiveness of new medical products, or at least not impede them.

In order to be effective, a compensation system must also exhibit a high level of acceptance among the service providers. In addition, it should be practical and transparent in order to keep the administrative and control costs low. Finally, a compensation system should be able to adapt to necessary changes.

V.E. Amelung, *Healthcare Management*, Springer Texts in Business and Economics, DOI 10.1007/978-3-642-38712-8_10, © Springer-Verlag Berlin Heidelberg 2013

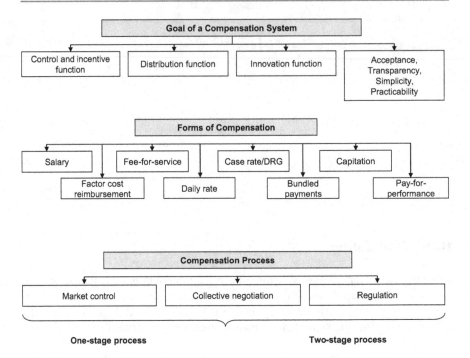

Fig. 10.1 Compensation systems

A compensation system is composed of **forms of compensation** as well as goals. These factors determine the unit of compensation which serves as the basis of assessment. Whether the services are outpatient or inpatient, the forms of compensation can be essentially traced back to the following ideal types of forms or basic forms:

1. Salary: The physicians receive a fixed salary for the services which they provide on behalf of a healthcare organisation (a hospital, a group practice, an MCO). The unit of compensation is the time period (basic salary for fixed time period).[1]
2. Factor cost reimbursement: The service providers receive compensation in the amount of the costs actually accrued in the treatment of their patients. The unit of compensation is the consumption factors (work, use of equipment or materials). In these cases the compensation follows retrospectively (cost-recovery principle).[2] The invoicing can be carried out on the basis of individual services or (retrospective) care rates.

---

[1] A basic salary for a fixed time period is also possible for hospital services. In this case, the hospital receives a budget, for example for a year, from which it has to finance all costs. In practice, however, hospital budgets are combined with other forms of compensation.

[2] In contrast to that, the remaining compensation forms are referred to as "prospective compensation forms" or "prices".

3. Fee-for-service: The service providers receive a certain compensation for each individual service provided to their patients.
4. Daily rate: The service provider receives a flat rate payment per day of inpatient stay.
5. Case rate and DRG: The service providers receive a flat rate payment for every treated case. These can also be differentiated according to foreseeable effort, i.e. according to age, severity of the illness or similar risk factors.
6. Bundled payments: The services necessary for the treatment of an individual case can be bundled into complexes – laboratory services, administrative services or operative services – and compensated with flat rate payments.
7. Capitation: The service providers receive a flat rate determined in advance for each insured person to whose treatment he is contractually bound. From this flat rate he must finance all services provided.[3] The flat rate can be differentiated, i.e. foreseeable differences in the service provider's use (based on age, sex or morbidity) can be considered when determining the amount of the capitation. In order to limit the service providers' losses or gains, deviations from the calculated expenses can also be evened out after the fact.
8. Pay-for-performance: The service providers receive a compensation amount corresponding to the success of his work. In a borderline case, this process implies that no payment is made in the case of failure, making the physician subject to considerable financial risk. The performance of the treatment is also not easy to measure. For that reason, this form of compensation is only used in combination with other forms – particularly capitation, case rate or salary.

The healthcare systems in most countries are characterised by mixed forms of compensation.

It is common in the managed care system that a service providers conclude provision agreements with multiple MCOs, which require different types of compensation, so that it cannot base its actions on one form of compensation. The general problem of complex compensation systems is that the control and incentive effects can counteract each other and it is difficult to maintain an overview.

Along with the form of compensation, a compensation system also consists of the **compensation process**, which helps to determine the type and amount of remuneration.

The form of compensation can first be determined via competitive market processes, i.e. through individual conclusions of contracts between a service provider and the service purchaser on the market. Those involved individually and selectively negotiate the compensation form as well as the amount for the contractually agreed-upon services ($\rightarrow$ selective contracts). One variation of the competitive determination of the amount of compensation is competitive bidding. Here, the

---

[3] The reference value is the potential patient. Sometimes the term is also used for the patient rate: a flat rate for the contacting patient. This is not the case here. Likewise, this does not refer to the capitation, which is discussed in the sense of financing healthcare.

conditions for a base of insured persons' care by a physician or hospital are tendered and bids for the amount of compensation are accepted. The most favourable provider is awarded the contract.

Even when it is clear that the lowest possible price is paid, it should be emphasised that considerable effort must be made in order to ensure quality. In addition, one must be aware that in such a model the quality that is actually delivered is not the highest quality possible but rather the lowest quality which is still acceptable.

Forms of compensation and the amount of compensation can also be established through state interventions (regulation). Examples for this include state tariffs or limiting the compensation amount through the use of a budget cap.

Furthermore, the compensation process can be administered by the service providers' self-governing bodies, and by the service purchasers (health insurances). The compensation amount and form are determined by bilateral negotiations between the associations (principle of collective negotiation).

In managed care systems in the United States, the basic principle is that both the form and the amount of compensation is individually negotiated between service providers and MCOs. However, it should be noted that regulating interventions in contractual freedom through laws and legal practise also exist here.

As already highlighted in the introduction, a main reason for the so-called "managed care backlash" lies in the excessive changes in the compensation systems. It clearly demonstrated that the nearly complete transfer of the financial risk to the service providers through the lump-sum compensation system is not target-oriented and has considerably destabilised the system. In the following sections these aspects will be explained more extensively.

10.2   Forms of Compensation

In the managed care environment, a wide range of compensation forms (reimbursement systems) have been implemented: salary, capitation, fee-for-service, bundled payments, case rate, reimbursement of factor costs and outcome-based or performance-based compensation, and pay-for-performance (P4P).

In practise, one usually finds a combination of different forms. This is not primarily justified by the fact that these should have been combined, but rather by the fact that the systems grew (e.g. through acquisition) and the opportunity did not arise to standardise the compensation systems. In addition, the organisation of the compensation system is largely dependent on the bargaining power of the partners, which can also be extremely varied within a system.

In MCOs, compensation systems with capitations and performance-based compensation are very significant. Many authors consider compensation with capitations to be a fundamental feature of managed care which separates this model of care from the traditional insurance system since the costs are reimbursed on the basis of fee-for-service.[4]

The forms of compensation for providers will first be introduced and then evaluated in the following section.

Salary

Physicians receive fixed monthly salaries primarily in the staff model HMOs (77.8 %, Sanofi 2012). However, in certain → network model HMOs a general capitation was negotiated, although within the confines of the group salaries were often the chosen form of compensation. Salaries are usually combined with a bonus system or even profit sharing, which allows for the participation of physicians in the economic success of an organisation. The profits of an HMO or just the medical costs can serve as reference values. Since the physicians themselves can only monitor the medical cost, these costs are better suited as reference values. A bonus is granted when the planned costs for the year or quarter are decided. The bonus for each physician is furthermore often linked to the fulfilment of other criteria for success (→ pay-for-performance).

Assessment

When physicians are hired and paid with a fixed salary, no incentives emerge for the unnecessary expansion of the volume of service. They are employees of an MCO which determines their range of tasks as they issue their job descriptions. There is a general interest in measures to maintain the patient's health with this form of compensation. Therefore, this compensation form ideally enables attentive and treatment-based care (Collier 2012). As far as administration is concerned, it is also a relatively simple compensation system. But there is a danger that waiting times could occur and patients will be referred to other service providers. For this reason, salaries are often combined with bonus systems.

Since the physician is an employee of an organisation, the services are dependent on the effectiveness of the organisation's internal control system and the company culture. This is why general statements about the benefits and drawbacks of this form of compensation are difficult to make.

---

[4] The term "fee-for-service" means a form of compensation in the strict sense. In a wider sense this term is used to refer to the traditional form of insurance.

Factor Cost Reimbursement

In the reimbursement system, providers are reimbursed for the costs incurred. The financial risk is carried solely by the service purchaser in this compensation form. Thus, it is necessary to monitor how reasonable the expenses are by proofing costs as well as performance.

This compensation form does not provide incentives for providers to produce economically. On the contrary, as inefficiency is a part of the expenses of the services provided, there is even an interest in increasing costs. This management interest is inevitably less oriented towards preventing costs than verifying and justifying them. However, monitoring appropriate costs is difficult because expenses are not an objective amount, but are rather subject to a certain creative freedom in their planning ($\rightarrow$ introduction). When all costs are reimbursed, however, there is an incentive to introduce expensive innovations in medical technology.

Assessment

Due to the negative incentive structures outlined in the aforementioned section, the expense reimbursement system is becoming less and less important. It can be primarily seen as a relic of the traditional systems of care. Nevertheless, there are sectors in which cost reimbursement can be useful, such as treatments in experimental medicine and in select service calculations for major facilities with maximal healthcare. In the former cases, other systems of compensation simply would not be efficient due to the innovative nature of the services.

Fee-for-service

The fee-for-service compensation is actually uncommon for the philosophy of managed care, since the morbidity risk and the moral hazard risk are assumed by the insurance company. However, this form of compensation is also widely used by MCOs. All forms of HMOs are compensated to a large extent through the fee-for-service compensation (Sanofi 2012).

The fee-for-service compensation is often additionally linked to criteria for success and combined with withholds in order to monitor the inherent tendency to unnecessarily expand services. In addition, there are fee caps in place mainly in $\rightarrow$ PPOs as an instrument to limit the increase in services. That means that the overstepping of planned costs – which also cannot be covered by withholds – leads to a linear reduction in fee-for-service amounts.

The fee-for-service compensation is based on the costs of the provision of services. This can depend on a medical practice's actual costs, which the physician invoices largely based on his own judgement (UCR: "usual, customary, and reasonable"). The compensation would then be the rough equivalent of compensation according to factor costs. It is compared with average values in order to assess whether the amount invoiced corresponds to UCR guidelines.

Between the various incentives, a fee-for-service compensation based on standardised costs (tariff system) is more practical. In managed care, compensation forms are used where the relative consumption of resources of a service is determined by points which are then separately calculated into a sum of money by multiplying the points with a conversion factor (RVS: relative value scale and resource-based RVS).[5] The adjustment of the point values follows according to the rate of inflation. Originally meant for the compensation of service providers by Medicare, the resource-based RVS compensation forms are also increasingly assumed by MCOs. While Medicare uses a conversion factor which is specified annually, private insurances use various conversion factors, for example for primary medical and surgical services, in order to recruit specialists with a higher compensation (Webster et al. 2007, p. 145; Knight 1998).

Assessment

Those physicians working to maximise their income and therefore acting rationally will try to increase individual services by raising the number of cases or the sum per case. Since the necessity of the provision of services in individual cases can barely be assessed, the physician is able to provide more services than necessary and assert his individual interest in a higher income. Further room to manoeuvre results from an appreciation of services (upcoding), in which the simple service provided is not invoiced, but rather the comparatively more complex service, or when a single service is split into multiple partial services which can be invoiced (unbundling).

Positive incentives are present when the costs per individual service are lowered. In practice, however, it is not possible for the prices of single services to reflect the actual costs of a medical practice due to the dynamic of technological advance. As a rule, the prices deviate from the cost structures, even when adjustments are periodically made to the tariffs. Therefore physicians have an incentive to provide services with prices relatively higher than the costs (cream skimming). This is particularly the case with services that require a large amount of medical equipment, since technical medical advances are particularly important in this context.

Daily Rates (Per Diem)

Daily rates compensate each day of a hospital stay, independent from the actual costs accrued per day. However, the lump sum can be differentiated in order to accommodate the various resources necessary: Instead of compensating the same

---

[5] This procedure is similar to the remuneration procedure for outpatient services in public health insurance in Germany.

amount per day, it can be lowered with the length of stay (degressive rate), as the costs of treatment per day also sink according to the length of stay. This flat rate can likewise be differentiated by unit or according to the type of hospital service provided, by compensating different rates for hotel services and the medical care services.

Daily rates should be differentiated according to the type of hospital and the varied case structure resulting from this. The basis of the differentiation is the formation of groups of the same kind of hospitals. These should be formed so that cost differences within the group are only due to differences in cost-effectiveness and not to differences in the case structure or the range of tasks. The respective groups can then be assigned to the same daily rate. In the United States the formation of groups takes place by comparing the same types of hospitals, the peer group (Carter et al. 1994).

Whereas hospitals have an incentive to reduce the costs per day, the same does not apply to the length of stay or the number of cases based on daily rates. The tendency to extend the number of days spent in the hospital can be limited through budgeting. The following relation applies:

$$\text{Budget} = \text{Daily Rate} \times \text{Planned Number of Cases} \times \text{Planned Average Length of Stay}$$

The budget of a period is the product of the case rate and the number of days spent in the hospital, which are respectively a product of the planned number of cases and the average planned length of stay. The daily rate should cover the planned costs per day. The costs are comprised of the variable costs, which differ according to the number of days, and the fixed costs, which remain unchanged. Thus, hospitals have an incentive to reduce the costs per day below the amount of the planned costs (economic efficiency).

Without budget limits, the hospital has an interest in raising the number of cases with this particular form of compensation, since while the variable costs increase, the fixed costs stay constant. Thus, the costs per day sink (fixed cost degression), while the daily rates remain constant. A revenue surplus then emerges. This effect is even more pronounced when proper case management or the general postponing of discharge from the hospital increases the average length of stay. The extension of length of stay lowers the costs per day not only due to fixed cost degression, but also because the variable costs per day also sink according to the length of stay.

The introduction of a budget is meant to limit these undesired effects. If deficits arise between the planned budget and the actual costs at the end of an accounting period because hospitals did not operate cost effectively or the lengths of stay were longer than planned, the hospital must assume the additional costs. However, it can keep the surpluses. In this case the hospital consequently assumes the financial risk of economic inefficiency and fluctuations in occupancy.

Assessment

With the daily rate, the hospital has an interest to reduce the costs per day. However, without budgeting, an incentive develops to extend single episodes of hospitalisation by increasing the number of cases and the average length of stay. As the daily rate is constant, the revenue increases while the costs per day sink due to the fixed cost degression effect. In addition, when the length of stay increases, the variable costs per day also sink. These effects can be managed in part by using a degressive daily rate or a budgeting of costs, however, problems arise here in the detailed management due to the information asymmetry to the benefit of the hospital. That means that the service purchaser does not possess the knowledge of the cost structure necessary to plan the degressive daily hospital rates and the balancing of the budget. Hence, the most significant monitoring instrument is the → utilisation review. Generally speaking, with the exception of psychiatry, daily rates have become considerably less important since they have exhibited major disadvantages and only minimal advantages.

Case Rates and Diagnosis Related Groups (DRGs)

In case rates, the individual case is the reference base for compensation. Due to the great discrepancies in the cost of treatment, when designing a compensation system based on case rates it is necessary to differentiate case rates. In doing so, different criteria can be used: The type of illness according to the main diagnosis, the seriousness of the illness or the complications which can be expected, the stage of the illness, the type of treatment and the age or sex of the patients.

In order to prevent excessive differentiation where each individual case is assigned a case rate, implying high administration costs and resulting in a cost reimbursement principle, patients should be classified into groups. The exact definition and differentiation of homogeneous groups is crucial to this process, as that is the only way to ensure a clear assignment of the individual case to a potential group. In addition to clinical similarity among the cases, an equal consumption of resources should also be considered.

The clinical similarity of the cases can be guaranteed by basing an illness classification system on the differentiation of groups, such as the ICD (international classification of diseases), a classification system that is periodically redacted by the World Health Organisation. Secondly, a differentiation can be made according to the treatment, for example according to the type of operation based on the ICPM (International Classification of Procedures in Medicine).

In a further step, the potential cases requiring the same amount of resources should be brought together in a group so that a uniform case rate can be assigned to them. The calculation of the relative cost of resources ("weights") can either be based on the statistical average values of costs or on the target costs aimed at optimal treatment paths determined by experts. However, actual values have the disadvantage that they perpetuate existing economic inefficiencies.

Case rates based on **DRGs** (diagnosis-related groups) have a particular signifi-cance as a case-orientated form of compensation in MCOs. DRGs belong to a diagnosis-based classification system which, along with the main diagnosis, takes into account the presence of secondary diseases and complications, the age of the patients and the type of treatment (operative or conservative) (Fetter et al. 1980). Originally intended as an instrument for medical documentation and quality assur-ance, it was first implemented as a case-related form of compensation with 468 DRGs for Medicare patients – currently there are 746 DRGs used by Medicare and 1,123 DRGs in Germany (Fleßa 2013) – and then it was increasingly adopted and expanded by MCOs (Cleverley et al. 2010).

The weights for the DRG-based case rates are calculated using statistical average values which are largely based on the length of stay. In this process the individual service providers make corrections to their systems. The prices of the case rates are determined through different procedures and vary from region to region and hospital to hospital (Cleverley et al. 2010; Carter et al. 1994). When a case exceeds the maximum of the length of stay or results in exceedingly high case costs, hospitals can invoice based on daily rates or moreover can be reimbursed for excess costs in order to protect themselves from financial risk. Thus, the hospital only bears the risk up to a pre-defined threshold.

Assessment

Case rates based on DRGs offer an incentive for the economical utilisation of resources, particularly to decrease the use of diagnostic assistance and shorten the length of stay per case. The savings through these measures can be considerable in individual categories of diagnosis.

One problem is the classification of patients with multiple diseases which, as has been mentioned various times, poses a considerable challenge to their care because the DRGs are based on the classification according to the main diagnosis. The error rate is quite high in these cases (Lee et al. 2011). Closely related to this is the problem of upgrading, i.e. patients are placed in case groups with a higher compen-sation which leads to a blurring of the case group definition (DRG creep) which is hard to avoid. In addition, cases can be unnecessarily divided into multiple single cases in order to attain higher total revenue. The risk selection of patients (cream skimming) cannot be ruled out when high-cost cases are turned away or referred because the costs of their care are unlikely to be covered by the case rate. In addition, there is a risk that patients may be discharged earlier, only in order to be hospitalised again as a new case. This problem of disproportionate referral is particularly significant for university clinics. With their superior care services, they are mainly confronted with the problem of having a higher than average case mix and being unfairly compensated by the DRG system. Correspondingly, in the Australian DRG system considerable sections of the DRG compensation system have been removed.

First and foremost, the decrease in quality has been criticised, for example discharging a patient too early ("quicker and sicker") or omitting necessary treatments. This can also be related to a cost shift in other systems of care (outpatient care, nursing and inpatient care institutions). For this reason → case management and concurrent review (→ utilisation review) are necessary in this system of compensation.

In addition, it must be considered that shortening the length of stay lowers the occupancy, so that the hospital will then attempt to increase the number of cases in order to cover the high fixed costs of a hospital. With case rates there is also the tendency to increase the number of patients – particularly those with a short length of stay. In managed care this can be monitored with a concurrent review (→ utilisation review). The integration in a budget can also limit the increase of cases.

Unlike the daily rate, a compensation system based on a case rate is associated with higher administration costs for the hospital and MCO (classifying and monitoring the classification of patients). The monitoring function, however, can potentially be carried out without additional costs in the scope of the → utilisation review or the → case management.

Bundled Payments

Bundled payments are a form of prospective compensation. They typically compensate services provided in connection with a specific episode of care with a lump sum. In contrast to the case rates (→ DRGs), which apply only to inpatient hospital stays, compensation through bundled payments includes additional stages of care. Depending on the specific arrangement, they can bundle acute treatments with preoperative diagnosis and also include rehabilitation and skilled nursing care, for example (Guterman et al. 2009). A further component allows the incorporation of treatment with medications into the bundle. For this reason, bundled payments are useful for overcoming the organisational separation of healthcare sectors and to facilitate cooperation between service providers. This compensation form aims to achieve higher quality and at the same time reduce healthcare expenses.

Even though bundled payments are considered relatively new, they make use of well known management instruments (Rosenthal 2008). Based on experience with other lump sum compensation systems, a series of requirements can be deduced which contribute to high quality and low cost care. First, bundled payments must adequately reflect the resources used for the treatment. A calculation of the prospective rate on the basis of actual costs should not be carried out, as this perpetuates economic inefficiency in the form of over-, under- and misuse. For this reason, existing models determine the expected consumption of resources for an episode of care according to evidence-based guidelines, and base the amount of compensation on these (Rosenthal 2008, p. 1199; Mechanic and Altman 2009). A further requirement is distributing the total compensation for the treatment among the providers involved according to the services provided. This also determines who benefits from potential savings (Chernew 2010, p. 1146). Here the use of guidelines is also key, as there is otherwise a risk that individual providers take on profitable parts of the procedure and avoid less profitable parts. In addition, previous experience with prospective compensation warns of possible misdirected incentives through bundled payments, such as the incentive of risk selection of patients (cream skimming) or the danger of a reduction in quality of services (Frisina and Cacace 2009). The transfer of individual services in service sectors that do not use bundled payments also poses a risk in this specific compensation form (Guterman et al. 2009). A series of these weak points can be addressed with relatively moderate modifications. Selection incentives, for example, are reduced by the risk adjustment of the rates, such as differentiation according to age and sex. Along with monitoring, a combination with other compensation systems, such as performance-based systems, is promising for quality assurance. In this case, the lump sum compensation through bundled payments is increased by a percentage calculated on the basis of the measured quality of structures, process or outcome (Rosenthal 2008). Thus, hybrid reimbursement systems that are a combination of multiple forms of compensation prove to be relatively more efficient than the pure forms (see Cacace 2010).

In the case of a fee-for-service with a capped budget, the incentive to provide unnecessary services is reduced since an unjustified expansion of services is associated with higher costs and no increase in profit. However, a "hamster wheel" effect" can arise. With the expectation of a possible linear devaluation of prices, more services are provided in the hopes that colleagues will restrain themselves (strategic behaviour). In this arrangement, the size of the group of physicians is important. When too small, the illness risks of the insured persons cannot be sufficiently pooled. A coincidental accumulation of patients with serious illnesses leads to an early exhaustion of the budget. On the other hand, if the group is too large, the individual physician is not aware of the other physicians included in the budget and, thus, no group pressure develops to encourage efficient behaviour.

Assessment

The evaluation focuses on the Geisinger Health System in the United States, which admittedly is an example of a particularly well-functioning model. As a vertically and horizontally integrated healthcare and insurance system, the Geisinger Health System includes the provision of a wide spectrum of services as well as their financing. Geisinger has compensated coronary artery bypass operations with bundled payments since 2006 through its ProvenCare programme. Beyond the operation and related hospital stay, the compensation includes all preoperative measures as well as postoperative follow-up treatment for up to 90 days. The amount of the basic compensation is calculated according to evidence-based guidelines. A surcharge is added to this which, based on empirical values, is calculated from half of the average compensation for complications. Therefore, the payment still assumes that it is possible to cut the complication rate in half. For quality purposes, the medical staff agreed upon 40 evidence-based procedures that must be performed on each patient (Rosenthal 2008; Mechanic and Altman 2009). After the first year of introduction, the evaluations actually reported an increase in quality as well as a reduction of the treatment costs through ProvenCare. After completion of the first year, 100 % of the patients had received the full set of 40 recommended quality service components. Their length of stay sank by 16 % and there was a simultaneous 10 % decline in readmissions rates. This led to 5.2 % lower hospital charges (Casale et al. 2007). More recent data presented by Geisinger even measured a 44 % decline in readmission rates within 18 months. Due to these very positive results, Geisinger expanded its recipe for success to treat additional diseases (Mechanic and Altman 2009). However, it should still be emphasised that according to expert opinion the success of ProvenCare is due to the unique structure of Geisinger to a large extent. This includes the high degree of integration, which also incorporates the financing of services, as well as their equipment with a highly efficient, computerised information and documentation system (Lee 2007). Thus, this model cannot be arbitrarily transferred.

Capitation

A recent study by Sanofi (2012) shows that the capitation compensation is implemented in almost all forms of HMOs. Particularly primary care physicians are compensated with capitations. Thus, 65.6 % of the IPA model HMOs, 60.2 % of the network model HMOs, 82.8 % of the group model HMOs and 55.6 % of the staff model HMOs make use of capitation (Sanofi 2012), whereby it must be emphasised that nearly all of the different systems can be implemented simultaneously, making it difficult to draw conclusions. In comparison to the Sanofi study from 2002, the number of HMOs that use capitations has increased significantly.

In the capitation system, the physician (or his medical organisation) receives a monthly lump sum per insured person, to whose care he is contractually obliged. In this way, risks that arise in the care of an insured person (moral hazard[6] of the insured person, risk of morbidity) are transferred to the service providers. They then partly assume the insuring function of the MCO (risk sharing). Depending on the way the contract is designed, this can result in a complete transfer of risk (risk delegation).

---

[6] This term refers to the risk of a change in behaviour of the insured person after the conclusion of the contract (too little prevention, inappropriate utilisation of services), in the furthest sense also changes in the behaviour of service providers ($\rightarrow$ introduction).

The calculation of capitation rates requires that the scope of the services provided by the physician be defined. In principle, the capitation can include all services necessary for the care of the insured person, including preventive and inpatient services as well as annex services (laboratory and radiology services or drugs). In this case, the physician bears the entire risk for all services provided and initiated (full risk capitation or global capitation).

In practise, however, certain services are often separated from the capitation, such as inpatient services or referrals to specialists (carve-outs). These services can in turn be compensated by the MCO in different forms (capitation, fee-for-service, case rates) (Kongstvedt 2013).

Although the goal of capitation is to transfer all risks to the service provider, the risks inherent in this form of compensation are often shared between the service providers and the MCO.[7] In this context, risks are on the one hand deviations in utilisation behaviour and in the morbidity of the insured persons in comparison with planned dimensions. In this case, the actual costs are higher (or lower) than the calculated costs, so that losses (or surpluses) can arise for the service provider. The smaller the pool of insured persons (panel) is, the greater the risk is for the service provider. On the other hand, the MCO faces the risk that the physician may transfer higher costs (cost shifting) to the outsourced services. This moral hazard behaviour becomes appealing for the physician when these types of services are compensated according to fee-for-service, since costs can be better transferred in that system.

A common form of risk sharing is **withholds**, which act as a form of reinsurance. The withholds form a percentage of the monthly capitations (e.g. 20 %) which are not initially paid, but rather used to finance excess expenses for further services, if necessary (referral to specialist, hospitalisation).

Another procedure is the setting up of risk pools (**capitation pools**). Capitation pools or risk pools are separate budgets for non-primary medical services performed by the primary physician such as specialist services, hospital services and annex services. The budgets are comprised of capitations for the given services. These are not initially paid to the service provider but rather represent a balancing of risks much like the withholds. If the actual expenses for a certain type of service remain under the given budget, these are first used to finance deficits in other budgets. Subsequently, outstanding surpluses are paid; physicians are responsible for compensating the remaining budget deficits. However, only the physicians with a positive balance in their own budgets receive payments.[8] That means that deficits are carried by all physicians together, and surpluses are individually distributed (Kongstvedt 2013).

If withholds and capitation pools are primarily concerned with limiting the risk of the MCO, then a limitation of the service provider's risk can be achieved by setting caps for unplanned excess expenses, such as expenses due to costly

---

[7] This adjustment to risks ex-post should be differentiated from the ex-ante consideration of the risks in the insurance structure by differentiating capitations (risk adjustment).

[8] In addition, criteria for success can be taken into account here.

individual cases (outliers). If these are exceeded, then the MCO bears the risk – in part or in full – by putting these excess costs in a fund (**stop loss**). The stop loss limits are often connected to the individual physician, whereby these may be differentiated according to the size of the panel. A higher limit can be set for physicians with a larger panel, as random influences can be better distributed in such cases (Kongstvedt 2001). Insurance for expensive individual cases can also be transferred to commercial insurance companies.

Assessment

In the case of higher physician compensation with capitations, the physician is motivated to act efficiently and to only perform services himself or arrange the services that he believes to be truly necessary (Amelung et al. 2005), since each additional action lowers his net income and reduces his leisure time. Capitations also facilitate the continuity of patients' care and require only relatively simple administration.

In this context, however, critics warn against a tendency towards insufficient care of patients. There is a justified danger of cost shifting and risk selection. However, a mechanism inherent to the system as well as the possibility of counter-active measures argue against these concerns: Firstly, because only a healthy patient is profitable for a physician in this system. Secondly, the MCO has the opportunity to carry out quality and service controls and to directly link the positive results with the compensation system or to publish them. This leads to a competitive disadvantage for the physicians who provide poor care to their patients. In this respect, this form of compensation theoretically promises relatively good results in terms of the costs as well as the quality of care.

However, in practise it has been shown that the scope of capitations is smaller; respectively, it has shrunk considerably (Robinson and Casalino 2001; Janus 2003) and its implementation requires much more effort than was originally thought. The use of capitation requires a considerable sense of judgement and it must not be ignored that the individual physician's as well as the physician group's ability to assume risk is very limited. Particularly problematic is the fact that the capitation rates were continually lowered until a point at which the service providers had to terminate contracts more or less out of necessity, since their costs were no longer covered. The results showed de facto that capitation is only suitable for large risk groups. That is why the associations of statutory health insurance physicians receive capitations for the outpatient sector, but not for the compensation of individual physicians. Thus, the problem is not the concept, but rather the appropriate application of capitations in the correct setting.

Due to their particular significance for managed care, pay-for-performance (P4P) and the closely related public reporting will be separately considered in the next section.

10.3   Pay-for-Performance (P4P) and Public Reporting

Pay-for-Performance

The compensation form pay-for-performance (P4P) is based on the achievement of pre-defined goals and the measure of their particular achievement level in comparison to the amount of compensation for the service provider. These goals, which are ideally developed by the service providers and purchasers together, may be related to the quality of the outcome, satisfaction, or other objective dimensions such as structure and process quality, patient satisfaction or efficiency criteria. An ex-ante agreement of binding and measurable goals is crucial to the pay-for-performance system and can have an immediate impact on a portion of compensation.

The starting point for the development of the concept was the release of the report "Crossing the Quality Chasm" (IOM 2001). The Institute of Medicine described the low observance of guidelines and quality standards in healthcare and that treatment costs varied starkly among different regions. They further elaborated that this could be counteracted with a quality-orientated compensation system[9] (IOM 2006a).

Pay-for-performance is a model motivating service providers to provide higher quality services and thus improve the patients' treatment results. This is based on the assumption that discrepancies in the quality of care by the individual providers are quantifiable. It enables the service providers who attain above-average quality to be better compensated than those with a lower quality (Qaseem et al. 2010, p. 366; Amelung and Zahn 2009, p. 25). Ideally the P4P models consist of a form of performance-based payment and public reporting: Hence, non-monetary incentives are added to P4P.

The rapid growth of this concept in the United States shows that it has become one of the most important managed care instruments in recent years (see Fig. 10.2). More than 50 % of HMOs as well as the Medicaid programme have integrated pay-for-performance into their compensation systems. Since 2006, there have also been pay-for-performance pilot projects in the public Medicare programmes (Gemmil 2007, p. 22).

Design of the Model

Due to the different objectives, the design of pay-for-performance programmes varies considerably. The concept has to be seen as a dynamic system that must be adjusted to suit the needs of the patients and service providers. However, there are four key elements present in every approach (Tanenbaum 2009, p. 720).

The central parameter is the definition of quality indicators that are to be measured. The development of valid indicators poses the greatest challenge

---

[9] Performance-based compensation, success-based compensation or pay-for-performance are referred to as synonyms. Quality-based compensation, however, already focuses on the decisive factor in the word.

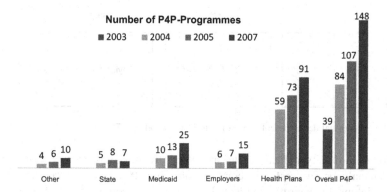

Fig. 10.2 Number of P4P programmes in the United States (according to Baker and Delbanco (2007))

for the pay-for-performance model. An approach emphasising participation, in which the service providers can be involved, is crucial for the acceptance and success of the model (Grumbach et al. 1998; Amelung and Zahn 2009, p. 25). There are essentially four areas used as quality indicators: Clinical performance, the use of information technology, efficiency criteria and patient satisfaction.

Parameters from evidence-based medicine are used as measurement values for clinical performance. For example, they refer to the HbA1c value in diabetes patients, a value giving the physician an indication whether the blood sugar of the patient is under control. However, it is controversial that particularly medical parameters are not only influenced by the service provider's treatment, but also by external factors such as the compliance of the patient (Amelung and Zahn 2009, p. 29f.; Kötter et al. 2011, p. 8). For this reason, there must be a high correlation between the degree to which the quality indicators are fulfilled and the results of the treatment. Since this aspect is so complex, surrogate parameters in the form of structural and process indicators are used. This is based on the thesis that by improving the performance processes, the quality of the results can also be improved (Donabedian 2005, originally 1966). When measuring the indicators related to the structure of care, the use of modern information technology is given priority, such as the use of electronic patient files. Investments in information technology can considerably enhance the communication between patient and service provider and prevent the occurrence of medical errors. For example, patients who are at risk due to chronic illnesses can be identified more effectively this way (Emmert and Schöffski 2007, p. 442).

The level of patient satisfaction is an important parameter for the evaluation of the quality of care. It considerably influences patient compliance and, consequently, the treatment results (Crow et al. 2002; Simpson et al. 2006). Through the continual further development and maturation of the model, indicators which reflect the use of IT, cost efficiency and processes are increasingly being replaced by outcome indicators (Fig. 10.3).

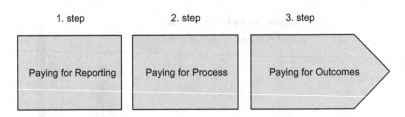

Fig. 10.3 Continual development (according to Underwood (2007))

Alongside quality indicators, the monetary structure must also be considered. P4P can only be successful in combination with other forms of compensation. Simply linking compensation with quality can lead to a complete loss of compensation when these goals are not reached. This would result in insecurity and demotivation among service providers. Thus a two-tier compensation form is used which is comprised of a fixed and a performance-based compensation component (Amelung and Zahn 2009, p. 27). The financial scope of the variable component fluctuates from less than 5–30 % of the income of the practice (McDonald and Roland 2009, p. 122). However, studies have shown that even a low amount of financial incentives for physicians leads to an improvement in quality[10] (Baker and Garter 2005).

The pay-for-performance model can either be aimed at a collective of physicians or an individual physician, or it can be introduced as a hybrid system. Rosenthal and Dudley (2007) defend the hybrid system as the optimal form. In this system, physicians monitor one another, for example in their referral habits. In addition, the risk of resource-intensive patients can be divided among the collective and aid in the prevention of the exclusion of high-risk patients (Rosenthal and Dudley 2007, p. 741).

Ultimately the question remains: At which degree of improved quality should additional payments be made? In principle there are the following possibilities (IOM 2006b; Cannon 2006, Amelung et al. 2009, p. 27; Cromwell et al. 2011, p. 46f.):

1. Absolute achievement of objectives
2. Relative achievement of objectives
3. Changes in comparison to the previous year
4. Comparison with a control group
5. A combination of previously mentioned four

In the first generation of P4P programmes, only the so-called absolute achievement of objectives was used, through which only the "top performers" were rewarded. This demotivated "low performers" and the differences in quality between the service providers became more pronounced. For this reason, combinations of benchmarks are currently used (Mannion and Davies 2008, p. 307; Rosenthal and Dudley 2007, p. 742). Thus, "high performers" who uphold

---

[10] Five to ten percent of the service provider's annual income improves the quality of care (Underwood 2007).

their high quality standard are rewarded. Nevertheless, low performers can also be motivated to continue to improve quality.

Like other forms of compensation, P4P also has its disadvantages. There is a potential risk that too strong of a focus on the quality indicators which are evaluated can lead to a neglect of other areas relevant to quality (tunnel vision). Motivation can also be negatively affected by additional bureaucratic strains. The exclusion of vulnerable patients and the selection of more cost-intensive patients can likewise result from success-based compensation if no adequate risk adjustment is in place (Biermann and Clark 2007, p. 1333f., Gemmil 2007, p. 23).

Case Study 5: Pay-for-Performance of Physicians or Physicians Groups in California: A Project of the Integrated Healthcare Association

The Integrated Healthcare Association (IHA) is an association of large Californian health plans, physician networks, hospital networks, the pharmaceutical industry, academics, employers and consumers (Janus 2003). On the executive board and in the work groups of the IHA, representatives from all interest groups come together to further develop healthcare in California through their collaboration. One reason for this collaboration is based on the fact that California health plans have often received below-average ratings in national comparisons of quality indicators based on HEDIS report cards. The IHA was created in 1996. It is currently carrying out three projects nationwide:

1. The further development of the purchasing of medical technology through the systematisation of available information about health technology assessment
2. Establishing a prevention programme to prevent obesity in cooperation with employers
3. Developing, implementing and evaluating a nationwide P4P programme[11]

History of the Development of the P4P Programme

Since the beginning of the 1990s, there have been separate projects carried out by individual health plans that have explored pay-for-performance of physicians with relatively small finance volumes. However, these increasing P4P "experiments" incurred the wrath of the physicians. They were overwhelmed with the different indicators from different health plans and had no opportunity to adjust their behaviour to the many indicators. Likewise, the variety of P4P programmes did not offer a transparent comparison of physician groups. Thus, a regional practice could be a "top performer" for diabetes treatment according to Blue Cross California's indicator set and at the same time only provide average care for diabetes patients according to the CIGNA indicator set. This problem led to the demand from physicians'

(continued)

---

[11] http://www.iha.org/p4ptoprf.htm

Case Study 5 (continued)
associations nationwide for a *uniform set of indicators* and *one* public report
card from the health plans. At the same time, physicians approached the IHA,
in which representatives from *every* interest group in the healthcare system
were represented. In 2000, the IHA founded a work group in which
physicians and health plans came together in order to draft an innovative,
uniform compensation strategy for the documented performance of physician
groups in California. However, the question of whether competing health
plans would cooperate on the development of a uniform set of indicators
remained. In September of 2001, the California Health Care Foundation
(CHCF) proposed comprehensive start-up capital for the technical development of a nationwide "quality incentive programme", provided that *all* large
California health plans take part and collaborate. Six large health plans[12] that
participated in the work group agreed to it. They gave the starting signal for a
uniform, long-term P4P project nationwide. Performance and invoice data
were evaluated for the first time in 2003. In 2004, physician practices
received the first bonus payments (Fig. 10.4).

The Measurement of Quality of Care in Practices
From the very beginning it was clear that a programme with such a large
scope[13] can only be implemented when the measuring indicators were limited
to *electronically available laboratory data, pharma and invoice data.* Data
from the participating health plans was collected for the project and very
large data sets were created. This enabled the first statistically significant
quality analyses of the individual physician groups and practices. When only
the data from the separate health plans is available, the number of cases in the
individual physician groups or practices is often too low to make reliable
conclusions. Correspondingly, quality data at the level of the individual
physician groups is evaluated and released with an unusually high degree of
detail in this programme. The physicians participate in "their" P4P project
which they helped initiate, largely on a voluntarily basis. The IHA's technical
committee and the cross-party steering committee annually revise and expand
the indicator set and the evaluation methods. In the seventh year of measurement, 2010, the indicator set depicted in Fig. 10.5 was used.

Except for the results of the "blood sugar value" (HbA1c) and the "cholesterol level" (LDL), the quality of the clinical domains was determined
using the invoice data which requires no knowledge of patient records. One
goal of the P4P programme is facilitating the use of *IT-enabled systems.* The

(continued)

---

[12] Aetna, Blue Cross of California, Blue Shield of California, CIGNA, Health Net and PacifiCare.

[13] Approx. ¼ of the Californian population is treated by voluntarily participating physicians.

	2003	2008
Participating health plans	6	8
Policyholders in the participating health plans	~ 7 Mio.	~ 11 Mio.
Participating practices	215	229
Physicians in participating practices	~ 40.000	~ 35.000
Quality indicators used	25	68
Σ Bonus payments through health plans	$ 38 Mio. (2004)	~ $ 52 Mio. (2009)

Fig. 10.4 The development of the IHA's P4P programme (IHA 2011)

Case Study 5 (continued)
indicator set has accordingly evaluated and rewarded the implementation of information technology since the beginning of the programme. Furthermore, *coordinated diabetes care* is also a part of the indicator set. The IHA would like to achieve a systematic, coordinated treatment of diabetes mellitus with it which will subsequently be applied to the treatment of other chronic diseases. In 2008, in response to pressure from the health plans, the first measured value for *appropriate resource use* was introduced. In 2009, five further ones were added – for example, the amount of generic medications prescribed.

The Compensation of Quality of Care in Physician Groups
The IHA makes recommendations for the compensation of measured quality of care. In addition to these recommendations, it explicitly recommends not only compensating the best, but also those physicians with significant improvements. Due to the careful observance of antitrust laws, however, it is up to the individual health plans to annually determine the amount and type of pay-for-performance for themselves. This varies from health plan to health plan and year to year, sometimes considerably. For example, Health Net invested $0.21 in monthly performance-based bonus payments per insured person in 2008. In contrast, Anthem Blue Cross provided a much larger budget which amounted to $1.50 per insured person per month.

The expected bonuses for the participating groups of physicians are dependent on the health plan for which they work and are difficult to calculate due to this. However, groups of physicians usually receive a bonus – which is calculated according to their position in the ranking – for each indicator in which they are among the best X%. In 2007 the additionally awarded bonuses amounted to an average of approx. 2 % of the entire compensation of all participating groups of physicians. In 2007 the health plans spent a total of $65 million on bonus payments for P4P programmes. The bonuses are financed through an increase in the premiums. Up until this point, there have been no payment deductions resulting from suboptimal care in the programme.

(continued)

		Cardiovascular • Annual Monitoring for Patients on Persistent Medications-ACEI/ARB, Digoxin, and Diuretics Diabetes Care • HbA1c Testing Musculoskeletal • Use of Imaging Studies for Low Back Pain Prevention • Childhood Immunization Status-24-mo Continuous Enrollment: Combination 3 Respiratory • Asthma Medication Ratio-Ages 5-64 Maternity • Unexpected Newborn Complications	Weighting: 50 %
PATIENT EXPERIENCE DOMAIN		1. Doctor-Patient Interaction Composite for PCPs 2. Doctor-Patient Interaction Composite for Specialists 3. Coordination of Care Composite 4. Timely Care and Service Composite for PCPs 5. Timely Care and Service Composite for Specialists 6. Overall Rating of Care Composite 7. Office Staff Composite 8. Health Promotion Composite	Weighting: 20 %
IT-ENABLED SYSTEMS DOMAIN		1. Implement drug-drug and drug-allergy interaction checks 2. Maintain an up-to-date problem list of current and active diagnoses 3. Maintain active medication list 4. Maintain active medication allergy list 5. Record demographics 6. Record and chart changes in vital signs 7. Record smoking status 8. Report ambulatory clinical quality measures 9. Provide patients with an electronic copy of their health information 10. Within-PO Performance Variations	Weighting: 30 %
APPROPRIATE RESSOURCE USE DOMAIN		1. Inpatient Utilization: Acute Care Discharges PTMY 2. Inpatient Utilization: Bed Day PTMY 3. HEDIS-based All-Cause Readmissions 4. Emergency Department Visits PTMY 5. Outpatient Procedures Utilization: % Done in Preferred Facilitys	Weighting: Shared Savings

LDL= low density lipoprotein (cholesterol level), MD= Doctor of Medicine

Fig. 10.5 Indicator set of the IHA and its monetary weighting of pay-for-performance in 2013 (IHA 2012)

Case Study 5 (continued)

The IHA annually releases a nationwide, uniform *report card* to document the performance of participating regional physician groups in addition to bonus payments. Insured persons, health plan employees and physicians can view their point values online for the *clinical domain* and *patient experience domain* in direct comparison.[14] The physician groups have the

(continued)

---

[14] http://opa.ca.gov/report_card/

Case Study 5 (continued)

opportunity to correct or comment on the results before they are published. The uniform and objective results as well as the potentially awarded "top performer" titles are an incredibly important negotiation and marketing instrument for the physician groups.

Results and Discussion

The clinical indicators have demonstrated a continual improvement in the average values. The surveying of patient satisfaction, however, revealed only marginal improvements. The most significant improvements were measured in the *IT-enabled systems domain*. For example, the number of physician groups with electronic access to laboratory results doubled. In addition, good IT performance correlated with good values in the clinical indicators. Furthermore, Damberg et al. (2005) demonstrated that particularly the ones at the bottom – that traditionally go away empty-handed – showed drastic improvement.

Despite these successes, the performance gaps have not yet been made up for with the P4P programme. Disappointed health plans say that the programme practises "teaching to the test" (IHA 2009, p. 25) without attaining genuine improvements. The physicians' focus on special indicators, which has been criticised, should be prevented in the future by expanding the indicator set. At the same time, the IHA emphasises that particularly the collection of further specific measurement values in the clinical domain is considerably dependent on improvement in the electronic accessibility of treatment data.

The IHA's compensation committee has also mentioned two problems in the current programme which are potentially responsible for the lack of success of the HEDIS assessment: (1) The nature and amount of the bonus payments vary too greatly between health plans and blur the well-defined, nationwide behaviour incentives. (2) With an average of approx. 2 % of the entire compensation volume, the bonus payments are too low overall. They should be raised to 10 %. This stipulation is impossible due to the increases of programme-based premiums which have already been implemented. Therefore, the IHA is currently focused on the newly introduced *appropriate resource use domain*, in which savings are shared with the physicians. Higher bonus payments should be financed by the more efficient use of resources with stable premiums in the future.

With the IHA's programme, decisive steps have been made towards transparent, comparative quality control at the physician group level in the United States. Through the unusual cooperation of physicians and health plans as well as the cooperation of health plans with one another in the IHA, for the first time in the United States a uniform set of indicators was

(continued)

Case Study 5 (continued)
developed and successfully implemented nationwide, along with the report
card and pay-for-performance.
    Source: www.iha.org
    www.opa.ca.gov

Alongside the United States, there are also pay-for-performance initiatives in
other countries. In the United Kingdom, there is a large P4P project integrated into
the compensation system for primary care physicians, the Quality and Outcomes
Framework. All in all there are few arguments against a stronger focus on performance in the compensation of medical services. However, the distinctive features must
be considered (Amelung 2007, p. 150). The different types of pay-for-performance
programmes and the varied settings in which they are implemented considerably
impede the evaluation of the model's effectiveness. According to the systematic
review by van Herck et al. (2010), the effects vary depending on the chosen design
and organisational structures as well as the political context into which it was
introduced. Therefore, success-based compensation can only be one of several
instruments to achieve improved quality of care.

**Case Study 6: Pay-for-Performance for Primary Care Physicians: The Quality
and Outcomes Framework**
The Quality and Outcomes Framework (QOF) is the largest P4P programme
in primary care worldwide, with the objective of improving the quality of care
in the United Kingdom. It was established as a part of the General Medical
Services contracts between the GPs and primary care organisations in the
United Kingdom. The program was implemented in 2004 and is a comprehensive and voluntary P4P program in which over 99 % of all GP practices
participate (Campbell and Lester 2011, p. 18). Even though the United
Kingdom's government intended to introduce a quality-based payment in
1986 already it was not until 2000 that the implementation of the P4P
programme actually began due to previous objections of the British Medical
Association, the physician's professional association in the United Kingdom,
against this form of compensation. Even though these objections began to be
overcome with the successful introduction of financial incentives for childhood immunization in 1990, they were still prevalent among healthcare
providers. Central triggering factors for the implementation of the QOF
were serious concerns about the quality of medical care. As a result, financial
incentives for improving quality were implemented. Furthermore, rewards
were connected to data collection, preventive strategies and the systematic
management of chronic diseases (Gillam and Siriwardena 2011, p. 1ff).

(continued)

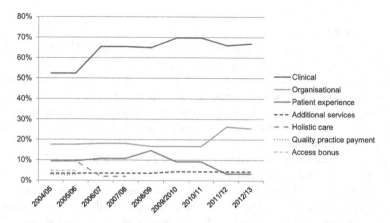

Fig. 10.6 Share of the indicators as percentage of maximum points available in the QOF (Source: own diagram based on Quality and Outcomes achievement data)

Case Study 6 (continued)

The QOF links 25 % of a GP's income to the achievement of a variety of indicators (Roland et al. 2009, p. 1). These can be subdivided into four domains: Clinical and organisational indicators, patient experience and additional services. The clinical indicators are strongly related to national guidelines, representing the major part of the QOF.

At the introduction of the QOF 146 indicators from the four domains mentioned above were applied. Periodically, these indicators are revised; new indicators are added while others are abolished. Equally, the maximum number of points available within the QOF can change from one period to another (Campbell and Lester 2011, p. 17). In the year 2012/2013, 148 were in use. For weighting these indicators a maximum of 1,000 points, each worth £133.76 in 2012/2013, can be achieved (BMA and NHS Employers 2012a, p. 7ff; 2012b, p. 20).

Before new indicators are introduced in the QOF they have to undergo a review process led by the NICE since 2009. Indicators are tested on reliability and the feasibility of data extraction. Further attributes which are important in the development of new indicators are their acceptability, attributability, meaning they have to be completely under the GP's control, feasibility concerning data availability and collection, reliability, sensitivity to change in order to discriminate between high and low quality of care, the indicator's predictive value concerning the quality of care as well as their relevance (Campbell/Lester, p. 21f.).

Thresholds indicate the range of achievement for individual quality indicators which have to be obtained to trigger payments. The thresholds

(continued)

Case Study 6 (continued)

vary from indicator to indicator and range from 40 % to 90 %. The current discussion of increasing the upper threshold further to 95 % is strongly criticized as being an austerity measure penalizing physicians who spend more time with their patients (Campbell and Lester 2011, p. 17; Aziz 2012).

The four domains, the clinical and organisational domain, patient experiences and additional services, have undergone massive changes in their relative importance since the introduction of the QOF. This can be seen both in the number of indicators in the domains as well as in the amount of points attributed to each of the domains (see Fig. 10.6).

In 2012/2013, indicators within the clinical domain[15] were organised according to 22 disease categories,[16] the organisational domain covered six areas[17] and the additional services domain was subdivided into four areas[18] whereas the patient experience domain only included one indicator since 2011–2012 (BMA and NHS Employers 2012a, p. 28ff).

Evaluation

An evaluation of the achievement data before the introduction of the QOF and after its introduction gives information on the dependence of improvements in certain indicators on financial incentives connected to these indicators. Doran et al. (2011) were able to show that improvements in incentivised indicators are significantly greater than improvements in non-incentivised domains. This might suggest a "teaching to the test", and hence a neglect of non-incentivised indicators, due to the QOF.

Even though the QOF might lead to physicians losing sight of non-incentivised measures, the P4P program leads to positive effects. Mortality is slightly reduced and hospital admissions for certain conditions included in the QOF were reduced (Gillam et al. 2012).

---

[15] Cervical screening, child health surveillance, maternity services, contraception.

[16] Secondary prevention of coronary heart disease, cardiovascular disease – primary prevention, heart failure, stroke and transient ischaemic attack, hypertension, diabetes mellitus, chronic obstructive pulmonary disease, epilepsy, hypothyroidism, cancer, palliative care, mental health, asthma, dementia, depression, chronic kidney disease, atrial fibrillation, obesity, learning disabilities, smoking, peripheral arterial disease, osteoporosis: secondary prevention of fragility fractures.

[17] Records and information, information for patients, education and training, practice management, medicines management, quality and productivity.

[18] Length of consultation.

Public Reporting

In the United States, the release of performance and quality data is a well-known and established principle. The implementation of public reporting in New York State already began in the 1980s and spread from there to other Western States (Faber et al. 2009, p. 1). However, it was first with the study "Crossing the Quality Chasm: a New Health Care System for the 21st Century" from the Institute of Medicine in the United States that interest in public reporting rapidly increased. In the investigation, considerable flaws were revealed, especially in the areas of transparency, security, patient orientation and effectiveness. In order to improve these sectors, instruments were needed which make the provision of services more transparent, but also provide incentives for a better quality of treatment. Public reporting is among these instruments.

Basic Principle

Public reporting is among the non-monetary incentive mechanisms. Through acknowledgement, appreciation and distinctions, attempts are made to influence the quality of treatment. In doing so the basic idea is that the competition between service providers can be stimulated when the insured persons have access to information about the quality of treatment and care. The patient can choose a service provider according to their needs, through which the autonomy and self-determination of the patient is reinforced (Amelung et al. 2009, p. 26).

In addition to its role as an aid in the decision-making process, public reporting is also used for external quality comparisons. As a result of the benchmark, the service providers must be motivated to minimise or eliminate certain negative incidents in the provision of services, and subsequently encourage the "competition" to follow their example. Using this mechanism can create more competition in healthcare and the quality of care in the entire healthcare system can be improved (Geraedts et al. 2009, p. 232).

Apart from the patients and service providers, public reporting also has a certain impact on the political level. The published information can enable better supervision in treatment and make it easier to identify areas in healthcare where change is necessary as well as inducing regulations.

Although numerous discussions have been carried out regarding this subject, there is little evidence investigating the impact of public reporting on quality. Fung et al. (2008) summarised the most recent findings in a systematic review. They described very inconsistent results about the benefits of public reporting on quality for the information gained within the United States. For example, reporting in hospitals led to an improvement in the quality of treatment and care, however, there are no uniform results in the outpatient sector and among health insurance companies. Some studies revealed positive effects while others registered little to no impact on healthcare services (Fung et al. 2008).

However, Cutler et al. (2004) were able to prove through a cross-sectional and a longitudinal study that hospitals with negative assessments lost market shares.

Along with the study regarding quality improvement, there is a lack of analyses regarding the use of data by patients, insured persons and relatives. Schwartz (2005) carried out one of the few available studies where they established that merely 11 % of patients in the United States who faced a major operation used public reports to compare the performance of hospitals.

Schneider et al. (1998) also analysed the impact of the available information. Patients were surveyed about the basis of their choice of surgeon and hospital before receiving bypass operations. Merely 12 % of the patients were familiar with the reports, and of these a mere 2 % used this quality data to make their decision.

Vaiana and McGlynn (2002) believe the low impact of public reporting is due to the poor preparation of information for the insured persons. The insured get most of their information from the experience of family, friends or acquaintances, or the nearest hospital is chosen for the examination without getting information about its security, efficiency and quality.

In order to raise the level of public interest in quality reports, they have to be written in a reader-friendly and trustworthy manner (Schaeffer 2006, p. 6). The public reports have to address dimensions of quality that are relevant to patients and they should be written in a manner understandable for lay people and be designed in an accessible and interesting way. Beyond information about performance and information relevant to them, patients particularly want to read personal reports which encourage trust in the data and reflect personal opinions (Marshall et al. 2004, p. 161; Schaeffer 2006). Current examples from the United States (e.g. California Office of the Patient Advocate, www.opa.ca.gov), however, show that the initial problems have been solved to a large extent.

Negative Incentives

Along with the many positive effects, unwanted negative effects can also result from public reporting. These include:

1. Gaming: Gaming refers to a service provider's change in behaviour, for example up-coding could be carried out in the main diagnosis or every possible co-morbidity could be documented in order to influence the risk adjustment (Scott and Ward 2006).
2. Tunnel vision: Tunnel vision describes limited perception. In this case the concentration is focused on the indicators to be measured, and in turn other important aspects are neglected (Marshall et al. 2004).
3. Ossification: Paralysis or fossilisation can arise when the service provider no longer uses new and innovative approaches out of fear of negative effects (Marshall et al. 2003).
4. Myopia: Short-sightedness leads to following short-term goals which in turn leads to the neglect of long-term criteria (Smith 1995).
5. Outsourcing/Avoidance of high-risk patients. The referral of very sick patients to other service providers as well as rejecting them is meant to lower the rate of complications and deaths in the quality reports (Scott and Ward 2006). This phenomenon has particularly been observed in healthcare systems influenced by market economies.

6. Misrepresentation: This refers to the deceptive, false representation of data (Smith 1995, p. 277ff.).

In order to prevent these undesired side effects, Marshall et al. (2004) recommend carrying out a suitable risk adjustment. Through the statistical processing, influential factors caused by different patient groups can also be taken into consideration in the quality of the results. This creates the precondition for a fair quality comparison and prevents the selection of high-risk patients. To ensure the acceptance and trustworthiness of the reports, it would be beneficial to carry out the compilation of public reports using standardised sets of indicators and have them assessed by an independent organisation. These measures could remedy the reports' negative consequences for service providers and insured persons (Hibbard et al. 2003, p. 92). Likewise, implementing financial incentives can prevent the negative effects of public reporting. In studies, the combination of public reporting and monetary incentives such as pay-for-performance exhibited more improvement in treatment quality than through public reporting alone (Lindenauer et al. 2007). This is true although the non-monetary effects of public reporting are considered to be a central parameter and public reporting offers many advantages over monetary incentives. It can therefore be reconciled with medical ethics and preserves the intrinsic motivation of the service provider. In addition, public reporting also attains the goal of minimising costs (Emmert 2008, p. 327).

Public reporting is still in the beginning stages in many countries, but the public demand for information is accelerating the further development of public reporting.

Conclusion

The ability of compensation systems to fine-tune behaviour is limited. The more the compensation is organised into lump sums, the larger the incentives are for physicians to choose patients according to their risks, to provide insufficient care and to shift costs. Innovations are only introduced when they clearly reduce the costs of diagnosis and treatment. On the other hand, the more the actual service provided is dependent upon the potential compensation, the higher the incentive is to render more services than necessary and to neglect cost-reducing efforts.

The empirical findings regarding the effects of compensation systems are not conclusive. There have been few studies on these effects up until now. On one hand, they show that lump sum compensation can reduce the use of services (Stearns et al. 1992). On the other hand, the compensation forms seem to have no significant influence on the use and cost of services in comparison with other factors such as the risk structure of insured persons or certain characteristics of the physicians and their practice (Conrad et al. 1998).

Therefore, compensation systems alone are not sufficient for steering behaviour. They need to be supplemented with additional managed care instruments and procedures, which guarantee the right choice of service providers ($\rightarrow$ selective contract), through $\rightarrow$ quality management measures and behavioural monitoring ($\rightarrow$ utilisation review).

Compensation form	Desired effect	Undesired effect
Salary	– Incentive to maintain the patient's health	– No incentives to use cost-effective measures – Long waiting times
Factor cost reimbursement	– Secure planning for the service provider – Facilitates innovation	– No incentive to use cost-effective measures – Expansion of services
Fee-for-service	– Performance-based compensation – Increases productivity and performance	– Undesired expansion of services – "Cherry-picking", e.g. preferencing services with medical devices
Daily rate	– Minimising of the costs per diem	– Expansion of the length of stay
Case rate / DRG	– No incentive to expand services – Incentive to use cost-effective measures	– Omission of desired services – Upgrading – Shifting of costs
Bundled payments	– No incentive for the expansion of individual services	– Scope of services only guaranteed through additional measures
Capitation	– Incentive to maintain patient's health – Incentive to use cost-effective measures – Low administration costs	– Risk selection – Shifting of costs – Endangering quality
Pay-for-performance	– Improved quality – Interest of physician and patient are largely the same	– Problems in measurement – High monitoring costs

Fig. 10.7 Compensation forms in comparison

Generally stated, MCOs have distanced themselves from the extreme shifting of risks in the past years. As important and practical as it may be to optimise incentive programmes, it is equally important to maintain a sense of proportion and not only concentrate on short-term goals. For example, it may be attractive in the short term for an HMO manager to reduce a capitation rate by 10 %. However, in the long term it may not be practical. If the physician or the hospital cannot survive on the agreed upon compensation, it is not in the interest of the HMO. The same is true of the very popular "negotiated discounts" which are primarily "rebate battles".

All in all it can be concluded that the challenge of an optimal compensation form for physicians (see Robinson 2001) has been inadequately solved and there is little hope that a compensation concept will be developed which can meet every requirement. In conclusion, the substantial advantages and disadvantages of all compensation forms are concisely summarised in Fig. 10.7.

The Institute of Medicine demanded in its study "Crossing the Quality Chasm" that compensation systems be used as a requirement for quality management. However, it is important to note that this is only one piece of the puzzle in a complex system of management instruments. The interaction of the individual elements is crucial for the success of the whole. However, the table also makes it clear that compensation systems must consist of multiple levels (e.g. DRG plus P4P, capitation plus fee-for-service etc.) in order to lessen the impact of the misdirected incentives in the dominant form of compensation.

Literature

Amelung, V. E., & Zahn, T. (2009). *Pay-for-Performance (P4P)- Der Business Case für Qualität?* DxCG-Study, Berlin.

Amelung, V. E., Voss, H., & Janus, K. (2005). Ökonomische Anreize in integrierten Versorgungssystemen – Grundlage für Nachhaltigkeit, Zufriedenheit und Motivation. In B. Badura & O. Iseringhausen (Eds.), *Wege aus der Krise der Versorgungssituation – Beiträge aus der Versorgungsforschung* (pp. 115–131). Bern: Hans Huber.

Aziz, Z. (2012, November 13) GP quality and outcomes framework indicator focus on the wrong issues. *The Guardian.*

Baker, G., & Delbanco, S. (2007). *Pay for performance: National Perspective. 2006 longitudinal survey results with 2007 market updates.* San Francisco: Med-Vantage Inc.

Biermann, A., & Clark, J. (2007). Performance measurement and equity. *British Medical Journal, 334,* 1333–1334.

BMA [British Medical Association], & NHS Employers. (2012a). *Quality and outcomes framework for 2012/13: Guidance for PCOs and practices.* http://www.nhsemployers.org/Aboutus/Publications/Documents/QOF_2012-13.pdf. Accessed 6 Feb 2013.

BMA [British Medical Association], & NHS Employers. (2012b). *The quality and outcomes framework frequently asked questions.* http://www.nhsemployers.org/Aboutus/Publications/Documents/QOF_FAQs_June_2012.pdf. Accessed 6 Feb 2013.

Cacace, M. (2010). *Das Gesundheitssystem der USA: Governance-Strukturen staatlicher und privater Akteure.* Frankfurt am Main: Campus.

Campbell, S., & Lester, H. (2011). Developing indicators and the concept of QOFability. In S. Gillam & A. N. Siriwardena (Eds.), *The quality and outcomes framework QOF – Transforming general practice.* Oxon: Radcliffe Publishing.

Cannon, M. F. (2006). Pay for performance: Is Medicare a good candidate? *Yale Journal of Health Policy, Law, and Ethics, 7*(1), 1–38.

Carter, M. G., Jacobson, P. D., Kominski, G. F., et al. (1994). Use of diagnosis-related groups by non-Medicare payers. *Health Care Financing Review, 16,* 127–159.

Casale, A. S., Paulus, R. A., Selna, M. J., et al. (2007). "ProvenCareSM": A provider-driven pay-for-performance program for acute episodic cardiac surgical care. *Annals of Surgery, 246*(4), 613–623.

Chernew, M. (2010). Bundled payment systems: Can they be more successful this time. *Health Services Research, 45*(5), Part I.

Cleverley, W. O., Song, P. H., & Cleverley, J. O. (2010). *Essentials of health care finance* (7th ed.). Sudbury: Jones & Bartlett Learning.

Conrad, D. A., Maynard, C., Cheadle, A., et al. (1998). Primary care physician compensation method in medical groups. *JAMA: The Journal of the American Medical Association, 279,* 853–858.

Cromwell, J., Trisolini, M. G., Pope, G. C., Mitchell, J. B., & Greenwald, L. M. (2011). *Pay for performance in health care: Methods and approaches* (RTI Press Publication No. BK-0002-1103). Research Triangle Park: RTI Press.

Crow, R., Gage, H., Hampson, S., et al. (2002). The measurement of patient satisfaction with healthcare: Implications for practice from a systematic review of literature. *Heath Technology Assessment, 6*(32), 1–244.

Cutler, D. M., Ilkmann, R. S., & Landrum, M. B. (2004). The role of information in medical markets: An analysis of publicly report outcomes in cardiac surgery. *The American Economic Review, 94*(2), 342–346.

Damberg, C., Raube, K., Williams, T., & Shortell, S. (2005). Paying for performance: Implementing a statewide project in California. *Quality Management in Health Care, 14*(2), 66–79.

Donabedian, A. (2005). Evaluating the quality of medical care. *The Milbank Quarterly, 83*(4), 691–729.

Doran, T., Kontopantelis, E., Valderas, J. M., et al. (2011). Effect of financial incentives on incentivised and non-incentivised clinical activities: Longitudinal analysis of data from the UK Quality and Outcomes Framework. *British Medical Journal, 342*, d3590.

Emmert, M. (2008). *Pay for Performance (P4P) im Gesundheitswesen, Ein Ansatz zur Verbesserung der Gesundheitsversorgung?* Burgdorf: HERZ.

Emmert, M., & Schöffski, O. (2007). Public Reporting des kalifornischen "Pay for Performance" der Integrated Healthcare Association (IHA). *Gesundheitswesen, 69*, 438–447.

Faber, M., Bosch, M., Wollersheim, H., et al. (2009). Public reporting in health care: How do consumers use quality-of-care information? A systematic review. *Medical Care, 47*, 1–8.

Fetter, R. B., Shin, Y., Freeman, J. L., et al. (1980). Case mix definition by diagnosis-related groups. *Medical Care, 18*(Suppl), 1–53.

Fleßa, S. (2013). *Grundzüge der Krankenhausbetriebslehre* Band 1, 3. Auflage. München: Oldenbourg Wissenschaftsverlag.

Frisina, L., & Cacace, M. (2009). Chapter XII: DRGs and the professional independence of physicians. In A. Dwivedi (Ed.), *Handbook of research on IT management and clinical data administration in healthcare* (Vol. I, pp. 173–191). Hershey: IGI Global.

Fung, C. H., Lim, Y., Mattke, S., et al. (2008). The evidence that publishing patient care performance data improves quality of care. *Annals of Internal Medicine, 148*, 111–123.

Gemmil, M. (2007). Pay-for-performance in the US: What lessons for Europe? *Eurohealth, 13*(4), 21–23.

Geraedts, M., Auras, S., Hermeling, P., et al. (2009). Public Reporting – Formen und Effekte öffentlicher Qualitätsberichterstattung. *Deutsche Medizinische Wochenschrift, 134*, 232–233.

Gillam, S. J., & Siriwardena, A. N. (2011). *The quality and outcomes framework: QOF – Transforming general practice.* Oxon: Radcliffe Publishing.

Gillam, S. J., Siriwardena, A. N., & Steel, N. (2012). Pay-for-performance in the United Kingdom: Impact of the quality and outcomes framework – A systematic review. *Annals of Family Medicine, 10*(5), 461–468.

Grumbach, K., Osmond, D., Vranizan, K., et al. (1998). Primary care physicians' experience of financial incentives in managed-care systems. *The New England Journal of Medicine, 339*, 1516–1521.

Guterman, S., Davis, K., Schoenbaum, S., & Shih, A. (2009). Using Medicare payment policy to transform the health system: A framework for improving performance. *Health Affairs 28*(2), w238–w250 (published online 27 January 2009).

Hibbard, J. H. (2003). Does publicizing hospital performance stimulate quality improvements efforts? *Health Affairs, 22*(2), 84–94.

IHA [Integrated Healthcare Association]. (2009). *Transparency report on 2008 health plan payouts.* http://www.iha.org/transpf/2008%20Transparency%20Report.pdf. Accessed 20 June 2009.

IHA [Integrated Healthcare Association]. (2011). *Approved MY 2011 P4P measurement set*, pp. 1–4, www.iha.org/pdfs_documents/pdf_california.

IHA [Integrated Healthcare Association]. (2012). *Final Measurement Year (MY) 2012 and approved MY 2013 P4P measure set.* http://www.iha.org/pdfs_documents/p4p_california/FinalMY2012_ApprovedMY2013_MeasureSets_111612.pdf. Accessed 25 Feb 2013.

IOM [Institute of Medicine]. (2001). *Crossing the quality chasm: A new health system for the 21st century.* Washington, DC: National Academies Press.

IOM [Institute of Medicine]. (2006a). *Rewarding provider performance, aligning incentives in Medicare.* Washington, DC: National Academies Press.

IOM [Institute of Medicine]. (2006b). *Performance measurement: Accelerating improvement (pathways to quality health care).* Washington, DC: National Academies Press.

Janus, K. (2003). *Managing health care in private organizations. Transaction costs cooperation and modes of organization in the value chain.* Frankfurt am Main: Peter Lang.

Knight, W. (1998). *Managed care. What it is and how it works.* Gaithersburg: Aspen.

Kongstvedt, P. R. (2001). Compensation of primary care physicians in open panel plans. In P. R. Kongstvedt (Ed.), *The managed health care handbook* (pp. 120–146). Gaithersburg: Aspen.

Kongstvedt, P. R. (2013). *Essentials of managed health care* (6th ed.). Burlington: Jones & Bartlett Learning.

Kötter, T., Schaefer, F., Blozik, E., et al. (2011). Die Etwicklung von Qualitätsindikatoren – Hintergrund, Methoden und Probleme. *Zeitschrift für Evidenz, Fortbildung und Qualität im Gesundheitswesen, 105,* 7–12.

Lee, T. H. (2007). Pay for performance, version 2.0? *The New England Journal of Medicine, 357*(6), 531–533.

Lee, M., Su, Z., Hou, Y., et al. (2011). A decision support system for diagnosis related groups coding. *Expert Systems with Applications, 38*(4), 3626–3631.

Lindenauer, P. K., Remus, D., Roman, S., et al. (2007). Public reporting und pay for performance in hospital quality improvement. *The New England Journal of Medicine, 356,* 486–496.

Mannion, R., & Davies, H. (2008). Payment for performance in health care. *British Medical Journal, 336,* 306–308.

Marshall, M. N., Romano, P. S., & Davies, H. T. O. (2004). How do we maximize the impact of the public reporting of quality of care? *International Journal for Quality in Health Care, 16,* i57–i63.

McDonald, R., & Roland, M. (2009). Pay for performance in primary care in England and California: Comparison of unintended consequences. *Annals of Family Medicine, 7*(2), 121–127.

Mechanic, R. E., & Altman, S. H. (2009). Payment reform options: Episode payment is a good place to start. *Health Affairs, 28*(2), w262–w271 (published online 27 January 2009).

Qaseem, A. (2010). Pay for performance through the lens of medical professionalism. *Annals of Internal Medicine, 152,* 366–369.

Robinson, J. C. (2001). The end of managed care. *JAMA: The Journal of the American Medical Association, 285*(20), 2622–2628.

Robinson, J. C., & Casalino, L. P. (2001, July/August). Reevaluation of capitation contracting in New York and California. *Health Affairs (Millwood),* Suppl Web Exclusives, w11–w19.

Roland, M., Elliott, M., Lyratzopoulos, G., et al. (2009). Reliability of patient responses in pay for performance schemes: analysis of national General Practitioner Patient Survey data in England. *British Medical Journal, 339,* b3851.

Rosenthal, M. B. (2008). Beyond pay for performance – Emerging models of provider-payment reform. *The New England Journal of Medicine, 359*(12), 1197–1200.

Rosenthal, M., & Dudley, R. (2007). Pay-for-performance, will the latest trend improve care? *JAMA: The Journal of the American Medical Association, 297*(7), 740–743.

Sanofi. (2002). Managed care digest series, HMO-PPO/Medicare-Medicaid Digest, Bridgewater.

Sanofi. (2012). Managed care digest series – HMO-PPO Digest 2012–2013, Bridgewater.

Schaeffer, D. (2006). *Bedarf an Patienteninformationen über das Krankenhaus, Eine Literaturanalyse.* Gütersloh: Bertelsmann-Stiftung.

Schneider, E. C., & Epstein, A. M. (1998). Use of public performance reports. A survey of patients undergoing cardiac surgery. *JAMA: The Journal of the American Medical Association, 279,* 1638–1642.

Schwartz, L. M. (2005). How do elderly patients decide where to go for major surgery? Telephone interview survey. *British Medical Journal, 331,* 821.

Scott, I. A., & Ward, M. (2006). Public reporting of hospital outcomes based on administrative data: Risks and opportunities. *The Medical Journal of Australia, 184*, 571–575.

Simpson, S. H., Eurich, D. T., Majumdar, S. R., et al. (2006). A meta-analysis of the association between adherence to drug therapy and mortality. *British Medical Journal, 333*(7557), 15.

Smith, P. (1995). On the unintended consequences of publishing performance data in the public sector. *International Journal of Public Administration, 18*, 277–310.

Stearns, S. C., Wolfe, B. L., & Kindig, D. A. (1992). Physicians responses to fee-for-service and capitation payment. *Inquiry, 29*, 416–425.

Tanenbaum, S. J. (2009). Pay for performance in Medicare: Evidentiary irony and the politics of value. *Journal of Health Politics, Policy and Law, 34*, 717–746.

Underwood, H. (2007). *Pay for performance: Value-based purchasing in healthcare.* Presentation Health Spring Meeting – Session 25, Seattle, UA.

Vaiana, M. E., & McGlynn, E. A. (2002). What cognitive science tells us about the design of reports for consumers. *Medical Care Research and Review, 59*, 3–35.

Van Herck, P., De Smedt, D., Annemans, L., et al. (2010). Systematic review: Effects, design choices, and context of pay-for-performance in health care. *BMC Health Service Research, 10*, 247.

Webster, L. A. H., Gans, D. N., & Milburn, J. (2007). *Financial management* (3rd ed.). Chicago: MGMA.

Young, W. W. (1991). Patient management categories. In G. Neubauer & G. Sieben (Eds.), *Alternative Entgeltverfahren in der Krankenhausversorgung.* Gerlingen: Bleicher.

Quality and Cost Management

11

In healthcare, a variety of different measures and instruments can be applied to manage both the quality and the costs at the same time. The following chapter will discuss the usefulness and effectiveness of applying specific instruments for quality and cost management.

In gatekeeping, most treatment episodes begin with a visit to an individually selected physician, the gatekeeper, who ensures a coordinated and cross-sectorial treatment process. Guidelines are used to standardise the provision of medical services and form the basis of clinical pathways, which coordinate the stages of the treatment throughout the different areas of care as efficiently as possible. Formularies are used to explicitly define which services are paid for, whereas the utilisation review is a case-by-case assessment of the services provided. Disease management, on the other hand, coordinates the care of patients suffering from a specific disease beyond the care provided by an individual service provider. In case management each individual patient's treatment is coordinated and evaluated across the different sectors. Differing from the methods mentioned before is demand management, which is used to directing the patients' utilisation of medical services. Besides limiting the demand for discretionary services, patient coaching aims at increasing the patients' self-competence. Ultimately, quality management is applied to increase the quality of the healthcare provision.

11.1 Gatekeeping

Basic Idea

The concept of gatekeeping means that each treatment episode – with the exception of emergencies and certain predetermined service sectors – begins with a visit to an individually selected physician. In most countries, gatekeeping is performed by general practitioners. There are, however, a few countries, for example France, in which gatekeeping can also be performed by specialist physicians. The insured delegates the decision to the gatekeeper of whether the necessary services will be

V.E. Amelung, *Healthcare Management*, Springer Texts in Business and Economics, DOI 10.1007/978-3-642-38712-8_11, © Springer-Verlag Berlin Heidelberg 2013

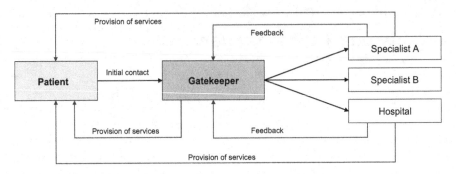

Fig. 11.1 Gate keeping system

provided by the gatekeeper himself or whether a referral to a specialist or a hospital admission is necessary.

The main idea of the gatekeeping principle is simple (Shi and Singh 2012). The gatekeeper should ensure a coordinated and cross-sectorial treatment process and, hence, function as a virtual clearing house. All treatments, whether provided directly or by referral, are coordinated by the gatekeeper. The gatekeeper also largely assumes the function of a disease manager in this context ($\rightarrow$ disease management). The assumption is that services can be provided at lower cost by gatekeepers. Their function therefore is to "protect" the healthcare system from an excessive overuse of expensive specialists and inpatient services. Figure 11.1 depicts the functions of a gatekeeper.

Gatekeeping is a prime example for the advocates of managed care (Brekke et al. 2005; Garrido et al. 2011) because it combines the aspects of improving quality through the optimisation of treatment processes and lowering costs through the management and coordination of the provision of services.

However, the concept has far-reaching consequences for the medical provision of services, since the role of the physicians, usually general practitioners, who act as a gatekeeper is changed in particular. The primary care physician no longer only represents the interests of the patient as in the traditional system, instead he is responsible for providing high quality services in a cost-efficient way. This change becomes especially clear when the gatekeeper is compensated with capitations ($\rightarrow$ compensation systems) and correspondingly carries the financial risk. Each unused service increases the individual benefits of the gatekeeper.

The gatekeeper plays a major role in developing managed care. Most HMOs implement a gatekeeper initially (Cleverly et al. 2010). However, particularly here the considerable differences in structure between the different healthcare systems should be taken into account. American healthcare is characterised by a surplus of specialists and a corresponding shortage of primary care physicians (Bodenheimer 2009).[1] This is intensified through the widespread and increased use of medical

---

[1] This amounted to 0.3 primary care physicians per 1,000 people in 2010 in the United States (OECD Health Data 2012), the OECD average in 2010 was 0.99.

technology (usually associated with high costs). Thus, gatekeeping is also an instrument for managed care organisations which helps to correct management mistakes (Grumbach et al. 1999; Bodenheimer et al. 2009, p. 52). Accordingly, gatekeeping in the United States is mainly discussed as an instrument used to reduce inappropriate "overtreatment" (Brekke et al. 2005). However, this also shows that the general increase in the amount of primary care practitioners in comparison to specialists is not necessarily related to gatekeeping, but may instead be the result of stronger service provision planning in respect to the range of services.

Beyond the American results, one can also learn from the extensive European experience in gatekeeping. Along with Great Britain, where the "fundholding general practitioner" was a significant management instrument, gatekeeping is also a widespread, tried and tested instrument in the Netherlands, Denmark and Switzerland (for the United Kingdom, see Forrest 2003; Roland et al. 2012; for Denmark see Andersen et al. 2011; for the Netherlands see Wasem et al. 2003; Schäfer et al. 2010; for Switzerland see Schwenkglenks et al. 2006; Berchtold and Peytremann-Bridevaux 2011).

Forms of Gatekeeping

Two types of gatekeeping can be distinguished. On one hand there is the "simple" gatekeeper who only assumes a sentinel function, and on the other hand the "capitated" gatekeeper, who, in addition to compensation via capitation fees, assumes the financial risk as well.

The "simple" gatekeeper is paid per service (fee-for-service). Correspondingly, this gatekeeper does not directly benefit from the economic success. Thus, in the course of gatekeeping, the scope of duties might change for the gatekeeper. The coordination and the supervision of treatment procedures, as well as additional administrative work gain in importance for the "simple" gatekeeper.

The situation of the "capitated" gatekeeper, however, is different. In its simplest form, the gatekeeper assumes the full financial risk (full risk capitation) for all medical services regardless of who renders them. In practise, usually the watered-down forms of full risk capitation are implemented as the risk for individual physicians is too high since they do not have a sufficiently large risk pool and are hence too dependent on random variables. Just a few patients can decide on the profit or loss of a physician's practise in this form of gatekeeping. In their systematic review, Garrido et al. (2011) also confirm that a complete transfer of the financial risk to the gatekeeper did not take place in any case.

Correspondingly, in practise two variations of models are typical: First, maximum payments are defined per insured in a risk pool. When a seriously ill insured person has already incurred more than a certain sum of expenses, they fall outside of the financial spectrum of responsibility of the gatekeeper. Here one can also refer to stop loss (→ compensation systems). However, in the United States it is more common that gatekeepers are only financially responsible for their own (primary care) services, not for the entire service spectrum. Even when this makes more sense for the approach – the physician only assumes the risk for their own services – the model loses significant control functions. This results in considerable incentives for the general practitioner to shift expensive patients to other service levels (specialists and particularly hospitals) – and precisely this should be prevented through the use of gatekeepers.

Significance and Mechanisms

First, the effective mechanisms on the quality side will be examined. The gate-keeper should ensure a holistic and balanced treatment process. Depending on the case, the interface problems of healthcare are resolved because the gatekeeper determines the form of treatment most suitable for each patient. In other words: the gatekeeper quickly solves the interface problems and ensures a coordinated flow of information between those involved. Because the gatekeeper receives all information, there is a high probability that they can see connections between diagnoses and can develop a suitable and holistic treatment plan. The gatekeeper also decides which specialist the patient will be referred to (not only which specialisation, but also the concrete specialist X or Y). Thus, he is considered the patient's "broker" (Eggers et al. 2008). In the case of an increase of multimorbidity and the rise of chronically ill, this function becomes more important and can be seen as a strategy to deal with changes in the disease panorama. In this process it is crucial that the gatekeeper takes responsibility for both the quality and cost-related results in some form.

Often the cost aspects can barely be distinguished from the quality criteria. Through his doorman role, the gatekeeper should ensure that no unnecessary specialist or inpatient services are demanded and supplied. This aims at decreasing costs and increasing quality at the same time. The gatekeeper no longer assumes any simply collegial role for the other service providers; he is now the contractor of the specialist and indirectly responsible for the specialist's revenue volume. Thus, the distribution of resources is delegated from the MCO to the level of the service provider.

The use of a gatekeeper leads to a reduction in information asymmetries for the MCO ($\rightarrow$ introduction), since the MCO can assume that the general practitioner is much more capable of deciding whether specific services are appropriate. The problem of controlling the quality of the specialists is also considerably reduced as the specialists rely on the gatekeepers' patient referrals and are correspondingly interested in a solution attractive to both parties in the long run (Brekke et al. 2005).

However, there is yet another hypothesis about the gatekeeping role which is important for the consideration of costs. A general practitioner can indeed provide many services performed by specialists. Because the gatekeeper has to compensate the specialist services from his budget (at least in the case of the "capitated" gatekeeper), the gatekeeper will closely examine whether they cannot provide the services themselves and ergo more affordably. A shifting from specialist to general practitioner should be implicitly facilitated. The role of the general practitioner will not only be revalued in terms of contents, but also in terms of quality. In order to prevent an undesired increase in the volume of services (first the visit to the gatekeeper and then to the specialist), obvious visits to specialists, such as routine examinations by the gynaecologist or paediatrician, are excluded here. In these cases the insured can visit a specialist without previously consulting the gatekeeper.

The implementation of a gatekeeper should also prevent the insured from so-called "doctor-hopping" (Linden et al. 2003, p. 696). This term is applied when a patient consults multiple specialists for one treatment. However, the actual significance of this phenomenon is debated. As previously mentioned, the limitation of unnecessary costs, which accrue from duplicate examinations, is also indirectly related. Through the gatekeeper's role as a coordinator, duplicate examinations can generally be prevented. It is their duty to provide the respective service providers with available examination results (e.g. x-rays or blood tests). In the best-case scenario this information would be made available online, i.e. the gatekeeper and other levels of care are connected with each other via a common network.

With the exception of the very watered-down form, gatekeeping is always related to budgeting on the lowest and thus the first level of service provision. This means that the gatekeeper receives a fixed ex ante monthly or quarterly lump sum per registered insured person – it is not the number of patients which is crucial to the gatekeeper's compensation.

Different studies with a high level of variation have examined the effects of gatekeeping. In the systematic review by Garrido et al. (2011) the effects of gatekeeping systems are investigated in comparison to "free access". The studies included did not show significant variations in the clinical result parameters or in the health-related quality of life. However, the majority of studies regarding healthcare expenses show that these can be lowered through gatekeeping. Depending on the study, the potential savings amount to between 6 % and 80 % of the entire healthcare expenses per person (Garrido et al. 2011, p. 34). However, we emphasise that a separation of the effects of gatekeeping from those of other factors in the healthcare model, such as financial instruments, was not existent.

Switzerland has been developing a network on the basis of the gatekeeping principle for several years. In this process, it is worth noting that there are no legal stipulations for such models of care. One of the oldest Swiss physician networks is MediX.

Case Study 7: MediX: A Swiss Physician Network
Initial Situation
The Swiss healthcare system is characterised by decentralised and strongly fragmented structures that impede the implementation of managed care

(continued)

Case Study 7 (continued)

elements.[2] Despite this, for over 20 years two different forms of integrated care have still been developed with remarkable success: On the one hand the health maintenance organisations (HMOs), on the other physician networks based on the gatekeeping principle. An increasing popularity has been observed among these managing forms of healthcare. While 25 % of the insured in Switzerland participated in such a model in 2008, in 2012 it already amounted to 58 % (Forum Managed Care 2012).

Healthcare Model and Quality Management

One of the first and currently largest Swiss physician networks is mediX Zurich. Founded in 1998, today it includes 95 physicians with their own practices, who are responsible for the care of 54,700 insured (average 2011). MediX Zurich is a selective network of GPs who are obliged to provide medical care that meets patients' needs and which is quality-based and cost-effective as well.

Under the mediX trademark, a second network in Bern was developed which more and more individual practices are joining (they remain in the ownership of the respective physician). Their objective is to establish a care brand considered to be exceptionally innovative, customer-oriented and reliable. They also strive to be a pioneer in the utilisation of information and communication technology in the care of the healthy as well as the ill and to sustainably promote healthcare and patient competence. The next step on this path is the development of a chronic care management for multimorbid patients in which specifically trained medical assistants and intelligent eHealth instruments assist the physician (team approach).

In order to establish itself as a pioneering care and quality brand in Swiss healthcare, mediX has developed stringent entry criteria. By entering into a mediX physician network, the participating doctors and practices commit to upholding the quality assurance guidelines. Among these is participation in at least 20 quality circles for physicians per year, the EQUAM certification of the practice (which is based on the EPA concept), collaboration on network projects as well as the willingness to disclose one's own economic viability. Transparency is also required for certain medication projects, for example when the substitution quota for the use of certain generic medications is collected. In addition, the umbrella organisation mediX Switzerland has over 70 of their own guidelines which are continually updated by network physicians and evaluated in the quality circles. Furthermore, they developed disease management programmes themselves or together with partners as

(continued)

---

[2] Written by Urs Zanoni.

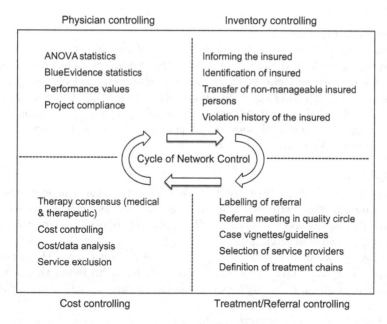

Physician controlling   Inventory controlling

ANOVA statistics

BlueEvidence statistics

Performance values

Project compliance

Informing the insured

Identification of insured

Transfer of non-manageable insured persons

Violation history of the insured

Cycle of Network Control

Therapy consensus (medical & therapeutic)

Cost controlling

Cost/data analysis

Service exclusion

Labelling of referral

Referral meeting in quality circle

Case vignettes/guidelines

Selection of service providers

Definition of treatment chains

Cost controlling   Treatment/Referral controlling

Fig. 11.2 Controlling in mediX Zurich (Strehle 2010)

Case Study 7 (continued)
well as their own software (databox) to measure and evaluate vital parameters for individual physicians and practices. Finally, there have been separate quality circles for the medical assistants for the last 2 years.

Insurance Model and Controlling
MediX Zurich/Bern offers a GP model together with the leading Swiss insurance companies. In this model the general practitioner takes on the function of the pilot through the complex healthcare system and supports the patient as the first contact person for all treatment decisions. Participating insured persons profit from additional services such as an around-the-clock emergency number, prevention services and health dossiers for preventive screenings and the most important everyday aches and pains.

When the insured persons choose a network physician as their first point of contact, they receive a financial incentive rebate on the obligatory basic insurance of 10–25 % (depending on insurer and place of residence). In turn, mediX Zurich/Bern concluded a capitation contract with the insured that delegates success and risk to the network level and not the physician level. The individual doctors receive compensation both for their efforts to

(continued)

Case Study 7 (continued)

ensure quality management and for their work in controlling; this compensation is based more and more on service criteria (pay-for-performance).

In order for the entire system to work as effectively and efficiently as possible, comprehensive controlling is in place (see Fig. 11.2). It is based on a web-based software available to each practice. Thanks to specialised workshops and continual support, all potential reservations against this controlling can be quickly overcome.

Assessment

The example of mediX distinctly shows how GP medical care can once again be shifted to the centre of healthcare. The organisation, which primarily consists of family doctors, is able to utilise the quality of the service providers and the provision of services as competitive factors. In doing so, mediX is on its way to establishing itself as a quality brand in Switzerland. The slight vertical integration up to now can be seen critically. In 2013 there should be concepts available regarding how one can incorporate specialists and inpatient facilities in the future.

Further information at: www.medix.ch

Assessment

It was already mentioned in the introduction that some of the managed care instruments are not innovations for some European healthcare systems, but rather also a rediscovery of traditional controlling elements. The gatekeeper is among these, and basically represents a revival of the traditional general practitioner system in Germany for example.

In doing so, gatekeeping addresses nearly all critical points of a fragmented healthcare system. Instead of the isolated treatment of a diagnosis, the continual support of the insured through "their" gatekeeper is in effect, ideally from before birth until death (although the physician will likely die beforehand). Through the long-term bond between the physician and patient which is crucial to gatekeeping, shifts between prevention and cures may be necessary. The call for stronger preventive measures (e.g. gatekeepers actively advocating that the insured stop smoking, do more sports, lose weight etc.) has gained a fully new dimension, as the gatekeeper has a financial interest in ensuring that their pool of patients is "in good health". However, this is usually rather an effective mechanism in capitation ($\rightarrow$ compensation systems), which has already been explained in depth.

In addition, there is considerable evidence that healthcare systems with such structures in place have total lower healthcare expenses than a system without them – which speaks volumes for the gatekeeping principle (Berchtold and Hess 2006, p. 20; Garrido et al. 2011, p. 34). However, the fact that it is quite difficult to clearly isolate the causes of low healthcare costs should be taken into account.

Supporters of gatekeeping declare that communication between general practitioners and the patient is better in general practitioner-oriented systems – however, it must be clearly emphasised that the discussion of this question is discussed extremely ideologically. However, this cannot be empirically demonstrated with an international comparison (Wasem et al. 2003, p. 4).

Along with the obvious strengths of gatekeeping there are also significant weaknesses. The freedom to choose physicians is a considerable criterion for patient satisfaction. Even when this is primarily concerned with a demand for freedom which very few take advantage of, it is highly valued by the insured. In this respect, gatekeeping is simply a limitation of the freedom to select physicians and will be difficult to justify in this manner. In other words, the denial of the freedom to choose physicians must be made attractive to the insured, either through more or better services in other areas of healthcare or through lower premiums. Thus, there is a trade-off relationship, i.e. limitation of freedom of choice must be combined with low premiums. However, the decisive weakness of the concept lies in this. Even when it is conceivable that a certain percentage of total costs can be saved through the consistent implementation of gatekeeping, the question remains as to whether these cost advantages overcompensate the necessary reductions of premiums or actually increase the volume of services. Without the corresponding incentives, the concept cannot be realized, since the qualitative aspects are difficult to impart particularly because the insured can also have their personal gatekeeper in a system with a free choice of physicians. There is no obligation for the insured to go directly to a specialist. As in gatekeeping, they can first consult their general practitioner each time. From the perspective of the insured, these advantages can be realised without limiting freedom of choice. Empirical studies from the United States have demonstrated that nearly all insured value the initial contact with a general practitioner who knows their health history (Grumbach et al. 1999, p. 264).

In addition, patient satisfaction is lowered by the additional effort which gate-keeping requires. Many insured often consider the consultation of a gatekeeper to be a nuisance. Particularly when they believe that they can determine which specialist they need to consult.

The insured will also see the new role of the general practitioner in a very critical light. While the insured previously had the feeling that physicians carried out more services than absolutely necessary ("at least it doesn't do harm") and considers this diligence as preventive care, this is now reversed. The danger of insufficient care becomes real for the insured. The insured persons must latently assume that they are treated too little instead of too much, since the gatekeeper covers each service. And the gatekeeper is also interested in maximising income or free time (individual maximizing of benefits).

Particularly the "capitation" variation represents an extensive re-orientation for general practitioners. The gatekeeper has a fixed income through the pool of patients and barely assumes an entrepreneurial risk, at least as long as the capitation rate is only based on the service spectrum. Thus, gatekeepers can no longer maximise their income, but only their free time. The more efficiently they manage their patient pools, the less effort there is and the more free time they have.

The main argument for supporting the concept with general practitioners, however, is that they now dominate the provision of services. The GP coordinates the budget, has information and can therefore extensively influence the treatment process. This is particularly important because the general practitioner has had a wallflower image up until now and tends to receive the lowest compensation.

However, the system also has grave disadvantages for general practitioners. The gatekeeper is put in a more uncomfortable position with considerable conflicts of interests, since on one hand the trust of the patient is limited and on the other hand the GP is virtually jointly responsible for the income of specialist colleagues. Furthermore, specialists will continually accuse the gatekeepers of providing too many services themselves, without having the corresponding qualifications. Gatekeeping shifts a large portion of the tension to the lowest level of the provision of services.

A decisive question for the final evaluation of the gatekeeping concept is how the threat of risk selection is approached. There are considerable incentives for the gatekeeper to "discourage" bad risks (for example through insufficient treatment which allows the patient to find another gatekeeper at the next possible opportunity) and to target good risks (according to area of residence, professional group etc.). This problem can only be solved when a risk-adjusted capitation premium ensures that there are no good or bad risks per se, or in other words, the composition of the pool of patients is not crucial to the economic success of a practice. Correspondingly, an extensive obligation to enter into contract must exist for the gatekeeper. These considerations show that through the shifting of the financial interests to the first level of service provision, external quality assurance measures ($\rightarrow$ quality management) become necessary in order to prevent gatekeeping from becoming merely a selection instrument.

In our opinion, there are two aspects in the discussion of gatekeeping regarding the strengthening of the GP's role which are not focused on enough. First, the thesis that the provision of services by GPs is less costly than specialist services should be critically questioned. The increasing specialisation in medicine – the number of specialised fields has multiplied in recent years – also has content-relevant causes. New methods of treatment almost inevitably require a specialisation. At the very least there are justified doubts as to whether a general practitioner is equipped to meet the requirement of being able to survey the entire spectrum of medical service provision and to stay informed of the technological and medical advances in all areas. If this is not the case, it could even result in an increase in treatment costs because the patients are either improperly treated (false diagnoses) or the referral to a specialist is made too late. At least in the Netherlands one assumes that the GPs will not be able to cover the entire service spectrum in the future and that specialisation will be necessary (Wasem et al. 2003, p. 26).

The second aspect points into a similar direction. In this discussion it is often ignored that medical education in general is not at all geared toward the management functions of the gatekeeper. Without the respective additional vocational training and qualifications as well as the reorganisation of the physician practices, this role can barely be assumed. Taking on coordination and controlling functions, for example, is also likely to lead to the appointing of disease managers in a group practice, who then assume these roles. The traditional organisation with "doctor plus receptionist" seems ill suited to implement effective gatekeeping.

In summary, it can be noted that gatekeeping is theoretically a very attractive concept that includes considerable possibilities for controlling as well as addressing increasing demands (in particular the optimisation of interfaces), also in the future. However, it should not be overlooked that institutions in the United States are once again distancing themselves from gatekeeping (Ferris et al. 2001; Lawrence 2001), and other systems are finding themselves in a position of crisis as well, such as the Netherlands (Wasem et al. 2003). On one hand this can be accounted for through the inappropriate limitation of freedom of choice and its extreme importance and on the other hand through the high demands of the service providers. As is the case in other managed care methods, finding a good compromise between the freedom of choice and controlling possibilities is crucial, and in particular the integration in adequate institutional arrangements ($\rightarrow$ integrated care systems).

With the increasingly established field of "patient coaching" the gatekeeper has non-medical competition which could lead to considerable changes. Especially the low-threshold and strong psychosocially oriented methods are suited to assume coordinating functions and pose no limits on freedom of choice. The relationship between the patient and patient coach shows more equilibrium than the doctor-patient relationship, which is characterised by linguistic barriers and hierarchies.

11.2 Guidelines and Clinical Pathways

Basic Concepts

In the realm of managed care, no other instrument has so many diverse variations of terms as that of the **guidelines**. In the European discussion, the terms guidelines, recommendations and statements are used; whereas in the American literature the terms algorithms, critical paths, practice parameter and clinical pathways are referred to (Amelung 1998, p. 3). Seventeen different clinical pathway terms were found alone in the English language after comprehensive literature research (De Bleser et al. 2006). The definitions of terms fundamentally differ regarding the degree of compulsion (from obligatory to recommendations), in regard to the scope (limited to a sector or cross-sector) and in the question of whether they are general or specific to the company (particularly clinical pathways can be seen as the implementation of company-specific settings).

In the following section only the term "guidelines" will be used, even when there are justified gradations between terms, since guidelines always deal with the standardisation of the provision of medical services. Case-by-case decisions will be replaced by general decisions. According to the general literature on management, this is considered to be a substitution of management by organisation. The connection between $\rightarrow$ utilisation review and guidelines also becomes apparent here: guidelines belong to the organisation – i.e. fixed rules are created – while utilisation review belongs to the management, in which decisions are made on a case-by-case basis.

In the scope of the managed care discussion, however, it must be made clear that this is a one-sided, medically oriented perspective and MCOs do indeed have varying objectives, namely regarding the reduction of costs. The physician or another service provider must "process" fixed treatment pathways, independently of whether or not they deem this form of treatment to be the most suitable.

Thus, Emanuel and Goldman (1998) rightly highlight the existence of two types of guidelines. First, there are those developed by physician associations and published in scientific journals, which allow for peer review and open discussion. Here there are also often guidelines which widely differ in the different associations and institutions which compete with one another.[3] Those guidelines developed by the public American Agency for Health Care and Policy Research in Washington, D.C. (www.ahcpr.gov) also belong to this category. This is similar to the association Arbeitsgemeinschaft der Wissenschaftlichen Medizinischen Fachgesellschaften (AWMF, association of the scientific medical societies in Germany). Beyond Germany, in 2002 the Guidelines International Network, G-I-N, was founded. It consists of more than 90 organisations and 127 individual members from 48 countries. Its repertoire includes a library with more than 7,000 internationally recognised guidelines (G-I-N 2013).

The second category is the confidential guidelines of MCOs, which primarily lower costs or are meant to create other competitive advantages, and are consequently not the object of controversy (Emanuel and Goldman 1998). In a competitive environment this type of service provision is a substantial factor for success, which therefore also makes it a "trade secret".

A hybrid form of both variations has gained significance in practise. This form includes guidelines for specialised consulting firms which may not publicly publish their guidelines for discussion, but are also not company-specific. The advantage for MCOs lies in the fact that most doctors are familiar with these guidelines.

Guidelines are without question one of the fundamental elements of managed care. Even though there are differences between the guidelines used and the scope of their implementation, they remain a major component for shaping the relationships between MCOs and the service providers.

Forms and Objectives of Guidelines

Before the different objectives are discussed here, a guideline – i.e. the management of hyperglycaemia in type 2 Diabetes of the American Diabetes Association (ADA

---

[3] A classic example is the question of mammographies for women under 50, on which points of view greatly differ.

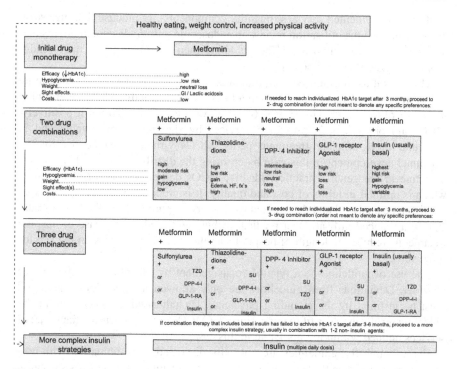

Fig. 11.3 Management of hyperglycemia in type 2 diabetes (Source: ADA (2012))

and the European Association for the Study of Diabetes – will be shown as an example (see Fig. 11.3).

This guideline was designed to facilitate the efficiency of this particular treatment plan for this reoccurring disease pattern. By precisely determining the steps of this process, it should be ensured that the treatment is carried out as fast as possible and at the same time that defined quality requirements are fulfilled.

The role of quality assurance, which is often highlighted as a central function, will not be discussed in more detail here because it is examined in the section → quality management. The role of guidelines as an internal controlling instrument, e.g. for training new employees, for internal coordination, coordination between companies or as a management instrument, will not be explored in further detail in this section. In the following section, the external controlling functions will be primarily discussed and the selection functions will be highlighted. Our focus is on the implementation of treatment forms with cost optimisation, product differentiation and the choice of contract partners.

MCOs primarily implement guidelines to manage quantity components. When a service is authorised via pre-authorisation utilisation review (→ utilisation review) – i.e. when it is determined that the service should be rendered – the review can then stipulate in which manner the service should be rendered. The MCOs thus determine not only the total volume of services (quantity), but also respectively the quality of implemented services (quantity components). In practise that means for example that via the utilisation review an endoscopic retrograde cholangiopancrea-tography would be authorised. The guideline then determines how many endo-scopic procedures should be performed.

The central assumption is that predefined quality levels can be provided more efficiently when physicians follow guidelines rather than individually determining the scope of treatment. This can be based on various factors. To put it positively, MCOs aid physicians in providing services by showing them suitable and in particular more efficient treatment paths. MCOs virtually assume the role of personnel development in this case by ensuring the distribution of evidence-based medicine in the general practice. Ideally, MCOs determine a form of treatment which is optimal in terms of cost and quality. It is crucial that the type of service provision be analysed and determined by the service purchaser. Guidelines usually signify a reduced utilisation of medical technologies and, in the case of hospital treatments, reduce the length of hospital stay through the compression the service provisions.

The use of guidelines is a type of "management by exception" for the service provider. Deviations from guidelines are only allowed in exceptional cases and must be justified by the attending physician. Unauthorised divergence from the guideline results in a loss of income, since the MCOs only compensate the scope of services defined within the guideline in this case.

Even though the guidelines are normally discussed in combination with cost reductions, in practise there are also examples that resulted in higher costs because a higher quantity component (increase in services) than usual was stipulated (Pauly 1995, p. 68). For this reason, MCOs should thoroughly assess whether a guideline will result in an increase of services, in regard to whether the expected improvements in quality justify the additional costs. Here it is already apparent that guidelines may not be considered solely an instrument for reducing costs.

The second aspect is the differentiation of products of an MCO. Through guidelines intended product differentiation (also external differentiation) can be documented. Guidelines primarily stipulate the quality of the process rather than that of the outcomes. Therefore, an MCO can strive to develop various services which differ in the actual operational organisation of their procedures. For example, the removal of gallstones is generally associated with a 3-day hospital stay. However, through a specialised process it is possible to reduce this stay to 1 day. While it requires a considerable amount of additional organisational work, it can still be interesting for an MCO to develop the aforementioned product and offer it to customers who can afford it. Likewise, it is conceivable to define guidelines for risk averse patients who want to have a higher than average number of tests performed. This would also mean additional work that must be compensated. Guidelines are suited to meet individualised requirements and willingness to pay and to counter the idea that product differentiation does not belong in healthcare.

The use of guidelines can also be seen as a criterion for the selection of contract partners ($\rightarrow$ selective contracting). While indicators for the quality of results are difficult to evaluate, it can be helpful to refer to the process quality and its stipulations. An MCO can, for example, only transact with service providers who use fixed guidelines and therefore must not implement any further quality assessments.

Areas of Application for Guidelines

A central question is which indicators require guidelines. This point is particularly relevant because the development of indicators involves high costs. There are four relevant aspects for MCOs:

1. Quantity and homogeneity,
2. Differences in cost and quality within the forms of treatment,
3. Degree of asymmetry between service providers and purchasers and
4. The lack of lump sum forms of compensation ($\rightarrow$ compensation systems).

First, guidelines only make sense for diagnosis or therapy forms that produce a significant volume of revenue (amount or cost per case). Classic examples include births, bypass operations, hip replacements, chronic diseases such as diabetes or treatments with high subsequent costs, such as for strokes. However, experience has shown that a large portion of medical services can be addressed with relatively few guidelines. The services must also be located in a relatively homogeneous spectrum, i.e. they must be very easy to standardise. Guidelines composed of a variety of exceptions are correspondingly complicated to manage and are difficult to establish in the first place. Considerably more medical services than generally assumed also fulfil these criteria. Although every patient has individual characteristics, the main elements of treatment to can be standardised to an extent without being detrimental to patient individuality.

Second, guidelines are only appropriate when the different therapy schemes show highly differing costs. For example, this may always be the case when there is a choice between cheaper outpatient care and more expensive inpatient care, or between treatment with medications and surgical treatment. Different forms of treatment, which do not differ in terms of costs or quality, do not have to be standardised. Through advances in medical technology, such as minimally invasive operations, the number of different forms of treatment with widely varying costs has increased.

The third aspect is the reduction of information asymmetries. Information asymmetries exist when it is difficult for a service purchaser to evaluate the provision of services, resulting in a controlling problem ($\rightarrow$ introduction). The more difficult it is to monitor the service provider in individual cases and the larger the potential that their own interests can be maximised, the more useful the implementation of guidelines is. In practical terms, this means that the provision of services becomes more transparent. These guidelines also make it possible for non-medical practitioners to monitor the provision of services. They can at least determine whether or not the treatment deviated from the guideline and whether the further explanation is necessary.

The fourth aspect concerns alternatives to guidelines. When there are lump sum forms of compensation, such as case rates (DRG), additional fees or capitation (→ compensation forms), the type of service provision is less financially relevant for service purchasers, since inefficiencies do not cost the purchaser anything. In this case only the quality of the results must be assessed (→ quality management) for which guidelines are suitable. In the case of lump sum forms of compensation, the service providers themselves have a great interest in developing and implementing guidelines since they can be used as a cost-monitoring tool.

In addition to aspects described in this section, there are three additional criteria from a medical standpoint. Firstly, guidelines are only appropriate when the available forms of treatment have some level of acceptance in the medical community; a form of diagnosis or therapy must exist upon which consensus can be reached. Second, guidelines are suitable for forms of treatment with high reputational or liability risks. Both risks can be nearly completely excluded by consistently applying the guidelines. In the United States a reduction of the liability risk through the use of guidelines has significantly increased their acceptance. Third, guidelines can be particularly easy to implement in treatment forms with a high degree of innovation because in these cases few "old practices" must be abandoned.

Assessment

A critical evaluation of guidelines is very difficult since guidelines can be implemented in many different ways where general statements are hardly appropriate. The subsequent graphic (Fig. 11.4) illustrates this principle (Amelung 1998, p. 23).

From the perspective of the service purchaser, guidelines, which lead to higher costs and better quality, are merely a matter of preference. One must consider the relation between additional costs and the increase in quality. Lower quality with (at the same time) low costs represents a reduction of the service package. The products available to the service provider are simply different than before the introduction of guidelines. The three fields in the upper right hand corner of the figure do not need to be discussed in more detail. There can be no interest in such strategies because they are detrimental to all participants. The same is true for the case when the quality and the costs are static. Here it is only the costs of developing the guidelines that have a negative impact. The three fields in the lower left corner can be considered as strategic factors for success.

All of these fields illustrate realistic forms for which corresponding examples can be found. It is not legitimate to focus on one field and correspondingly argue in a positive or negative way. Here we will not further discuss quality aspects (→ quality management), but rather the management functions. This separation is solely based on the attempt to avoid redundancies. Subsequently, several important conclusions on guidelines will be discussed.

Guidelines and → utilisation reviews should be considered in the following context since they signify a far-reaching limitation of freedom in therapies and diagnosis for the service providers. First, which services can be rendered is often

		Quality		
		higher	*same*	*lower*
Costs	*higher*	preference decision	negative	negative
	same	positive	insignificant	negative
	lower	star	positive	product differentiation

Fig. 11.4 Guideline cost/quality matrix

determined based on check lists, and then the execution of an externally provided treatment pattern follows. Through the development of the guidelines, crucial decisions are made about who is authorised to define the type and scope of the provision of services. Thus, guidelines also determine the balance of power between the purchasing and provision of services.

In other words, guidelines signify the introduction of this type of managed care and results in the abolishment of the "blank check" for the service purchasers, i.e. the complete delegation of responsibility for the type and scope of the provision of services to the service provider. The initial evaluations are quite convincing. Therefore, in the case of heart attacks the length of hospital stay could be reduced by 16.5 % without a loss of quality. Comparable studies for liver excisions showed similar potential for lowering costs (Roeder and Küttner 2006).

Like all management instruments, guidelines require incentive and penalty mechanisms for their implementation. They are only adhered to when non-compliance has direct consequences.

In the United States, the implementation of guidelines is affected by three factors: First through the considerable threat of malpractice cases (liability risk). Because of this, physicians have an increased interest in limiting their risk of liability as much as possible. The consistent utilisation of guidelines usually suffices as proof of appropriate treatment. This is an aspect that has become increasingly important. Second, the market power of MCOs is crucial. The greater their power is, the easier it is to implement guidelines – particularly guidelines aiming to reduce costs. The third factor is that only the services that are covered by a guideline are compensated by the MCOs. There are no problems with an increase in volume through the physician as long as this does not lead to higher costs for the MCO.

Although the guidelines are not discussed much in this context, they are a nearly optimal instrument for limiting services. Because the scope of services is clearly fixed, and this does not necessarily have to be the "optimal" scope, services can be easily limited. Regardless if the services are carried out for a pregnancy or for preventive health examinations, on one hand it is a medical question and on the other hand a question of the desired scope of services.

Guidelines which are developed by the MCOs simply as internal documents require particular attention: The participating physicians must sign so-called "gag rules" stating they are not allowed to reveal the guidelines they follow to their patients (Emanuel and Goldman 1998). Emanuel and Goldman assert that all guidelines should be examined and authorised by a neutral, interdisciplinary body. This would also be a component of a quality review ($\rightarrow$ quality management). This demand can be seen as a reaction to very problematic guidelines such as "24 h delivery" guidelines. This guideline defined processes according to which a woman giving birth should leave the hospital within 24 h. However, this would lead to much resistance among the population and the political representatives.

In comparison to other managed care instruments guidelines possess a major advantage. Service providers can hardly criticise guidelines created by neutral or state institutions. This is because the basic idea of developing standards for optimal patient care can be agreed upon. Even when it is often argued that these oversimplify the treatment processes, there is a consensus that developing standards is indeed practical (Robinson and Steiner 1998, p. 149). Some physicians also tend to deny that their colleagues are practising the trend in the field. Thus, guidelines are a managed care instrument that can be implemented without considerable opposition from the service provider.

Despite the overall positive management function, the question remains unresolved as to whether the considerable effort to develop and implement guidelines is relative to the potential cost savings or quality increases. Surveys of American physicians have shown that only 18 % of their working methods have changed and that only 22 % are convinced that guidelines can save costs. However, 67 % found that they should be implemented to "penalise" other physicians (Robinson and Steiner 1998, p. 149f.). Here it is apparent that new management instruments need a considerable amount of time in order to establish themselves in practise. It can be assumed that guidelines will represent an absolute given and that a treatment not based on guidelines is unthinkable.

DRGs make it necessary to implement process cost accounting and, if necessary, target costing (Amelung 1998). In addition to the restructuring of the accounting, optimising processes and implementing clinical pathways are logical steps to follow based on this conclusion.

It can be assumed that the use of guidelines will play a key role in the expected discussion of quality and the heightened creation of transparency. This is also because guidelines are a quality instrument that can be easily assessed. However, this is contradicted by the fact that the possible applications are limited with the increasing significance of multimorbid patients (Boyd et al. 2005, p. 722).

11.3 Formularies

Fundamental Concepts and Effective Mechanisms

Formularies represent the explicit service definition from the perspective of the service purchaser. Instead of deciding case-by-case ($\rightarrow$ utilisation review),[4] general rules determine which services, in particular medications, are financed. Thus, formularies are largely an addition to $\rightarrow$ guidelines, in which treatment methods can be stipulated. It is not specified how a treatment must be carried out exactly, but rather how it should not be carried out. This is achieved by non-inclusion of the treatment or medication in the formularies. In the following section, only formularies for medications will be discussed, as only these have a practical relevance for managed care.

In the managed care context, formularies are management instruments for each individual MCO in relation to their service providers and insured persons. The implementation of the formularies is related (1) to the assumption that there are many medications or treatment procedures that are completely ineffective; (2) that the same effectiveness can be achieved with a smaller amount of resources and that (3) they do not belong in the service area of the respective MCO. At this point, it becomes clear that this is an instrument with various intentions, all of which must each be separately considered. The goals in implementing formularies range from an increase in efficiency to product differentiation in a competitive environment.

Six strategic goals can be pursued with formularies:
1. Product differentiation in respect to other MCOs,
2. Lowering of costs through the substitution of branded products with generics,
3. Implementation of cost-effective medications,
4. Quality assurance through more effective, evidence-based medications and the exclusion of ineffective pharmaceuticals,
5. Development of market power in relation to pharmaceutical manufacturers and
6. The reduction of medication consumption.

These strategic orientations must not necessarily exclude one another, but rather they can complement each other. In addition the compilation of formularies must be considered as well as the consequences for those concerned. For this process, it must be determined whether the list in question is an open or closed list. In the case of an open list, the prescription of a medication not included on the list must be justified, while in the case of a closed list the prescription is excluded. In addition, there is the possibility of choosing a hybrid form, i.e. to make a total of three categories. The first category includes products which are completely covered, the second those in which co-payments must be paid and the third category of products must be generally paid by the insured (Cassel 2008, p. 129). In Austria, for example, this system is used for the payment of pharmaceuticals. Let us now consider the

---

[4] In the scope of the utilisation review, the sub-form of drug utilisation reviews plays an important role. 90.4 % of all HMOs use this form of utilisation review (Sanofi 2012).

strategic objectives of formularies. Using a formulary, an MCO can create a differentiation of insurance products. The inclusion or non-inclusion of medications with a large presence in the media, such as Xenical or Viagra, is an excellent instrument for the presentation of a product. In principle, relatively homogeneous health insurance products can be clearly distinguished here. In contrast to the variations in treatment forms (purchasing or not purchasing), many formularies are not only suited for product differentiation, but also for communication policy. On one hand one can communicate based on the length of the formularies ("With us you can receive everything you need"), and on the other hand one can particularly communicate about the financing of the most discussed innovations. Through these examples it is also apparent that mandatory prescriptions are not the crucial criteria, i.e. medications for which prescriptions are mandatory due to their toxicity must not be included on the lists.

The second goal is the consistent substitution of branded products with generic products which are generally much less expensive. Physicians tend to prescribe familiar medications with which they have had extensive experience and which, due to the patent periods, are typically name-brand products. Physicians are also more comfortable prescribing patients well-known branded products instead of no-name generic products which always have the image of being a cheap copy. The significance of the personal connections between physicians and pharmaceutical company representatives will not be further discussed here.

The third and fourth aspects lead in a similar direction. On the one hand formularies are meant to ensure that cost-effective and optimal quality medications are chosen. In this way the MCO also takes on an educational role for the service provider. The different forms of medication are systematically analysed and examined for economic efficiency and effectiveness. For the individual physician, this results in a reduction of complexity and an improvement in the quality of provision of services. In addition, the physician saves time because they no longer have to deal with pharmaceutical company representatives. However, the physician's discretionary leeway should also be limited. For example, formularies prevent the prescription of medications that are only prescribed so that the patient "at least got something". Many patients expect these forms of prescriptions since the absence of a prescription is often seen as a denial of services.

The fifth aspect is the development of market power in relation to the pharmaceutical industry (Shapiro 1997, p. 265). Firstly, procurement management is considerably professionalised, i.e. studies can be carried out on different forms of therapy and the market can also be better analysed. Secondly, the pharmaceutical manufacturers are put under pressure by the question of inclusion and non-inclusion. However, this is only of limited relevance because the inclusion should be based on medical criteria. The third criterion is more important. By reducing the amounts of medications, not only are less medications are consumed, the demand is also shifted. Fewer medications are required in larger amounts. Through this effect, MCOs can attain economies of scale through procurement (Cassel and Friske 1999, p. 535).

The reduction of medication consumption in general should also be considered here. Formularies consistently pursue the goal of driving ineffective products from the market. By not purchasing certain products and product groups, the volume of medications is reduced.

In the 1990s, 96 % of providers used open medication lists and nearly 50 % used closed medication lists (Blissenbach and Penna 1996, p. 377). In view of the rising costs for prescription medications, HMOs have also implemented a four- to five-level co-pay system. According to the "Co-pay Tier Design", those insured with HMOs can choose different co-payments for medications. The insured can access a medication list where is 33 % of medications are open in "tier one", while in "tier three" it is 74 % (Sanofi 2010). Thus, it is one of the classic instruments of managed care. The utilisation differs widely between MCOs. The stronger the degree of loyalty of the service provider to the service purchaser and the larger the MCO is, the more important the formularies are. 100 % of the staff model HMOs and only 65.9 % of the IPA model HMOs use formularies. The lower percentage of formularies among IPA model HMOs is an example of the idea that IPAs are in the position "to protect" their members from the far-reaching influence of MCOs.

MCOs no longer primarily compile formularies and handle the procurement of medications, but rather specialised consulting firms have taken over this responsibility (→ pharmacy benefit management). Pharmacy benefit management (PBM) companies are companies originally founded as purchasing associations to take on this function. Their advantages are in two areas: Firstly, they can attain economies of scale in the compilation of formularies. For example, the development of ten formularies for MCOs is only minimally more expensive than if the MCO had developed them themselves. Secondly, they bundle the purchasing power to a great extent and are able to negotiate much higher rebates. In the meantime 13.6 % of the HMOs use the formularies developed by PBM (Sanofi 2012).

Assessment

As is the case of nearly all managed care instruments, one cannot make a generalised judgement about formularies. Whether formularies contribute to a lowering of costs and/or an increase in quality depends on the strategic intentions.

Formularies can doubtlessly have very successful effects on the cost structure when it can be determined that the most affordable respective medication is included. It cannot be expected that physicians are familiar with the most cost-effective variations of medications used in treatment. While the regulatory authorities only examine whether a medication is effective and not whether or not it is efficient, the service purchasers have to carry out their own cost-benefit analyses (→ evaluation procedure).

Formularies can also make an important contribution to → quality management. Assuming that formularies not only eliminate uneconomical medications from the selection but also those which are ineffective or less effective, the quality of the provision of services can be significantly increased. In the American discussion, it is nearly unanimously emphasised that formularies can improve quality (Blissenbach and Penna 1996, p. 378).

It has been mentioned multiple times that the acceptance by the service providers is an important criterion for the success of managed care instruments. This is where the main weakness of formularies lies. It can hardly be expected that physicians prefer for insurance companies to dictate which medications they are allowed to prescribe. This would doubtlessly be seen as an imposition upon their freedom in treatment and would be particularly difficult to implement when the physician has to orient themselves based on different formularies from different MCOs. Thus, it can be assumed that the effect of formularies largely depends on the organisational structure. In a staff model HMO it would pose no problem to implement closed formularies. In addition, MCOs make sure to include their physicians in the compilation of the lists. Empirical studies have shown that 87.7 % and 84.8 % of the selection committees are made up of physicians and pharmacists, respectively (Sanofi 2010, p. 47).

Formularies lead to an administrative burden which is not negligible. They will only be recognised and implemented by physicians when they are based on sound analysis. A particular problem in this process is that they lag behind, virtually by definition. New, possibly very effective medications first reach the service providers after a delay, since they have to go through an additional review process. Especially in the case of diseases for which there are not yet sufficient therapies, such as Parkinson's or Alzheimer's, it is absolutely not realistic that a medication which has been announced for months is not directly made available to patients suffering from these diseases. The supplements to existing formularies, which restrict the comprehensibility somewhat, offer the only feasible method. Thus, it is no wonder that 52.9 % of the HMOs revise their formularies every quarter (Sanofi 2010, p. 47).

In an increasing transformation of operative treatments towards forms of medication therapy, formularies also represent a very effective rationing instrument. Without wanting to discuss the theory of rationing in itself, it must be mentioned that through nonpurchasing, as in the case of controversial AIDS therapies, the treatment spectrum is limited to the level of the individual MCOs.

Another core problem is the lacking evidence basis of many treatment forms. It must be simply accepted that, in the cases of many forms of diagnosis and therapy, we are unaware of their true efficiency. This is also true for the medications that are actually implemented.

The last aspect to be addressed is the effect of formularies within the pharmaceutical industry. There is no question that formularies promote manufacturers without own research activity. As a result, manufacturers conducting research must shift their sometimes very high volume of research and development to patented products and especially to products without competition. This inevitably leads to an increase in the price of medications in niche markets and product innovations. An alternative strategy is the transformation of a pure medication manufacturer to an integrated problem solver (Reuter 1997, p. 332ff.; Janus 2003). This means that a service packet is developed which, along with the medications, also includes further training, medical technology and other products. Products that are essentially comparable to one another should be differentiated through the creation of added value. This is a typical strategy for mature markets with strong predatory competition.

11.4   Utilisation Review and Management

Basic Concepts

Direct intervention in the type and scope of provision of services is a crucial element of managed care. **Utilisation review** is a key instrument for this process (Zelman and Berenson 1998, p. 73ff.; Shi and Singh 2012; Cleverley et al. 2010, p. 159ff.).

In utilisation review, the suitability of medical services is evaluated based on individual case studies. The service providers must systematically disclose services planned or carried out to external assessors and must, in some cases, relinquish their freedom of diagnosis and treatment. Three questions are central to utilisation review (Dranove and Spier 2003):

1. Do the patient's symptoms lead to the assumption that certain medical services (e.g. magnetic resonance imaging) should be carried out in order to correspond to the treatment process (in other words, "to do the right thing")?
2. Is inpatient treatment necessary for the patient or are there other suitable forms of treatment (place and also level of service provision)? and
3. When inpatient treatment is unavoidable, how long should the patient stay in the hospital (i.e. "do things right")?

From the perspective of the service purchasers, it is emphasised again and again that utilisation review is not only an instrument for cost control, but that quality is also improved through the systematic assessment of the suitability of examinations (Christianson et al. 2008, p. 1368). However, in practise the focus is still on the prevention of inappropriate services and therefore remains focused on cost control. There is good reason for this as international studies show that 51 % of hospital admissions are inappropriate (Duncan 2008). In a Commonwealth Fund survey, 20 % of German patients and 18 % of American patients affirmed that they underwent unnecessary duplicate examinations (Schoen et al. 2005). Older studies assume significantly higher percentages, as the savings potential was not yet fully utilised. Thus, Wickizer estimates that 35 % of days spent in the hospital are inappropriate (Wickizer 1992, p. 104).

In contrast, **utilisation management** is not a case-by-case evaluation. The aggregated services of a physician, for example, are compared with the results of the best physicians (best practice) or with the statistical average. According to management theory, the key characteristics of utilisation management correspond to benchmarking ($\rightarrow$ quality management).

Utilisation review as well as utilisation management both require service providers to justify services that are planned or have already been carried out.

Thus, the service purchasers now rely on systematic analysis as opposed to trust. This goes hand in hand with a shift in the balance of power from the service providers towards the service purchasers. Under the assumption that only 50 % of the patients receive the treatment considered necessary (McGlynn et al. 2003), this development is understandable.

The concept of utilisation review originated from the cost-cutting laws of the Nixon administration in the early 1970s. Despite considerable opposition from medical associations, so-called Professional Standards Review Organisations (PSRO) were implemented for the public programmes Medicare and Medicaid ($\rightarrow$ introduction) (Ginzberg 1996, p. 17; Brown 1996, p. 2; Sultz and Young 2010, p. 248) in order to evaluate the compliance with medical standards. Even when these organisations were not able to contribute to a thorough reduction of costs, the concept of the instrument was successfully established.

Forms of Utilisation Review and Utilisation Management

In practise, utilisation review and utilisation management have given rise to a wealth of different forms and approaches. Figure 11.5 displays an overview of the most important forms.

In light of their practical significance, the prevailing forms of reviews are pre-admission review and pre-authorisation review as well as concurrent review.

Pre-admission review, which is also referred to as pre-certification review, generally precedes inpatient hospital admission. The service provider, usually a specialist or general practitioner, cannot make a decision regarding admission on their own, but must obtain the authorisation of the service purchaser. In the first step, admission enquiries are usually decided by nurses[5] working according to standardised protocols, rather than the physicians themselves. Physicians are first contacted by utilisation review to decide upon the individual cases when conflicts arise (Mullahy 2010). At the same time, the maximum length of stay (MaxLOS)[6] is often fixed, although this depends on the form of compensation ($\rightarrow$ compensation systems). Insurance companies do not compensate hospital stays that exceed the maximum length of stay.

Pre-authorisation review manages the use of diagnosis and therapy forms as well as medical aids in outpatient care. In this case the physician is also unable to decide independently whether a PET can be carried out, for example, but must have it authorised beforehand. Pre-authorisation review concentrates on the limited number of very expensive treatment forms, e.g. the use of new imaging procedures. It does not necessarily only consider the unjustified expansion of services, but can also expose an undersupply of services.

---

[5] In the US there are two types of nurses with vastly different qualification profiles. Registered nurses (RNs) complete a degree, while nurse practitioners complete a professional training course.

[6] Maximum length of stay, usually based on the ICD-10.

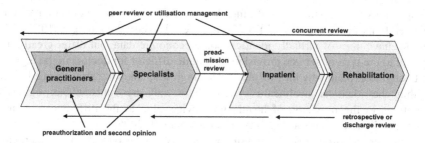

Fig. 11.5 Utilisation review, utilisation management in the value chain

Second opinion programmes are closely related to the preauthorisation review. Instead of a classic review process, the opinion of another doctor is required. The operation can only be carried out when both physicians agree upon a diagnosis. Second opinion programmes are consequently not only a controlling instrument, but can equally be considered as a quality assurance instrument (Green and Rowell 2011; Geraedts 2013). Katz (2006, p. 31f) emphasises that the second opinion should come from similar but not identical fields of medicine, and always recommends second opinions when interventions are elective, when the diagnosis is rare and diffuse, when risks and benefits cannot be adequately represented, when the services have very high costs and generally when there is not sufficient confidence in the diagnosis or treatment.

In the case of **concurrent review** the service providers submit a treatment plan and then the suitability of said treatment plan is assessed. A concurrent review assesses, for example, whether the duration of hospital stay is appropriate and if the planned examinations during the stay are necessary. Concrete discharge planning and the organisation of subsequent forms of treatment play an important role in concurrent review (Kongstvedt 2013).

The **retrospective** or **discharge review** is a classic ex-post control of the provision of services. The respective treatment or portions of treatment are considered and assessed for economic efficiency. Thus, the treatment can be analysed on the basis of patient records, i.e. whether or not the physician complied with the guidelines or whether there are considerable deviations from the peer groups. The retrospective or discharge review is the basis for warnings or the termination of contracts in the scope of → selective contracting. It is common for particularly costly cases to be assessed for suitability after the fact and also allows a comparison between patients' files and invoicing (Kongstvedt 2013; Shi and Singh 2012).

Peer review and **utilisation management** differ considerably from the previously mentioned forms of utilisation review as they deal less with the controlling aspects but rather with the learning effects (Kongstvedt 2013). Peer review is the analysis of individual cases together with colleagues. One's own provision of services is discussed with peers and should promote a constructive dialogue and initiate a continual process of improvement (→ quality management). Utilisation management differs from all other forms of review that have been discussed, since it concerns the entire provision of services instead of individual cases that are compared over a certain period of time. A common example is the old comparison of operations in the regions of Boston and New Haven (Wennberg 2010). Both regions have a set of virtually identical socio-economic data, but differ greatly in respect to the type of service provision. It is quite difficult for doctors in the region of Boston to explain why they display such a high frequency of certain procedures. Within the identical healthcare system there may be considerable regional variations in the provision of healthcare services due to the differences in the physicians' enthusiasm for these services (Dixon et al. 2006).

However, the simple comparison of hospital stays can also result in considerable pressure to justify decisions and is comparable to benchmarking ($\rightarrow$ quality management). Utilisation management can relate to physicians, hospitals, populations or diagnoses. Beyond their informing function, the results of utilisation management can facilitate selective problem solving. The practices or hospitals with significantly poorer results then have to undergo a re-engineering or reorganisation process.

Importance and Effective Mechanisms

Utilisation review has a great significance in practise in the United States. In the following section, it will be briefly outlined which and whose services actually go through utilisation review, and which consequences result from this review.

In a large-scale survey in the United States, Remler et al. (1997, p. 200) found that among 59 % of the doctors the length of hospital stay was evaluated within the utilisation review, among 45 % of them the location was reviewed and among 39 % the suitability of the services was evaluated. It is also striking that among surgeons utilisation reviews are carried out much more often. This could primarily be due to the fact that the largest savings potential is expected in the surgical sector.

Robinson and Steiner (1998, p. 125 ff.) discovered that 95 % of MCOs implement at least one form of utilisation review and 62 % use four of the five most important forms. Utilisation management is used by 74 % of the MCOs. The use of this instrument can thus be considered to be characteristic for American MCOs.

However, there are considerable differences in terms of which service sectors undergo reviews, particularly preauthorisation reviews. It is of special importance to conduct a preauthorisation review for expensive procedures (Duncan et al. 2008). Due to the high administrative costs of a review procedure, the MCOs concentrate on selected areas.

Utilisation reviews have proven to be successful: They have shown that the duration of inpatient stay was too long in 67 % of the cases. Under the application of utilisation reviews the hospitals stays can be reduced by 50 % (Duncan et al. 2008). In recent years, the implementation of utilisation reviews has become particularly established in the pharmaceutical sector. While only 2.6 % of IPAs use second opinion programmes to influence the prescription behaviour of physicians, 94.3 % of the IPAs use drug utilisation reviews (Sanofi 2012).

Empirical results show that the potential of utilisation reviews does not lie in the savings through rejected services. However, it cannot be concluded for this reason that utilisation reviews are not suitable as management instruments. Even when services are not rejected, the inhibition threshold for unsuitable services has been considerably raised. Even the justification pressure alone has positive results. In an older study Wickizer (1992, p. 117) asserts that through utilisation reviews hospital admissions can be lowered by 12 %, hospital costs can be reduced by 14 % and total medical expenses can be lowered by 6 %. In a comprehensive, long-term study, Rosenberg et al. (1995) demonstrated the effectiveness of second opinion programmes. It was also proven here that it is not the rejections but the mere existence of the instrument that is primarily responsible for the savings. The second opinion programmes were seen by the patients as an improvement in quality, which is a very clear indication regarding the low level of patient-doctor trust.

The review instruments preceding the provision of services also have the advantage (from the service purchaser's perspective) that more precise prognoses regarding the cash flows are possible and are therefore suitable as an instrument for short-term financial planning (Kongstvedt 2013). The larger the sample is, however, the more drastically the significance is reduced by the law of large numbers.

Payne et al. (1991, p. 474) emphasise that utilisation review can be viewed not only as an external instrument, but that it should also be used by service providers as an internal management instrument. Thus, a hospital can determine which physicians or services are particularly efficient or how the management instruments have affected efficiency (evaluation function).

Assessment

Utilisation review and utilisation management belong without a doubt to the most important instruments of managed care (Robinson and Steiner 1998, p. 19). Through the direct and consistent influence that service purchasers have on the provision of services – directly or indirectly via utilisation review organisations (UROs)[7] – utilisation review can be characterised as fundamental reorganisation of the distribution of duties between the provision and purchasing of services. Because they are dependent on the "authorisation" of the service purchaser, doctors lose a great degree of freedom of choice. What is more serious is that they must continually justify decisions; not only to patients, but also to the service purchaser. Thus, utilisation review inevitably leads to the reconception of the doctor-patient relationship. The patient is faced with the problem that their physician is in a conflict of roles and must equally consider the requirements of utilisation review. Moreover, the patient's trust is rightly limited.

---

[7] In practise, in the US many consulting firms have been established in recent years, which specialise in carrying out utilisation reviews and management. Their crucial advantage is that they have very large quantities of comparable figures and can thus better assess whether physicians or treatments diverge from the norm (→ MCO).

An often-criticised point is that utilisation reviews lead to an enormous increase in bureaucracy in the provision of services. Schlesinger et al. (1997, p. 108) aptly state that American physicians are the most "second-guessed and paperwork-laden physicians in Western Industrialised democracies". This conflict was intensified even more because at least in the first step of the review process the physicians have to deal with personnel who are not necessarily qualified in the field and who simply work their way through check lists. It can be generally assumed that per service enquiry the utilisation review takes 15 min for the physician as well as for the insurance.

The argument that utilisation reviews, like → guidelines, almost inevitably lead to "cookbook medicine" is of greater concern. This can on one hand be beneficial as well as improve quality, since MCOs will make sure that state of the art forms of treatment are promoted when they develop review programmes. In this way, utilisation reviews also contribute to the diffusion of medical innovation. On the other hand, there are also justified fears that individual specific characteristics are not sufficiently considered.

Despite the points of criticism mentioned, it must be stated that utilisation review represents a significant factor for the success of managed care. Only when the service purchasers intervene in the decisions of service provision is it possible to attain far-reaching changes. Utilisation reviews show that transparency and know-ledge about controlling can bring about a considerable change in behaviour rather than concrete decisions (e.g. rejected admissions). However, it must be emphasised that this is only possible when statutory insurance companies massively invest in care research and the development of further competence. Utilisation review and utilisation management are core elements in the concept of smart purchasing. Smart purchasing, however, requires that the service purchasers as well as the service providers develop competencies in order to meet this new challenge and allow healthcare to become a market with purchasers and sellers.

11.5 Disease Management and Chronic Care

Introductory Remarks

A relatively small portion of the insured causes a large part of the healthcare expenses (Rebscher 2006). Thus, there is a necessity to specifically improve the quality and the costs of healthcare for these groups of insured. This is where disease management comes in.

Disease management can be defined as an organisational method that coordinates and improves the healthcare of groups of patients over the course of a disease and beyond the limits of the individual service provider (Kongstvedt 2013). It is a system of healthcare interventions and communication methods coordinated with each other for population groups with health problems, and in which the cooperation of the patient is essential (Disease Management Association of America 2004). Disease management aims to improve quality and bring about a reduction in costs for the care of patients with chronic illnesses (Bodenheimer 2000).

Disease management is a structured answer to a series of problems that arise in many healthcare systems: a fragmented and non-coordinated healthcare system, an overemphasis on acute care, particularly regarding inpatient treatment; a neglect of prevention as well as unsuitable forms of treatment. Individual components that focus on acute treatment can be considered a component management model. The component management model is based on the idea that by minimising the costs of component processes the overall costs can be lowered (Zitter 2001). However, this assumption has not proven to be true. Healthcare experts estimate that in American healthcare 25–40 % of all costs accrue due to insufficient quality in the treatment chain. Even though they cannot be precisely quantified, efficiency reserves in other healthcare systems are similar, albeit propably slightly lower.

The philosophy of disease management is based on the assumption that the systematic, integrated, evidence-based, long-term care of identifiable risk groups of patients with chronic, high-cost illnesses is more effective and less expensive than the episodic, fragmented care of individuals. In this way, a shortage or surplus of care as well as improper care can be reduced. Disease management aims to change the behaviour of service providers and patients (Kongstvedt 2013). Unlike → case management, in disease management the group of people affected by certain illnesses is in the foreground rather than the expensive individual case with a complex illness profile. However, as a patient management method, case management is an important element of disease management (Duncan 2008).

Disease management assumes that each disease has a recognisable life cycle and a typical economic structure, so that experiences with the quality management of industrial value-added processes can be successfully applied to healthcare. Thus, disease management is similar to the innovative approaches of → quality management.

Elements of Disease Management

The essential elements of disease management are (DMAA 2004; Huber 2005; Nuovo 2007; Peytremann-Bridevaux and Burnand 2009):

1. Integrated healthcare delivery systems without traditional boundaries between specific medical fields and institutions (physician's practice, hospital, caretaking and rehabilitation organisations) which coordinate healthcare over the entire course of a disease;
2. A knowledge base that comprehensively informs about the prevention of complications, treatment and the alleviation of a disease (→ evidence-based medicine) and that continually integrates the results of → health systems research. For example, they also influence the → guidelines;
3. A sophisticated clinical and administrative information system to analyse treatment patterns. This information system establishes the economic structure of a disease and determines which type of care should be implemented by whom and

in which way in a certain phase of a disease. The information system is based on IT and network technologies;

4. A compensation system which takes the results of treatment (outcomes) into account for the basis of compensation (→ compensation systems);
5. The application of → quality management methods to continuously improve and develop the information system and healthcare. This includes process and outcome assessments and programme evaluations;
6. Measures for patient information, promotion of health and patient education in order to increase patient compliance in the treatment process and in order to reduce the health risks of the insured. The measures can take behaviour changing programmes into account;
7. Identification and risk stratification processes for population groups;
8. Service provider cooperation models in order to include physicians and supporting service providers.

There are general criteria for the selection of a disease for disease management by a purchaser or a managed care organisation (MCO): A broad scope of treatment patterns among patients and doctors, the high costs of disease, an accumulation of preventable complications and low patient compliance. Further criteria include treatment patterns with numerous referrals from general practitioners to specialists, the possibility of developing guidelines and a good ability to control diseases through disease management (Kongstvedt 2013).

Disease management is particularly suitable for diseases that have been well researched, particularly if evidence-based treatment protocols are available and for which treatment outcomes can be evaluated. Among these are diabetes, heart diseases, cancers, stroke, asthma, skin diseases, osteoporosis, back pain, depression and certain infectious diseases. Most HMOs already implemented programmes for asthma, diabetes and high-risk pregnancies at the end of the 1990s (Gold 1999).

Stages of Disease Management

A disease management programme can be understood as a system of controls (see Fig. 11.6).

The following questions should be answered at the initial stage of developing a disease management programme (Ellrodt et al. 1997; Eichert et al. 1997):

1. Should all manifestations or severity levels of a disease be included in the programme, or only certain ones? If all of them are to be included, nuanced treatment concepts should be developed (patient segmentation).
2. Which areas of medicine, health consultants, case managers, pharmacologists, and physiotherapists but also representatives of the service purchasers and patients should be included in the programme (establishing the team)?
3. What are the critical, i.e. costly, interfaces of treatment?
4. Which interventions are suitable for improving clinical and economic results?
5. How can these results be collected and evaluated?

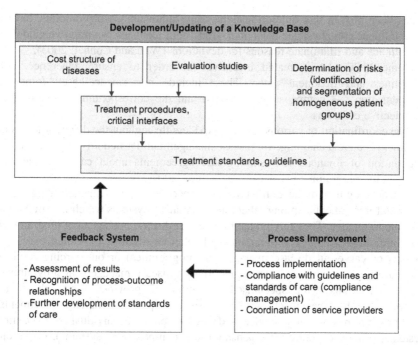

Fig. 11.6 Stages of disease management (Following Neuffer 1997)

Data about the current treatment patterns, the treatment results and the cost structures are necessary in order to answer these questions. Data collection is usually carried out using comprehensive information systems. The clinical and economic effectiveness of prevention and treatment methods can partly be gathered from the available evaluation studies ($\rightarrow$ evaluation process) and should be determined through studies with the highest possible level of evidence ($\rightarrow$ health systems research). In addition, $\rightarrow$ guidelines developed by well-respected organisations and associations should be evaluated.

Building upon this knowledge base, diagnosis and treatment standards will be developed for prevention, diagnosis, acute therapy and rehabilitation. To achieve widely accepted guidelines, this process requires the implementation of extensive and variously structured information in a suitable, easy to implement way. These guidelines often form the basis of clinical pathways to coordinate the stages of patient treatment throughout different areas of medicine. Clinical pathways reflect the goals of the patients and service providers and include the ideal organisational and scheduling processes in order to accomplish these goals as efficiently as possible.

Guidelines and treatment pathways should be implemented in the next step with the help of a well-structured presentation, such as a handbook or summaries of the most important recommendations. Including important colleagues from an early point in all stages of disease management increases the chances of their success, as it has been proven that opinion leaders, being innovators and promoters, have a great influence on physician behaviour. Consistent feedback can improve guideline compliance and illuminate reasons for deviations (Wan and Connell 2003).

Some MCOs have created incentives in order to ensure adherence with guidelines and treatment paths. These include performance-based forms of compensation ($\rightarrow$ compensation systems) and the corresponding structuring of $\rightarrow$ selective contracts.

The coordination of various service providers throughout the different levels of treatment is a great challenge for disease management. Particularly important is the negotiation of financial risk sharing and agreements about case management between the programme partners (Draper et al. 2002).

The development of these structures and processes requires time and a high level of capital investments, among others in information systems which not all MCOs are able to finance. They rely on taking over the disease management programmes (or components of these programmes) of other institutions (so-called carve-out models or carve-out disease management programmes) or outsourcing services and starting joint ventures. Companies offering disease management programmes are organisations with specialised networks of providers and which are compensated for specialised services – such as psychotherapeutic treatments, drug programmes or dental services – depending on their individual compensation systems, usually capitation compensation ($\rightarrow$ compensation systems). Carve-out organisations typically carry out their services for HMOs and large companies with their own insurance companies (Zitter 2001) or also for hospitals (Bodenheimer 2000). Unlike disease management, in which the MCO takes on an active role, responsibility is completely handed over to an independent organisation. Like an MCO, the carve-out organisation can be a loose network of service providers who seldom cooperate with one another or a highly integrated organisation in which different professions constantly work together. Effective cost control is indeed possible in loose organisational forms, although coordinated efforts are more difficult for guaranteeing and improving quality to the same extent in integrated forms (Plocher 1996).

In the last phase of the disease management process, the measures implemented are assessed and evaluated. The most important clinical and economic results as well as the factors that influence them should be collected. This includes process variables such as the implementation of regular controls ($\rightarrow$ utilisation review) or patient consultation, which could be correlated with the result variables like the restoration of the ability to work or health indicators of quality of life ($\rightarrow$ evaluation procedure).

New Orientation of Disease Management

MCOs increasingly realise that cost-effective and high quality treatment of the insured requires a stronger orientation towards health risks and health promotion. This new orientation in disease management, which closely incorporates primary

Chronic Care Model

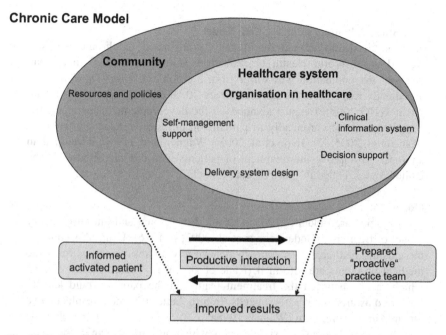

Fig. 11.7 Chronic care model according to Wagner (1996)

medical care, is known as (population based) health management or also as chronic care management (see following case study). It aims to maintain the health of the insured pool by lowering risk factors, detecting diseases, preventing disease-specific complications and evaluating the success of the measures implemented (Schlette et al. 2005).

Particular importance is placed on health risk appraisal of the insured. Health risk appraisal is a method to evaluate the morbidity or mortality risk of a person over a certain period of time. It serves to motivate individuals to take on personal responsibility for their health, to make decisions about their health behaviours and to appropriately take advantage of the range of medical services offered. In addition, health risk appraisal represents an instrument to identify high-risk groups as potential participants in disease management programmes (NBCH 2006). The data of the insured provide efficient and exact estimates concerning future risks and expected costs, so that programmes can be developed accordingly.

The segmentation of patients into risk groups also forms the basis for chronic care management. Multidisciplinary outpatient teams of nurses directly include patients in this process (Wagner 2000).

The chronic care model (Wagner 2000) also emphasises the involvement of patients. It compares improvement strategies which have proven successful in five elements (see Fig. 11.7) and builds upon three principles:
1. Exact definition of optimal care,
2. Concrete process for systematic change, and
3. Effective improvement strategy.

Case Study 8: Wagner's Chronic Care Model

62% of all deaths around world can be attributed to chronic diseases. According to World Health Organisation estimates, in 2020 more than 60 % of the population will suffer from a chronic disease. These patients are already responsible for approximately 70 % of healthcare costs (Harris 2013; WHO 2005). Despite advances in the developments of therapies, the complex needs of chronically ill patients do not receive adequate attention (Kane et al. 2005; McGlynn et al. 2003). Wagner et al. (1996) developed an approach to improve the treatment of patients with chronic diseases in the United States, called the chronic care model.

Model

The chronic care model (CCM) is a multidimensional and interdisciplinary model of treatment (Bodenheimer et al. 2002, p. 1776). Using this concept, the existing healthcare structures which largely address therapies for acute medical problems are reformed (Kane et al. 2005). The consistent contact which results between the treatment team and the patient would lead to increased awareness of patient needs. In turn, better treatment results can be attained in the long term (Wagner 1998a, p. 2).

Wagner et al. identified six elements which help to reorganise the treatment of chronically ill patients (Wagner 1996). These include self-management of the patient, organisation of service providers, guideline-oriented support in medical decision-making and medical information systems. While these four factors relate to the physician practices, there are two additional external factors: community and organisation in healthcare (Bodenheimer 2009, p. 21). Together, these six elements lead to a "productive interaction" between an informed and active patient and the proactive service provider (see Fig. 11.7) (Hroscikoski et al. 2006, p. 317).

Patient Self-Management

Self-management helps patients to master daily challenges of a chronic disease. Patients are empowered to adapt their behaviour to their individual health status and, thus, take control of their disease. This requires the patient and medical team to create a plan together with attainable goals that help the patient to recognise and overcome barriers (Wagner et al. 2001, p. 70; Nuovo 2007). Long-term improvement can only be achieved together with an informed and motivated patient (Solberg et al. 2006, p. 312).

Organisation of Service Providers

In restructuring the practice organisation, the central parameter is the responsible delegation of duties. In particular, duties should be increasingly delegated to non-medical personal "health coaches" (Bodenheimer 2009,

(continued)

Case Study 8 (continued)
p. 21). They organise and lead patient workshops in order to facilitate self-management for those with chronic diseases, thus relieving the physician so that they are able to intensively attend to the needs of acute treatment cases (Patlak et al. 2008).

Support in Clinical Decision-Making
Evidence-based guidelines aid the service provider in making decisions about the optimal therapy of chronic diseases. Thus, they should be integrated into daily treatment schedules (Bodenheimer et al. 2002, p. 1776). Along with guidelines, there should also be a stronger focus on the involvement of specialists. Access to expert knowledge and the inclusion of specialists ensures and facilitates effective treatment (Epping-Jordan et al. 2004, p. 300).

Clinical Information Systems
Clinical information systems offer the service provider useful and timely information about the patient. Through the use of a patient registry, the treatment team can compile current patient information and depict long-term medical histories (Amarasingham et al. 2009). In addition, by developing quality management practices the practice group can receive information about its own performance and allow these results to inform future treatments (Dlugacz 2006).

Organisation of the Provision of Healthcare and the Community
The healthcare community includes all service providers, such as hospitals, medical care centres and outpatient physician practices. Through the networking and cooperation between different service providers with public and community resources, such as self-help groups, chronically ill patients can be empowered and the quality of treatment can be improved (Bodenheimer 2003, p. 65).

Study Results
Since the development of the chronic care model (CCM) there have been countless studies, particularly in the United States, about the effectiveness of the concept. For example, an improved quality of life was attained as well as improving clinical endpoints for diabetes mellitus patients (Strickland et al. 2010; Jenkins et al. 2010; Vargas et al. 2007). Adams et al. (2007) found similar results for the indication of chronic obstructive pulmonary disorder. In their systematic review they proved that the implementation of CCM elements resulted in a lower rate of hospitalisation and shorter hospital stays in comparison to the control groups. In another study by Coleman et al. (2009) all studies since 2000 were compared and analysed. The results

(continued)

Case Study 8 (continued)
showed that not only could significant improvements be documented in the practice procedures, improved treatment results were also documented, independent of the type of chronic disease. This model of care did not just have positive effects in the treatment of chronic diseases. Studies by Hung et al. (2007) showed that by using self-management components the concept can also influence high-risk behaviour such as the consumption of tobacco or unhealthy diets.

Evaluation
The results of the study show that the chronic care model can improve the primary medical treatment of chronically ill patients. However, the current state of care still shows room for improvement. The complex needs of patients with chronic diseases should be in the foreground and included in therapy; only when the patient is enabled and motivated to manage their own disease can long-term success be attained (Bodenheimer 2009). In comparison to disease management, which focuses on the communication between disease management companies and the patient, the chronic care model also aims to reorganise the physician's practice (Coleman et al. 2009). Barriers which exist from the perspective of the service provider must also be overcome to successfully implement care management processes. The barriers mentioned include lacking financial and personnel resources, insufficient clinical information systems, physicians' heavy work loads and compensation which fails to take quality of performance into account (Black and Elliott 2012).

Critical Assessment of Disease Management and Chronic Care Management

Disease management offers cost advantages for a MCO due to the continuity of treatment and the close cooperation with service providers. However, disease management has higher administration costs and investment expenditures in order to develop a computer-based information network. The potential effectiveness and savings in service costs have been critically evaluated recently and place higher demands on the methods of evaluating disease management programmes (Fitzner et al. 2005; Beyer et al. 2006). Meta-analyses show the efficiency of disease management programmes for selected disease patterns and in connection with the severity of the insured's diseases (Gonseth et al. 2004; Krause 2005). Stock et al. (2010) investigated the effectiveness of disease management programs with elements of the chronic care model for patients with diabetes mellitus. After a follow-up of 4 years (2003–2007), significant differences between participants and non-DMP participants were identified. In the intervention group, the average drug and hospital costs were $600 lower than in the control group, the lower hospitalisation rate achieved in the disease management programme participants demonstrated the greatest savings effect. Moreover, mortality among non-participants (4.7 %) was twice as high as the DMP participants (2.3 %) (Stock et al. 2010). Similar results were obtained in the German Elsid study. In addition to lower mortality, the female DMP participants especially benefited in terms of quality of life in comparison to non-participants. Yet, male DMP participants estimated their quality of life as lower than non-participants (Miksch et al. 2011).

Since up to 20 % of all members annually change in some MCOs, they are forced to develop disease management programmes which recover investments quickly. Thus, certain disease patterns are hardly paid attention to, although their inclusion in disease management programmes could increase chances of middle and long-term improvement of the quality and efficiency of care. For this reason, it is nearly impossible to make statements about the long-term results of existing programmes.

The outsourcing of disease management services has been controversially discussed. The problem with carve-outs is that they limit the coordination function of primary medical care and, by involving patients in different programmes (different providers), the continuity of treatment is interrupted (Bodenheimer 2000; van der Vinne 2009). In doing so, this could undermine a significant goal of disease management. Particularly elderly, multi-morbid patients require well-coordinated, consistent treatment which cannot be carried out through a series of carve-out programmes.

Some of these providers are associated with pharmaceutical manufacturers. They increasingly offer commercial disease management programmes. The pharmaceutical companies no longer see themselves as mere producers of pharmaceuticals, instead they respond to the criticism of the pharmaceutical industry price policy by actively engaging in healthcare by expanding their value chain. In the last 15 years pharmaceutical companies in the United States, and to a certain extent in Europe, have developed different programmes, including programmes for diabetes, prenatal or palliative care, the management of terminal liver failure and for the treatment of stroke patients, patients with asthma, depression, migraines and certain types of cancer. "Anti-kickback" rules are designed to prevent pharmaceutical companies from establishing programmes that are primarily used as a sales channel for products, for instance (AHCA 2013).

Because the providers of carve-out programmes take additional funds away from healthcare in the form of company revenue, their opponents advocate the establishment of in-house disease management programmes that involve and aid service providers to a larger extent (Bodenheimer 2000). Disease management offers physicians and other service providers involved in disease management opportunities in evidence-based medical treatment and intensive specialist cooperation. In contrast, this poses disadvantages such as the limitation of freedom of therapy and possible conflicts between fulfilling patient wishes and the requirements of disease management.

Patients can expect improvement in the quality of treatment as well as stronger participation in the treatment process in an ideal disease management scenario.

Advantages and Disadvantages of Disease Management from the Perspective of Interest Groups		
	Advantages	**Disadvantages**
Service purchasers	- Higher cost-effectiveness - Continuity of treatment - Improved cooperation with service providers	- Higher administrative costs - Requires investments in the information system and needs time - Can result in rigidities and block innovations
Physicians	- Opportunity to work effectively and in cooperation - Good, stable relationships with other service providers - Good access to information - Increased professionalism	- Threat to freedom to act in therapy - Reduction in status - Conflict in interests between patient wishes and guidelines - Can reduce trust in the doctor-patient relationship
Patients	- Better treatment results - More and better information - High level of patient participation - Continual provision of care - Preventive care has high priority	- Limitation of services - Excessive demands in decisions and responsibilities - Low degree of willingness to be „monitored" - Risk that costs are focused upon more than quality, since they are easier to measure

Fig. 11.8 Advantages and disadvantages of disease management

On the other hand, health behaviour monitoring associated with disease management can be seen as disadvantageous. The patient must be won over as a partner in order to ensure effective disease management (van der Vinne 2009).

In the overview provided in Fig. 11.8 the advantages and disadvantages of disease management are depicted from the perspectives of different interest groups (following Hunter and Fairfield 1997).

11.6   Case Management

Introduction

Case management is a collaborative process in which the possibilities for a patient's treatment are planned, assessed, implemented, coordinated, monitored and evaluated across sectors. The quality and cost-effectiveness of care should be facilitated through communication processes and the optimal use of available resources (Schwaiberger 2002; Löcherbach et al. 2003; Wendt and Löcherbach 2009; Mullahy 2010).

In contrast to → disease management, → demand management and → patient coaching, case management is geared towards the multidisciplinary management of complicated, high-cost individual cases within a defined time frame. However, there is always partial overlapping between the methods listed. Focus is placed on high-risk patients, patients with potentially fatal injuries or those with chronic diseases. Typical disease patterns which are treated within case management include: AIDS, stroke, transplantations, head injuries, severe burns, high-risk pregnancies and births, spinal cord injuries, neuromuscular diseases and certain mental diseases. Other criteria for case management include prolonged hospital stays or repeated surgical procedures as well as case costs which exceed certain critical values (e.g. case costs higher than US $30,000). Additional applicability criteria could include treatments counteracting each other which have a cumulative effect or long-term treatment with analgesics or antidepressants (Mullahy 2010).

In the United States case management has a long tradition, and its roots lie in treatment of the ill by nurses and social workers. With the expansion of managed care it has gained importance and is increasingly considered a part of → disease management (Ward and Rieve 1997).

Case managers are primarily hired by service providers in managed care systems, particularly service providers whose compensation system is based on capitations (→ compensation systems). Here they work in hospitals as members of the hospital discharge team, in rehabilitation clinics or in residential care organisations. HMOs, insurance companies and TPAs[8] also hire case managers.

In addition, there are freelance case managers and case managers who work with other organisations. Case managers work for service providers as well as for service purchasers, and can also be directly employed by patients or their families (Mullahy 2010).

Nurses, who are trained accordingly, largely assume the functions of a case manager. Based on their training, they are able to provide clinical management in line with guidelines and qualified support in the patient's self-management (Cohen and Cesta 2005). Their services either span a wide spectrum or they specialise in certain diseases or patient groups.

Case management displays a certain relation with → gatekeeping, in which a patient also has a specific point of entry into the system of care which is monitored by a person responsible for coordinating the process of care that follows. However, case managers differ from gatekeepers in that they do not carry out treatments, make diagnoses, prescribe medications or develop medical treatment plans.

A patient can be involved in case management via a retrospective case evaluation or prospectively (Ward and Rieve 1997). The latter approach is particularly used for patients for whom operations are planned. Their case managers work closely with the hospital personnel responsible for planning discharges in order to reduce the length of stay. Furthermore, they organise the transition into residential care in either rehabilitation or nursing institutions. Patients who have been admitted to the hospital multiple times or who have gone to the emergency room frequently are identified in retrospect. Case managers develop outpatient care programmes for them with the aim of reducing the expenses of hospital services. They often involve patient education at home, which can be one element of a case management programme organised and financed by a hospital. These programmes include

---

[8] TPAs (third party administrators) designate all organisations which assume administrative tasks such as case management or invoicing for MCOs, employers or other insurance companies.

support for health-related lifestyles and patient compliance. Thus, retrospective case management in particular displays similarities with → disease management.

Range of Tasks of the Case Manager

Case managers typically fulfil three important roles: (a) assistance in medical treatment, including psychological support, (b) advice regarding financial difficulties and (c) consultation regarding work-related issues during a case of illness (Mullahy 2010; Cesta et al. 1998; also see Fig. 11.9). Their focus is on treatment-oriented activities.

Treatment Activities

The treatment-related duties of a case manager include all activities which are meant to ensure that the patient receives effective medical and nursing care. In particular, they include the following individual activities (Mullahy 2010; Cesta et al. 1998):

1. Communication with the patient in the hospital, rehabilitation facility or at home. Case managers speak with patients to find out whether or not the diagnosis and treatment instructions were understood. Medication compliance should be assessed and, if necessary, the home furnishings should be examined to see if modifications are required. When necessary, psychological consultation and support is provided for the patient and their family. Additional patient education particularly aims to improve compliance (e.g. in medication therapy) and to promote health-oriented behaviours.

2. Communication between the case manager and the medical treatment team (physicians, nurses, physiotherapists and psychotherapists) to answer the following questions: Which diagnosis was determined, which treatment steps are planned, what is the potential treatment result and are complications expected? Acquiring a second opinion may be necessary in order to clarify a complex medical profile or to prepare alternatives to the current or planned treatment. Second opinions can also be necessary when there is a conflict between potential treatment plans, in the case of questionable treatments or when the current treatment proves unsuccessful. The case manager then continues to cooperate closely with the doctor in the subsequent steps of treatment.

3. In discharge planning, all of the services necessary for discharging or transferring the patient (transportation services, nursing services, communal services etc.) must be arranged and coordinated. The aim of discharge planning is to shorten the length of stay.

4. In addition, case managers discuss the purpose, quality, costs and performance of medical equipment with representatives and product providers as well as service providers in residential care.

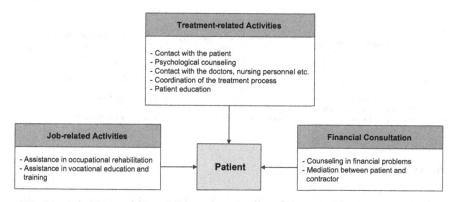

Fig. 11.9 The case manager's range of tasks

Financial Consultation

Financial consultation includes the procurement of offers from communal and non-profit institutions that provide care services and medical equipment free of charge. In addition, purchasers are contacted in order to clarify the assumption of costs for certain treatments and case managers serve as intermediaries between the service provider and purchaser in the case of a conflict. If necessary, the case manager also provides support in the patient's (or patient's family's) financial issues, including advice regarding the household budget.

Work-Related Activities

The case manager's work-related activities include contacting the employer in order to become informed about the expectations of the employer and the needs of the patient. Then, the case manager speaks with the physician responsible for treatment regarding the results. On the basis of this discussion, the case manager can advise the patient regarding their occupational reintegration and vocational training and provide support during recovery.

Case Management Procedure

An effective case management is based on standardised critical paths. Originally developed in engineering, critical paths have become increasingly widespread in healthcare since the 1970s, particularly in the standardisation of clinical treatment procedures. A critical path optimises the individual steps of a treatment process and its sequence through doctors, nurses and other participants. The processes can be depicted through different methods of representation. The goal is to reduce the use of resources and delays and to improve quality. Thus, critical paths also dictate

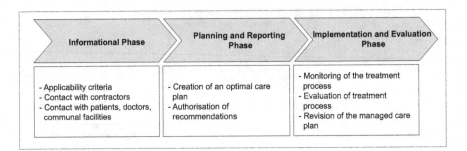

Fig. 11.10 Stages of case management

crucial points in time for the beginning of an intervention. They are typically developed for diagnoses and procedures with high costs, risks and higher revenue.

The case managers are responsible for the coordination, monitoring and evaluation of the patient's treatment along the critical path (Coffey et al. 1992; Cohen and Cesta 2005). The sequence of case management along a treatment path can be divided into an informational phase, a planning and an evaluation phase (Mullahy 1996; Cesta et al. 1998, see Fig. 11.10 following Mullahy 1996).

Informational Phase

At the beginning of the informational phase, a review of the cases for which the case manager is responsible for must be carried out. The requirements of the contractor and the previously mentioned criteria for case management guide this process. The concrete goals of case management can be derived from these for individual cases.

The assumption of costs and the technical details of care should be clarified in discussions with the purchaser. Subsequently, discussions should take place with the patient, their family, the treating physician and other people and organisations active in the treatment process in order to gather the necessary data for case management. If necessary, the employer, providers of medication products and local institutions as well as non-profit organisations may be contacted.

Planning and Reporting Phase

The case manager drafts a care plan based on the needs of the patient which includes recommendations as to how these needs can be met economically and with high quality. These recommendations are then discussed with the patient, the physician and further involved persons in the treatment process.

The case manager provides the contractor with an initial report with recommendations. The report designates points of focus based on the requirements of the contractor and is regularly supplemented. If the case manager is an employee of a HMO then the medical activities are in the foreground. If the contractor is the patient's employer, however, the case manager will place more value on recommendations for the restoration of the patient's capacity to work in the report.

The report can include a cost-benefit analysis ($\rightarrow$ economic evaluation procedure). The cost-benefit analysis includes a summary of the type of interventions, the costs of the case management and the savings (negotiated rebates, reduced use of services, devices and medication products). It should demonstrate that case management results in savings which are higher than its costs. The recommendations of the case manager are summarised in a report which must be agreed upon by the contractor; otherwise the recommendations must be revised.

Implementation and Evaluation Phase

As long as the contractor agrees to the recommendations, the case manager is responsible for successfully implementing the plan. This requires the service provider to be monitored with regular telephone calls and visits. It also involves an evaluation of the desired treatment outcomes in the individual phases of care and the planned sequence. If necessary, the plan should be revised after consultation with the contractor.

Evaluating Case Management

A series of empirical studies (Wagner 1998b; Gensichen et al. 2006) has shown that case management carried out by nurses is very effective, particularly in the treatment of chronic diseases (diabetes, coronary heart disease, depression). Patient education by the case manager, compliance with guidelines and communication with physicians, the delegation of critical tasks to the case manager (planning of care, compliance monitoring, supporting self-management of the patient) as well as collecting and analysing the data relevant to the case management are responsible for this phenomenon.

Case management can also be very effective in planning the discharge of patients. This was shown by a study in which an intervention group of elderly multimorbid patients were treated using critical paths during and after a hospital stay and were compared to a control group. The results showed that in the intervention group the readmission rate was lower, their stay after readmission was shorter, the level of patient satisfaction was higher, their functional status was better and the overall costs of the hospital services were lower (Naylor et al. 1999).

On the other hand, certain deficits can be seen in particularly unprofessional case management. The case manager's support can be limited to telephone contact. In addition, in the conflict between the patient's and the contractor's interests there is always the danger that the case manager could neglect the interests of the patient in favour of the economic interests of the contractor (Mullahy 2010).

11.7   Demand Management

Along with the management of services using gatekeeping and case management with one defined physician, telephone or online information and consultation services play a role in the English National Health System as well as in the Dutch, Danish, Swiss and other healthcare systems. This type of care differs from patient coaching because it is a direct form of service provision. However, the boundaries are rather fluid.

Besides providing efficient healthcare, this type of care also takes an increasing demand for quick, easily accessible medical advice into account, either only outside of office hours or even around the clock. One important development for the service provider is that emergency medical services – for example in the United Kingdom or the Netherlands – are often no longer organised by a few cooperating practices, but rather by large physician associations. In the Netherlands, for instance, it is organised by 40–120 resident physicians who usually provide a professional telephone consultation team (Moll van Charante 2006). The service providers strive to minimise the burden on individual doctors and the amount of house visits outside of their office hours through such telephone consultations.

In the case of demand management, specially trained nursing professionals as well as physicians are available for telephone calls, make a triage of the symptoms,[9] offer information about the illness and tips for self-treatment or, when they are not sufficiently qualified, transfer the call to (specialist) physicians and explain further steps for the diagnostic clarification or treatment path (Lattimer et al. 2000). In the Netherlands the "telephone nurses" refer to comprehensive protocols about the most important disease patterns, which are compiled by the Dutch college of general practitioners for these telephone consultations. In the United Kingdom there is a "decision support software" available to the specialist nursing staff. In Switzerland physicians answer calls for the medical telephone consultation centre "Medgate" or "Medi24" (www.medgate.ch; www.medi24.ch).

A triage of symptoms and counselling on methods of self-treatment or about additional diagnosis or treatment paths is designed to manage and improve access to service providers. Telephone contact with a patient can also be used for follow-up exams or for carrying out preventive or screening measures. In the case of serious chronic diseases a telephone hotline consultation service can also be implemented as a part of case management ($\rightarrow$ case management). Demand management provides the patient with the opportunity to get additional advice – e.g. before non-emergency operations – or to get a second opinion beyond first inquiries on the situation of their illness.

---

[9] For example (1) Emergency admission, (2) Doctor visit immediately, (3) Doctor visit < 24 h, (4) Routine doctor visit, (5) Self-treatment.

Case Study 9: NHS Direct

One of the largest telephone and internet-based health consultation systems is NHS Direct in England, which was created in 1997. Contrary to the "usual" consultation hotlines organised by physician associations (often outside of office hours), NHS Direct is organised nationally, centrally and across sectors. Approximately 4.4 million calls are annually served in 31 contact centres around the clock by 3,000 employees. More than a third, 1,200 of the employees, are nurses (Kumar and Snooks 2011; NHS Direct 2012). For the hearing impaired there is a text messaging service. NHS Direct is also available via interactive digital television in approx. 16 million English homes. In an easy-to-navigate menu, over 3,000 pages of information are available about the NHS system and finding doctors. In addition, "taking care of yourself" films are available on topics such as asthma, diabetes, smoking, nutrition, childhood illnesses, pregnancy, preventive measures etc. 24 million users access the NHS Direct website each year, 10 million people use the Health and Symptom Checkers on the NHS Direct website annually. Along with information about the NHS system, the website offers an easily understandable medical encyclopaedia and a self-help guide for health questions which recommends whether or not NHS Direct or an ambulance should be called on the basis of simple yes-no questions. In addition, in 2009 a check-up system was developed for issues of mental illness which is used annually by over five million online users. Since May 2011, a NHS Direct app can be downloaded on web-enabled smartphones to use a mobile symptom checker (NHS Direct 2011).

The NHS Direct telephone hotline is divided into four programmes, according to which the callers are individually counselled.

1. Urgent Care

A new patient calls with an urgent problem. They are either directly connected to emergency services or a doctor, or have a detailed interview with a specialist nurse, who performs a triage or provides appropriate healthcare information.

2. Long-Term Conditions

In line with disease management ($\rightarrow$ disease management) NHS Direct provides initial disease diagnoses and screenings for the early detection of chronic diseases. After a diagnosis from a physician, information is provided regarding how to deal with pharmaceutical, lifestyle and prevention programmes with the goal of strengthening the effectiveness of the patient. According to an internal risk stratification scheme, in the case of serious illness the NHS Direct nurses are available as "care managers" and initiate treatment paths, make emergency physician appointments and follow-up examinations in close cooperation with primary care trusts and individual physician practices.

(continued)

Case Study 9 (continued)

3. Secondary Care

In the case of a planned hospital stay, with the agreement of the patient, NHS Direct receives data about the patient and the case of illness or disease. Before the operations NHS calls the patient to ask whether they are prepared for the operation and, if necessary, arranges further examinations. This makes pre-operation clarifications convenient for the patient (from home), frees up hospital resources or uses them more efficiently and reduces unnecessary hospital admittances. After discharge from the hospital, particularly patients with high-risk or chronic diseases are contacted with follow-up calls. In order to prevent readmission to the hospital, information about post-operative self-treatment is provided, patient compliance with medication is monitored and appointments are arranged for follow-up examinations. These accompanying services are also meant to increase the capacity of outpatient operations.

4. Dental Care

Since 2007, NHS Direct has also offered dental consultation services in five centres throughout the country. Furthermore, this service provides information about oral hygiene and the alleviation of pain and recommends dentists.

NHS Direct reports that 54 % of the callers were completed within NHS Direct without the need of consulting a GP. 22 % of the callers were advised to immediately see a GP. Another 10 % were advised to go directly to an emergency department. An ambulance was immediately called for 5 % of the callers. 9 % of the callers came under other case categories, such as chronic disease or pre-/post-inpatient care. In 2010/11, 1.6 million general practitioner visits, one million emergency admissions to the hospital and 120,000 ambulance calls could be prevented by the NHS Direct service, resulting in savings of an equivalent of US $252,8 million (NHS Direct 2011).

For further information about NHS Direct see: www.nhsdirect.nhs.uk.

Study Results for Demand Management

According to a review of nine evaluated studies of hotline assistance, 50 % of the callers were sufficiently helped without immediate medical attention (Bunn et al. 2005). Telephone consultations also reduced the workloads of the resident physicians. The number of emergency admissions (Bunn et al. 2005) or hospital admissions (Moll van Charante 2006), however, remained the same.

In his somewhat older study, Lattimer (1998) examined the telephone hotline service (consultation by nurses) of a British physician association (55 physicians, approx. 97,229 patients) and assessed the emergency admissions and mortality. Neither of the statistics increased or decreased remarkably through the intervention of "telephone assistance" which can, thus, appear safe or harmless. In addition, he demonstrated that as a result of the telephone consultations the number of medical telephone consultations in "primary care centres" decreased by 38 % and doctors' house calls decreased by 23 %.

In another study, Lattimer (2000) determined the costs of running a telephone hotline, compared the savings to the reduced service costs and calculated a positive balance. However, the cost-benefit savings did not benefit the medical operators of the telephone consultation association, but rather mainly the NHS.

10.4 % of the registered English insured use the telephone hotline operated by nurses (Lattimer et al. 1998). In the case of the Swiss hotline, Medgate, whose service is available to a pool of insured from four health insurances, only 1.3 % of the insured took advantage of the service to speak directly with a physician (Berchtold et al. 2004). The compliance values were also investigated for Medgate. Thus, 72 % of the callers followed the recommendation "seek out a doctor"; 65 % followed the recommendation "self-treatment"; 100 % followed the recommendation "emergency"; 93 % the recommendation "doctor appointment in 24–48 h" and 19 % followed the recommendation "doctor visit in 48 h or more". Thus, patient compliance primarily depends on the immediacy of the recommendation. Therefore, patient compliance is highly dependent on the urgency of the aforementioned recommendations.

The compliance rate in urgent cases makes it clear that managing services with demand management is indeed possible. Now the next difficult step is to more closely examine the effects on service costs.

Assessment

A Swiss study about the acceptance and benefits of telephone medical assistance confirmed that the full potential of demand management has yet to be fulfilled. The study identified that merely 5 % of those surveyed use the service and that over 62 % did not know whether their health insurance offered telephone consultation (Schwarz 2006).

The evaluation of demand management is also ambivalent. There is consensus that in principle demand management is a useful instrument. In most healthcare systems coordination and communication are central weak points and these are precisely the focus of demand management. As convincing and attractive as the demand management method is, the "business case" is equally problematic. Glancing into the past shows that while the business model of demand management was celebrated years ago, in many aspects it failed. Spectacular market exits such as that of Medvantis are only examples of this. It is largely due to the fact that there is a lack of personal responsibility in the current structures and among patients there is no willingness to pay. In addition, many services offered at the beginning did not have staff with necessary qualifications in order to play a significant role as new service providers, and were rather considered "infotainment". Along with the specialist qualifications which represented a sine qua non, absolute independence is crucial.

In the middle term it can be assumed that demand management will play a significant role in healthcare, as it is a method very much in line with managed care that raises quality and optimises costs.

11.8   Patient Coaching

The method of patient coaching is similar to demand management in many respects. Even though the instruments used overlap in many aspects, the decisive difference is that patient coaching is a system of intervention based on the individual which is meant to increase self-competence. An informed and engaged patient is an essential component of high-quality healthcare (Coulter and Ellins 2007). For example, the more initiative patients take and the more control they exercise in discussions with physicians, the fewer sick days they have to take (Kaplan et al. 1989). Moreover, insured persons with limited health know-how generally have a lower health status compared to those who are well informed. They are admitted into the hospital more often, use preventive measures less often, disregard treatment behaviour requirements more frequently and as a result suffer more often from medication- or treatment errors (IOM 2004).

The opportunities available in modern curative medicine are an important factor for healthcare. Depending on the circumstances, uninformed insured paying little attention to their health behaviours as well as informed, engaged insured with highly complex diseases may both be unable to effectively take advantage of such opportunities (see SVR 2005, p. 23).

In a meta-analysis, Coulter and Ellins (2007) selected and analysed the effectiveness of strategies to inform, educate and involve patients. The meta-study surveyed 129 systematic reviews of patient-oriented measures to boost patients' personal health competence. The term "patient coaching" became established as a collective term for interventions focusing on strengthening a patient's ability to actively contribute to their own health.

Over the course of managed care, MCOs already use instruments such as → disease management, → case management and → demand management. First and foremost these instruments serve to aid the coordination and cooperation between multiple participating service providers. The patient should be guided through the treatment process with various service providers on the basis of evidence-based medicine guidelines and receive the correct treatment in a cost-effective way at the right time and place. Even when the compliance of a patient is essential for the realisation of such care, in the case of these instruments the organisational coordination between service providers is in the foreground. The three procedures mentioned are based on a rather paternalistic understanding of the physician-patient relationship. The patient delegates the responsibility for their disease to the doctor and passively tolerates the inflicted treatment. In turn, the authorised physician can – supported by disease management, case management or demand management programmes – freely choose their resources and can independently determine the successful treatment (Klusen and Meusch 2009).

Patient coaching measures are meant to encourage the insured to take better care of themselves and, in cooperation with physicians, to particularly take active responsibility for their health and contribute to a successful treatment. In this way independent service providers and insurance companies which offer nationwide patient coaching programmes help promote patient autonomy.

Specifications of Patient Coaching

The term "coaching" was coined approximately 20 years ago in the context of measures to develop personnel in free-market companies for middle and senior managers. Apart from the activity of an in-depth discussion or a consultation, the term has not been defined more precisely up to now. At the same time, coaching is now offered in nearly every area of life.

Coaching is carried out with insured or patients in one-on-one sessions or in groups; personally, on the phone or via internet-supported devices. The contact person is usually a trained nurse. Occasionally physicians or trained amateurs also assist the insured (O'Connor et al. 2008). Generally, a patient coach provides no information regarding diagnosis or therapy. This is also a major difference in comparison to demand management as it is practised in Switzerland. The physicians from those hotlines not only perform remote diagnoses, they also issue e-prescriptions for example. In the case of medical specialist questions, the physician transfers the caller to the respective specialists. The physician also refers to available guidelines or decision algorithms for guidance in frequently asked questions (Schmid et al. 2008). In general, the following goals are pursued in patient coaching (following Coulter and Ellins 2007):

1. Improving general knowledge about health and of ones own health state
2. Increasing awareness of ones own state of health and promoting health-conscious behaviour
3. Support in (difficult) medical decisions according to the concept of participative decision-making
4. Promotion of active and informed participation in the treatment process and the efficient use of healthcare services
5. Promotion of patient compliance.

The goals, type, content and intensity of coaching depend on one hand on the knowledge and needs of the individual. On the other hand, the design of coaching largely depends on the current health or illness status of the patient.

Figure 11.11 illustrates the large spectrum of possible coaching activities. Wellness and lifestyle management tasks are usually widely spread among the entire population of insured with relatively low frequency of contact. It deals with programmes to combat stress, improve nutrition and fitness activities, for back training, quitting smoking etc. As a part of health coaching, a coach can arrange a unique combination of such activities with the insured and monitor patient compliance. In doing so, the measures for primary prevention – possibly

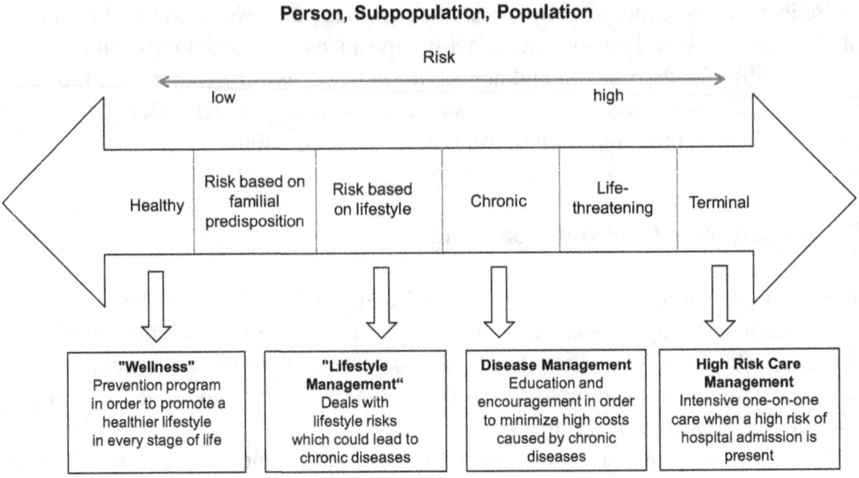

Person, Subpopulation, Population

Fig. 11.11 Stratification of the population of insured according to disease severity and accordingly adapted coaching concepts (following Klein 2009)

specifically for certain risk groups according to profession, sex or age – are implemented in an ideal way, tailored to the individual.

One can primarily refer to patient coaching when a middle to long-term disease is present. The degree of contact to a coach increases according to the severity of the disease. Relatives are included in the process, particularly in the case of a serious or even terminal illness which is often associated with a high level of nursing care.

Insured who could most benefit from coaching for a limited time are identified through an analysis of the health insurances' master data on the insured. Patient profiles are compiled from socio-demographic data, possibly chronic or other diseases, use of pharmaceuticals, inpatient or outpatient services and specific costly procedures.[10] In the next step of compiling the patient profile, probabilities for repeated admission, first admission, incapacity to work, chronification and further complications and cost risks are determined. From these factors the intended population with the highest potential for success in health coaching can be determined (Temmert 2009).

In a second step the coaches – specially trained nursing personnel – call the insured and build up a personal, empathetic relationship with the insured. Usually the insured are assisted for 6–18 months at individually varying intervals. At the beginning of coaching, information from the guidelines is provided which pertains to the respective diagnosis as well as further information helpful to the individual situations. After the patient agrees to and registers in the coaching programme and initial clarification is provided, the coaches document the treatment process and help organise it. Accordingly, prior to doctor's visits patients are provided with

---

[10] Such as artificial respiration.

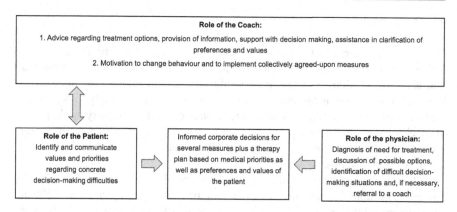

Role of the Coach:

1. Advice regarding treatment options, provision of information, support with decision making, assistance in clarification of preferences and values

2. Motivation to change behaviour and to implement collectively agreed-upon measures

Role of the Patient:
Identify and communicate values and priorities regarding concrete decision-making difficulties

Informed corporate decisions for several measures plus a therapy plan based on medical priorities as well as preferences and values of the patient

Role of the physician:
Diagnosis of need for treatment, discussion of possible options, identification of difficult decision-making situations and, if necessary, referral to a coach

Fig. 11.12 The role of the coach in participative decision-making (following O'Connor et al. 2007)

relevant information and, if necessary, individual patient preferences will be assessed. The patients should then be in the position to confidently and assertively reach a decision together with their physician. The desired preparation and follow-up of physician consultations can lead to a reduction of necessary doctor visits, since the decision-making process between doctor and patient is thus shortened and the "correct" treatment is carried out "immediately". In addition, when choosing a doctor, coaches can highlight physician compliance with comparable quality criteria to the patients (Fig. 11.12).

The advisor role of the coach becomes more important when a patient is required to make difficult decisions. This could include, for example, decisions about the type of treatment for breast or prostate cancer or osteoarthritis.

The coach monitors the compliance with therapy and gives suggestions and advice accordingly through telephone contact after a consultation. In addition, the goal of a coach in their role as motivator is to generally motivate and encourage the patient to develop and maintain health-conscious habits. Psychotherapeutic methods and a variety of results from studies regarding motivation research can be used for this purpose. The patient should be guided as to how one can go from a stage of denial to a stage of inner realisation and that furthermore a change is necessary and how it can be brought about.

Coaches also point out possible preventive methods in all stages of health or illness. This includes early-detection measures in the area of secondary prevention which help at preventing the manifestation of diseases such as intestinal cancer. Likewise, in the case of already present diseases, scientifically proven measures for tertiary prevention are recommended – i.e. to prevent further complications, an escalation or a renewed occurrence (e.g. a heart attack). On the basis of the data analysis Accenture, a management consulting company can carry out "coaching campaigns", i.e. a careful implementation of prevention measures and goals for certain risk groups (Accenture 2007).

Assessment

Central to the success of a patient coaching programme are the factors which include building up a trustful relationship to the patient and the accurate identification and stratification of at-risk patients through an elaborated data analysis. A better quality as well as the prompt availability of data increasingly makes better analyses possible. Building up a trustful relationship and the voluntary participation in coaching seem to pose no problems. According to Gold and Kongstvedt (2003), for instance, 95–97 % of the approx. 60,000 patients contacted participated in a Healthways programme in Minnesota.

In the Healthways programme the development of costs was divided into two cohorts. The annual costs per person could be decreased by approx. $500 in comparison to the average by reducing emergency admissions and inpatient admissions. In this study, an investment in patient coaching of one dollar generated $2.90 in savings (Gold and Kongstvedt 2003).

11.9   Quality Management

Preliminary Remarks

The goal of quality management is to improve the quality of services and to lower the degree of diffusion of quality in the provision of services. For this purpose, incentive systems and organisational models are developed on the basis of quality objectives. Particularly in the case of restructuring an organisation or purchasing healthcare services, systematic quality assessments of medical care are necessary (McGlynn 1997). As managed care instruments primarily aim at cost reduction in the provision of services, the quality assessment gains an important control function.

In order to achieve a definition of "quality" in relation to health services, managed care literature frequently uses the definition provided by the Institute of Medicine. According to this definition, quality is the degree to which health services for individuals and populations correspond to desired health outcomes. These outcomes must be based upon current professional knowledge (Blumenthal 1996).

Quality management includes a more detailed definition based on how healthcare executives understand, explain, and improve the quality of healthcare and the health of their patients within the environment of their individual organisations (Kelly 2003).

The following features are characteristic of the quality management approach (Al-Asaaf 1998):

- Quality is multidimensional and takes on different meanings for the various parties involved in healthcare. Thus, defining quality objectives and priorities in quality management is necessary. These objectives will ideally be decided on jointly by all parties in order to achieve maximum acceptance. Since quality is

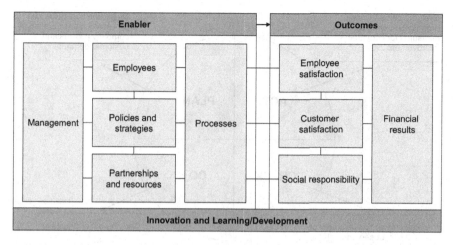

Fig. 11.13 The EFQM model (according to www.efqm.org)

earmarked, the result is the requirement of the precise formulation of goals in quality management.

- Quality management is based on standards and an appropriate data basis. In every phase of quality management, data is collected using statistical methods that should be compared to reference values.
- Quality is a result of numerous individual processes within an organisation. Therefore, the intersections of these particular processes require special attention (overlap management).
- Quality management is coordinated with cost management. Poor quality attracts consequential costs (disease costs, administrative costs). On the other hand, quality improvements generally presuppose increased costs (investment costs, control costs, financial incentives). Therefore, the relationship between quality and costs must be optimized.

Modern approaches to improvement in the quality of healthcare, e.g. the EFQM-Model (Fig. 11.13) require the completion of three major objectives, the so-called "Triple Aim". Behind the concept is the assumption that high-quality care can only be achieved if the system is restructured as a whole with linked targets (Berwick et al. 2008). The objectives are:

1. Improvement in the individual perception of healthcare,
2. Improving the health of the general population and
3. Reducing the per capita costs of individual healthcare services.

The closed loop is usually referred to as a PDCA cycle, according to Deming, and is divided into a quality planning phase ("plan"), the implementation ("do"), the quality control ("check") and a quality improvement phase ("act") (Fig. 11.14).

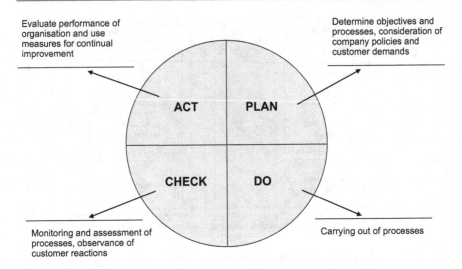

Evaluate performance of
organisation and use
measures for continual
improvement

Determine objectives and
processes, consideration of
company policies and
customer demands

Monitoring and assessment of
processes, observance of
customer reactions

Carrying out of processes

Fig. 11.14 The PDCA cycle according to Deming

Quality Planning ("Plan")

Identification of Customer-Relevant Quality Requirements

In the context of quality planning it is established who will implement what and with which resources. Effective quality planning is based on the recognition of the customer's needs. Methods to communicate customer needs include the collection and processing of complaints, surveys about customer satisfaction, interviews and the development of a suggestion programme. Quality management can concentrate on the aspects of service provision that are integral for customer satisfaction based on the data that these measures provide about customer needs and quality requirements.

Thereby, five types of MCO customers should be distinguished: The service provider, with whom selective contracts take place, the service purchaser (insurer), the employer and the patient as well as internal customers. The internal customers make up the interface of the internal organisation units and services which can be seen as reciprocal relationships.[11] Quality management must take the differing importance of customers into account. It is not uncommon that 80 % of the revenue stems from 20 % of external customers. Even within one category of customers, customers of differing priorities must be considered (Siren and Laffel 1998).

Along with the identification of customer needs, another element of quality planning is the development of an indicator system to depict quality.

---

[11] In another sense the public and state authorities or associations can also be customers, which assess quality according to ethical criteria or according to their conformity with legal and self-imposed norms.

Determination of Goals and Processes

The requirements of quality planning provide the basis for developing concrete goals for the quality management of an MCO. Customers' relationships to the service providers are based on contracts that define service goals, delineate measures to reach these service goals and include performance-based forms of compensation. The quality preferences of the insured and the employers are particularly aimed at easy access to service providers and the extent of the services provided. In addition, these customers value early detection measures, prevention programmes and high quality service (Siren and Laffel 1998). Thus, MCOs have an interest in assessing, improving and communicating quality based on the objectives agreed upon in contracts. For this reason, contracts with service providers must contain agreements regarding the quality data to be provided and instruments for quality assessment and improvement.

Instruments

In order to reach the concrete goals of quality management, MCOs must choose points of focus in line with the expectations of customers which are derived from a strength and weakness analysis based on performance comparison. A system of quality control and support should then be developed to build upon this. The following procedures are suitable for this:

Quality Circles

Quality circles are a method taken from industry which includes employees in the promotion of quality. They are based on voluntary initiative and serve the continual sharing of experiences between colleagues about topics and problems that they choose themselves. Collegial work groups, moderated by a specially trained person, make up the core of the quality circle idea. In the context of quality management, quality circles pursue the goal of promoting motivation to ensure high quality and to increase the competence to solve quality problems through the exchange of information (Bungard et al. 1992; Protzman et al. 2011). An example of a topic in such a quality circle are treatment problems that could arise.

Audits

The main objective of audits is learning from mistakes. The system of medical audits is based on a committee of specialist doctors who periodically examines a certain number of patient files based on random sampling to determine the completeness, consistency and correctness of medical, nursing and other services. In this process, diagnoses, therapies or medication use can be checked, for example. The audit committee should analyse possible errors and provide suggestions as to how these errors can be prevented in the future.

Along with medical audits, quality management entails organisational audits, e.g. those according to DIN EN 9001:2008. The actual difference from clinical audits is the interdisciplinary involvement of all participants in the process and the consideration of the consequences for the patient's quality of life. As it is not possible for everyone to be concerned with audits, even for purely technical reasons, they are often carried out in quality circles.

Tracers

Tracers are selected indicators upon which the strengths and weaknesses of the treatment and care processes used are evaluated. When a number of diagnostic and therapeutic processes are available, the tracer concept focuses on representative elements and uses these to make conclusions about the quality of the whole. Thus, tracers are concerned with indicators which monitor individual quality aspects and, based on this assessment, the overall quality (Kessner et al. 1971).

A tracer diagnosis must be frequent, reproducible and scientifically generally applicable. For example, in one clinic computerised surveys were filled out for all patients with inguinal hernias and after their discharge they were made available to an external point of collection. Because the collection point manages data for multiple clinics, the differences in quality – for example in the context of benchmarking – could be made apparent.

Statistical Quality Controls

The statistical quality controls are based on specific methods of deviation or variation analysis (Blumenthal 1993; ACMQ 2005). In this way control charts visualise information about whether the deviations of certain quality characteristics of the benchmark and desired values are coincidental or whether they are systematic deviations which require intervention. Flow charts which depict the steps of a treatment provide evidence about potential causes of systematic deviations. The deviation analysis provides information about the causes of the rates of wound infections, for example. In primary care, in which the patient displays relatively stable conditions (healthy or chronically ill), the deviation analysis can provide information about whether the changes in condition are within the normal range or display systematic deviations.

Profiling

Profiling identifies the treatment pattern of an individual provider over a certain period of time and for a certain population of insured. This custom profile can be compared with that of the medical department or with the standard. In this process, the costs of quality management are not in the foreground but rather the quality profile of the services. The results of the profiling are made available to those concerned in order to aid them in improving treatments.

Guidelines have been developed for this profiling (Siren and Laffel 1998; ACMQ 2005). Profiles must be analysed for a certain population, and they must contain a sufficient number of monitored cases. Furthermore, they should be adjusted according to case structure. The profiling must finally be analysed for such a small unit that responsibilities can be determined. Examples of profiling indicators are: Average waiting times, length of stay, number of hospital admissions, number of transfers outside of the network, number of emergency admissions, satisfaction of the members and orientation to → guidelines.

Comparative Evaluation of Quality

Another step in quality planning is the evaluation of the quality indicator values determined by comparing them with the professional standard or the standard of "best practice". The appropriateness review, the peer review, benchmarking and the outcomes assessment (Siren and Laffel 1998) are used as instruments to compare the performance of a quality management.

Appropriateness Review

The appropriateness review examines the extent to which an MCO provides necessary treatments and prevents unnecessary ones. This method of quality evaluation is especially applied in the case of elective operations as well as controversial, not evidence-based or costly procedures, e.g. bypass operations. The indication for the recommended operation procedures is compared with a list of consensual indications which has been compiled by a physicians' association or the MCO itself. The assessment of suitability can encounter method-related problems, however. The data is distorted by the case structure and there is as of yet too little evidence-based information. The MCO can set minimum quality standards for expensive diagnoses as a response to this, in order to determine processes with higher degrees of use. Positive trends in clinical indicators of the appropriateness review can be determined for the customers.

Peer Review

Peer review is the analysis of the treatment of a patient carried out by peers. The cases intended for peer review either result from grave deviations from specific indicators or through the evaluation of medical reports. The treatment documents, the diagnosis and treatment procedures and the use of resources are particularly discussed here.

On the one hand, the limits of peer review are due to the fact that compliance with standards can impede innovation. On the other hand, studies have shown that consensual decisions among the peers only have a slightly higher probability than entirely random decisions.

Outcome Assessment

Critical activities are evaluated in outcome assessment. An outcome assessment can be carried out, for example, for the ten most common or most expensive diagnoses or procedures. With the aid of the outcome assessment a quantitative comparison can be made between treatment programmes, the typical progression of a chronic illness can be depicted or variances in the results can be determined as evidence of process deviations.

The outcome assessment comprises three core activities: The assessment of outcomes at certain points in time, the continual monitoring of outcomes in order to recognise causal relationships and outcome management, i.e. the application of knowledge gained in order to achieve better results (Siren and Laffel 1998; Kongstvedt 2013).

Benchmarking

As an instrument of quality management, benchmarking is a process used to compare individual organisations with the most successful organisations (best practise companies) on the basis of quality-oriented comparative values and benchmark values. Benchmarking can be applied to clinical processes as well as to the service processes of an MCO. The information obtained from such service comparisons enables an organisation's own strengths and weaknesses to be recognised. Benchmarking not only provides information for the MCO, which gains insight into its ability to compete, but also for its customers (Hackman and Wageman 1995).

In practise there are three types of benchmarking which can be distinguished from one another, even when they partly overlap (Gift and Mosel 1994; Mullner 2009). In internal benchmarking, successful processes within a department of an organisation are used as benchmarks for other departments. Competition benchmarking is concerned with the continual comparison of an organisation's own capability with that of the best competitor. This type of benchmarking is more elaborate and usually cannot be carried out without an exchange of information between competitors.

In cross-branch functional benchmarking, procedures and techniques are investigated that can be applied outside of the healthcare sector. Examples include hotel reception or restaurant, delivery relations in the car industry or the organisation of data processing, appointment planning and the allocation of a car rental company. When using solution concepts from other branches, the problem and solution structures must be adapted to the specific problem situation of MCOs. A particular variation of this type of benchmarking is collaborative benchmarking. Here service providers gather together in a network in order to realise competitive, functional benchmarking concepts which are internal to the network (Gift and Mosel 1994).

In the process of comparison in benchmarking one should make sure that the objects of comparison usually display differences in the patient structure (age, sex or severity of disease) which are out of the MCO's control or out of the service provider's control. The objects of comparison are thus there in order to adjust the factors of influence and to prevent poor decision-making.

Along with the development of a quality assurance and quality control, the implementation of measures improving quality is a further task of quality management. Once the objectives have been chosen, e.g. an increase in the rate of vaccinations in small children, the processes are adjusted in order to reach the goal, possibly in this case by implementing a recall or reminding system.

Quality Implementation ("Do")

In this phase the changed processes are implemented, such as treatments, according to newly implemented → guidelines within a group of service providers or compliance with new service principles.

This phase begins after an agreement on the quality planning is reached. In this phase, measures for monitoring quality improvement are defined and methods for improving the quality are implemented (Dlugacz 2006).

Quality Inspection ("Check")

Assessing Quality

After the implementation of processes, the effectiveness of the improvements and necessary modifications is assessed. This requires an assessment of quality using the quality indicators. The assessment and evaluation of quality can be carried out within the organisation as part of the internal quality management or also through external organisations. Structural quality indicators include physician certification, compliance with security regulations or equipment approvals. It is expected that a higher standard of structural quality has a positive effect on the treatment results. Regulation authorities prefer structural criteria because they are easy to collect and document. However, the structural criteria are not differentiated enough to guarantee more than the minimum standards for the provision of services.

Within the basic structural conditions, service provision processes are carried out whose quality can be individually determined. The process indicators include the patient-based activities of an MCO as well as the number of transfers to other care networks, the number of early detection screenings performed, the existence of treatment pathways or → guidelines. Along with the patient-based process criteria, the administrative process criteria should also be included. Relevant quality characteristics include access to the service provider or service quality.

Finally, quality can be directly measured based on the outcome. The outcome indicators are related to the actual objective of the care process: The improvement of patients' health conditions.

Among the outcome indicators in quality management MCOs prefer patient satisfaction (Siren and Laffel 1998). Patient satisfaction can correlate with clinical outcomes, the environment in which the care takes place and the interpersonal relationship between patients and physician or nurses. However, factors of satisfaction alone cannot adequately describe the outcome of care. Factors of health-related quality of life would provide more comprehensive information (→ evaluation process) which are however very complex to collect. Thus, MCOs are reluctant to use them as outcome factors.

However, the outcome indicators only partially determine the causes of insufficient quality management (→ health systems research). Furthermore, quality defects can first be recognised when damages have already incurred and therefore do not allow clear conclusions to be drawn about the triggering processes. For these reasons, along with the outcome indicators, structural and process indicators should also be evaluated in quality management (Donabedian 1992).

In 2006 in Germany the National Association of Statutory Health Insurance Physicians (KBV) developed a set of quality indicators and parameters for outpatient care. With the help of these sets, data regarding the quality of the outcome could be

	ADHS	Aids/ HIV	Dementia	Practice Management
Indicator	- Diagnosis criteria - Initial prescription - Follow-up contact - School assistance	- Hepatitis C state - Determination of viral load - Reduction of viral load	- Depression screening - Laboratory diagnostics - Monitoring of medication - Assistance services	- House visits - Medication allergies - Discussion of critical results - Emergency medication - Patient survey - Vocational training

Fig. 11.15 Selected indicators of the German KBV Sets (KBV 2013)

collected along with the already assessed structural and process quality. There are currently 48 quality indicators, among others for different chronic diseases, prevention and practice management. The majority of the indicators (s. Fig. 11.15) originate from internationally recognised indicator systems (KBV 2013).

In the United States, the National Committee for Quality Assurance (NCQA), an independent non-profit organisation, is responsible for the national collection, analysis and publication of certain performance measurement figures. When creating their indicator systems, the MCOs orient themselves towards the HEDIS indicators (see Fig. 11.16) which the NCQA developed ($\rightarrow$ contract design). MCOs, which also transact with Medicare and Medicaid, base their quality management on the quality standards developed by the CMS[12] in the Quality Improvement System for Managed Care (QISMC).

A report concerning the quality of healthcare is published annually on the basis of the data voluntarily provided by the MCOs in the HEDIS programme (National Committee for Quality Assurance 2011). The determination of the insured persons' satisfaction is carried out in the Consumer Assessment of Healthcare Providers and Systems (CAHPS) programme, the survey instrument which the Agency for Healthcare Research and Quality (AHRQ) uses. An accreditation of the MCOs is carried out by the NCQA as a supplement to the performance measurement. In the several-day inspection of the MCO by an interdisciplinary team of physicians and managed care experts, there are discussions with the employees responsible and the team inspects routine documents as well as patient files. Together with additional information, the outcomes form the basis for certification results on a five-level scale. The accreditation which builds upon this is generally valid for a 3-year period. One of the most comprehensive accreditation systems was established by the Joint Commission on Accreditation of Health Care Organizations (JCAHO) in the United States, which likewise carries out external inspections and accreditations of healthcare facilities (Gerlach 2001).

---

[12] The CMS (Centers for Medicare & Medicaid Services), previously known as the HCFA (Health Care Financing Administration) is a national authority which manages the Medicare programme and monitors the Medicaid programmes of the individual states.

	applicate to:		
	Medicaid	Commercial	Medicare
Childhood Immunisation Status	X	X	
Adolescent Immunisation Status	X	X	
Breast Cancer Screening	X	X	X
Cervical Cancer Screening	X	X	
Chlamydia Screening in Women	X	X	
Controlling High Blood Pressure	X	X	X
Beta-Blocker Treatment After A Heart Attack	X	X	X
Comprehensive Diabetes Care	X	X	X
Use of Appropriate Medications for People with Asthma	X	X	
Follow -up Atfer Hospitalisation For Mental Illness	X	X	X
Antidepressant Medication Mangement	X	X	X
Medical Assistance With Smoking and Tobacco Use Cessation	X	X	
Flu shots for Adults Ages 50–64 (First Year Measure)		X	

Fig. 11.16   HEDIS data set 2013 (Extract, source: www.ncqa.org)

Implementation of Quality Improvement Measures ("Act")

In the implementation phase of quality management the measures to improve quality should be introduced as new regulations. Feedback then follows. This feedback phase can also be referred to as the evaluation phase. The evaluation phase forms the basis for a new initial phase of the quality improvement process with the planning of additional improvement measures. This is definitely necessary when the programme was not successful. However, even if the programme was successful, the circle can begin again in order to fulfil new or unnoticed patient needs.

The task of implementing the outcomes of a quality management programme requires various talents and abilities, as this is not possible without changing the organisational structure. The complexity of the organisational forms of MCOs also makes adjustments necessary. This task is overwhelming for individuals. So-called quality improvement teams, comprised of members from different disciplines and different functional areas, could better deal with the complex challenges such as innovations and changing customer needs. In addition, they boost confidence in mutual abilities and thus ensure that mutual goals are realised. In MCOs quality improvement teams can be comprised of MCO managers, representatives from insurances (purchasers), members and service providers who determine quality objectives. They can also be comprised of cross-functional teams which determine the specific needs of a group of insured and then develop and test recommendations for e.g. guidelines based on their findings (Siren and Laffel 1998; Meltzer et al. 2009). This task can also be carried out by quality circles.

The quality management of an MCO should also involve patient education programmes. Such programmes include health risk appraisal measures ($\rightarrow$ disease management) as well as company healthcare promotion and informational material regarding individualised healthcare support.

Assessment

The evaluation of quality management differs depending on the perspective of the interest group (stakeholders).

From the perspective of the MCO, an effective quality management creates advantages over competitors. The interest of the insured and the service providers is satisfied with a range of high quality care services to meet patients' needs. As long as a quality improvement also reduces the consequential costs of insufficient quality, the prices of insurance services can be reduced and the compensation of service providers can be increased.

On the other hand, the development and maintenance of an effective quality management system is associated with investments in information technology and higher administration costs which must be weighed against the advantages. It should be noted that while the insured have high price sensitivity, they do not equally value an improvement of quality due to information deficits. Experience from the United States shows that below-average quality affects decisions, while it does not matter how above-average the health insurance is (also see Scanlon et al. 2008). Thus the MCO is required to ensure transparency through marketing measures. In the United States these can include report cards which supply customers with information about cost and quality on the basis of comparable indicators so that customers can choose an insurance provider (Epstein 1998). Report cards (public reporting) are released online by the National Committee for Quality Assurance (NCQA). They are based on the results of different sources of data collection and the evaluations which are divided into categories such as access/service qualified service providers or the promotion of health and certification status. However, it must be mentioned that report cards can also contain major risks. Physicians behave rationally when they turn away particularly problematic patients who could possibly influence their rating negatively (Werner and Ash 2005). Exclusion criteria are particularly necessary for this reason.

Literature

Accenture. (2007). Accenture Gesundheitscoaching. – Accenture Gesundheitscoaching – Krankenversicherungen betreten Neuland, Werbebroschüre. www.accenture.com. Accessed 16 Jan 2013.

ACMQ [American College of Medical Quality]. (2005). *Core curriculum for medical quality management*. Sudbury, MA: Jones and Bartlett.

ADA [American Diabetes Association]. (2012). Management of hyperglycemia in type 2 diabetes: A patient-centered approach – position statement of the American Diabetes Association (ADA) and the European Association for the Study of Diabetes (EASD). http://professional.diabetes.org/News_Display.aspx?TYP=9&CID=90136. Accessed 4 Dec 2012.

Adams, S., Smith, P. K., Allan, P. F., et al. (2007). Systematic review of the chronic care model in chronic obstructive pulmonary disease prevention and management. *Archives of Internal Medicine, 167*(6), 551–561.

AHCA [American Health Care Association]. (2013). *The Federal anti-kickback statute.* http://www.ahcancal.org/facility_operations/ComplianceProgram/Pages/RiskPoliciesProc.aspx. Accessed 22 Feb 2013.

Al-Assaf, A. F. (1998). *Managed care quality – A practical guide.* Boca Raton: CRC press.

Amarasingham, R., Plantinga, L., Diener-West, D., et al. (2009). Clinical information technologies and inpatient outcomes: A mutliple hospital study. *Archives of Internal Medicine, 169*(2), 108–114.

Amelung, V. E. (1998, June). Guidelines: Standardisierung medizinischer Leistungserstellung? Eine kritische Analyse. In H. Fischer et al. (Ed.), *Management Handbuch Krankenhaus*, 13. Ergänzungslieferung. Heidelberg: R.v. Decker's.

Andersen, R. S., Vedsted, P., Olesen, F., et al. (2011). Does the organizational structure of health care systems influence care-seeking decisions? A qualitative analysis of Danish cancer patients' reflections on care-seeking. *Scandinavian Journal of Primary Health Care, 29*, 144–149.

Berchtold, P., & Hess, K. (2006). Evidenz für Managed Care: Europäische Literaturanalyse unter besonderer Berücksichtigung der Schweiz: Wirkung von Versorgungssteuerung auf Qualität und Kosteneffektivität, Arbeitsdokument des Obsan 16, Schweizer Gesundheitsobservatorium, Neuchâtel.

Berchtold, P., & Peytremann-Bridevaux, I. (2011). Integrated care organizations in Switzerland. *International Journal Integrated Care, 11*(Special 10th Anniversary Edition), e010.

Berchtold, P., Spycher, S. T., & Guggisberg, J. (2004). *Evaluation der Telefonberatung durch Medgate – Management Summary.* Bern: College für Management im Gesundheitswesen.

Berwick, D. M., Nolan, T. W., & Whittington, J. (2008). The triple aim: Care, health, and cost – The remaining barriers to integrated care are not technical; they are political. *Health Affairs, 27* (3), 759–769.

Beyer, M., Genischen, J., Szecsenyi, J., Wensing, M., & Gerlach, F. M. (2006). Wirksamkeit von Disease-Management-Programmen in Deutschland – Probleme der medizinischen Evaluationsforschung anhand eines Studienprotokolls. *Zeitschrift für ärztliche Fortbildung Qualitatssicherung Gesundheitswesen, 100*, 355–363.

Black, H. R., & Elliott, W. (2012). *Hypertension: A companion to Braunwald's heart disease* (2nd ed.). Philadelphia: Saunders.

Blissenbach, H. F., & Penna, P. M. (1996). Pharmaceutical service in managed care. In P. R. Kongstvedt (Ed.), *The managed health care handbook* (3rd ed., pp. 367–387). Gaithersburg: Aspen.

Blumenthal, D. (1993). Total quality management and physicians' clinical decisions. *JAMA: The Journal of the American Medical Association, 269*, 2775–2778.

Blumenthal, D. (1996). Quality of health care, Part 1. *The New England Journal of Medicine, 335*, 891–894.

Bodenheimer, T. (2000). Disease management in the American market. *BMJ: British Medical Journal, 320*, 563–566.

Bodenheimer, T. (2003). Interventions to improve chronic illness care: Evaluating their effectiveness. *Disease Management, 6*(2), 63–71.

Bodenheimer, T. (2009). Das Chronic Care Modell auf dem Prüfstand. *Care Management, 2*(6), 21–23.

Bodenheimer, T., Wagner, E. H., & Grumbach, K. (2002). Improving primary care for patients with chronic illness. *JAMA: The Journal of the American Medical Association, 288*, 1775–1779.

Bodenheimer, T., Grumbach, K., & Berenson, R. A. (2009). A lifeline for primary care. *The New England Journal of Medicine, 360*(26), 2693–2696.

Boyd, C. M., Darer, J., Boult, C., et al. (2005). Clinical practice guidelines and quality of care for older patients with multiple comorbid diseases – Implications for P4P. *JAMA: The Journal of the American Medical Association, 294*(6), 717–724.

Brekke, K. R., Nuscheler, R., & Straume, O. R. (2005). *Gatekeeping in health care* (CESifo working paper no. 1552), Category 9. Industrial Organisation.

Brown, L. D. (1996). *American health care in transition: A guide to the perplexed*. Washington, DC: Grantmaker Assistance Program.

KBV [Kassenärztliche Bundesvereinigung]. (2013). http://www.kbv.de/23546.html. Accessed 23 Feb 2013.

Bungard, W., Wiendick, A., & Zink, K. J. (1992). *Qualitätszirkel im Umbruch: Experten nehmen Stellung*. Ludwigshafen: Ehrenhof.

Bunn, F., Byrne, G., & Kendall, S. (2005). The effects of telephone consultation and triage on healthcare use and patient satisfaction: A systematic review. *The British Journal of General Practice, 55*, 956–961.

Cassel, D. (2008). Kassenspezifische Positivlisten als Vertragsgrundlage in der GKV-Arzneimittelversorgung. In E. Wille & K. Knabner (Eds.), *Wettbewerb im Gesundheitswesen*. Frankfurt am Main: Chancen und Grenzen.

Cassel, D., & Friske, J. (1999). Arzneimittelpositivlisten: Kostendämpfungsinstrument oder Wettbewerbsparameter? *Wirtschaftsdienst, 1999/IX*, 529–537.

Cesta, T. G., Tahan, H. A., & Fink, L. F. (1998). *The case manager's survival guide: Winning strategies for clinical practice*. Missouri: St. Louis.

Christianson, J. B., Ginsburg, P. B., & Draper, D. A. (2008). The transition from managed care to consumerison: A community level status report. *Health Affairs, 27*(5), 1362–1370.

Cleverley, W. O., Song, P. H., & Cleverley, J. O. (2010). *Essentials of health care finance* (7th ed.). Sudbury: Jones and Bartlett.

Coffey, R. J., Richards, J. S., Remmert, C. S., et al. (1992). An introduction to critical path. *Quality Management in Health Care, 1*, 45–54.

Cohen, E. L., & Cesta, T. G. (2005). *Nursing Case Management, from essentials to advanced practice applications* (4th ed.). St. Louis: Elsevier.

Coleman, K., Austin, B. T., Brach, C., & Wagner, E. H. (2009). Evidence on the chronic care modell in the new millenium. *Health Affairs, 28*(1), 75–85.

Coulter, A., & Ellins, J. (2007). Effectiveness of strategies for informing, educating, and involving patients. *BMJ: British Medical Journal, 335*, 24–27.

De Bleser, L., Depreitere, R., De Waele, K., et al. (2006). Defining pathways. *Journal of Nursing Management, 14*(7), 553–563.

Disease Management Association of America [DMAA]. (2004). *Definition of DM*. www.dmaa.org/definition.html. Accessed 2 Feb 2004.

Dixon, T., Shaw, M. E., & Dieppe, P. A. (2006). Analysis of regional variation in hip and knee joint replacement rates in England using hospital episodes statistics. *Public Health, 120*, 83–90.

Dlugacz, Y. D. (2006). *Measuring health care: Using quality data for operational, financial and clinical improvement*. San Francisco: Jossey.-Bass.

Donabedian, A. (1992). The role of outcomes in quality assessment and assurance. *Quality Review Bulletin, 18*, 356–360.

Dranove, D., & Spier, K. E. (2003). The theory of utilization review. *Contributions to Economic Analysis & Policy, 2*(1), 1–21.

Draper, D. A., Hurley, R. E., Lesser, C. S., et al. (2002). The changing face of managed care. *Health Affairs, 21*(1), 11–23.

Duncan, I. (2008). *Managing and evaluating healthcare interventions and programs*. Winsted: ACTEX Publications.

Eggers, S., Römer-Kirchner, A., & Schmidt, R. (2008). *Management Handbuch Pflege: Grundlagen des Case Managements*. http://www.fh-erfurt.de/soz/fileadmin/SO/Dokumente/Lehrende/Schmidt_Roland_Prof_Dr/Publikationen/Grundlagen_Case_Management.pdf. Accessed 20 Feb 2013.

Eichert, J. H., Wong, H., & Smith, D. R. (1997). The disease management development process. In W. E. Todd & D. Nash (Eds.), *Disease management. A system approach to improving patient outcomes* (pp. 27–59). Chicago: American Hospital Association.

Ellrodt, G., Cook, D. J., Lee, J., et al. (1997). Evidence-based disease management. *JAMA: The Journal of the American Medical Association, 278,* 1687–1692.

Emanuel, E. J., & Goldman, L. (1998). Protecting Patients Welfare in Managed care: Six safeguards. *Journal of Health Politics, Policy and Law, 23*(4), 635–659.

Epping-Jordan, J. E., Pruitt, S. D., Bengoa, R., et al. (2004). Improving the quality of health care for chronic conditions. *Quality & Safety in Heath Care, 13,* 299–305.

Epstein, A. M. (1998). Rolling down the runway: The challenges ahead for quality report cards. *JAMA: The Journal of the American Medical Association, 279,* 691–696.

Ferris, T. G., Chang, Y., Blumenthal, D., et al. (2001). Leaving gatekeeping behind – Effects of opening access to specialists for adults in a health maintenance organization. *The New England Journal of Medicine, 345*(18), 1312–1317.

Forrest, C. B. (2003). Primary care gatekeeping and referrals: Effective filter or failed experiment? *BMJ: British Medical Journal, 326*(7391), 692–695.

Garrido, M. V., Zentner, A., & Busse, R. (2011). The effects of gatekeeping: A systematic review of the literature. *Scandinavian Journal of Primary Health Care, 29,* 28–38.

Gensichen, J., Beyer, M., Muth, C., et al. (2006). Case Management to improve major depression. *A Systematic Review Psychological Medicine, 36,* 7–14.

Geraedts, M. (2013). Die ärztliche Zweitmeinung bei der Therapiewahl. In Krankenhausreport 2013, Mengendynamik: mehr Mengen, mehr Nutzen?. Berlin: Schattauer.

Gerlach, F. (2001). *Qualitätsförderung in Klinik und Praxis – Eine Chance für die Medizin.* Stuttgart: Thieme.

Gift, R., & Mosel, D. (1994). *Benchmarking in health care: A collaborative approach.* Chicago: American Hospital Association.

G-I-N [Guidelines International Network]. (2013). www.g-i-n.net. Accessed 20 Feb 2013.

Ginzberg, E. (1996). *Tomorrow's hospital.* New Haven: Yale University Press.

Gold, M. (1999). The changing US health care system. *The Milbank Quarterly, 77,* 113–137.

Gold, W., & Kongstvedt, P. (2003). How broadening DM's focus helped shrink one plan's costs. *Managed Care, 12*(11), 33–34, 37–39.

Gonseth, J., Guallar-Castillón, P., Banegas, J. R., et al. (2004). The effectiveness of disease management programmes in reducing hospital re-admission in older patients with heart failure: A systematic review and meta-analysis of published reports. *European Heart Journal, 25*(18), 1570–1595.

Green, M. A., & Rowell, J. C. (2011). *Understanding health insurance: A guide to billing and reimbursement.* New York: Delmar Cengage Learning.

Grumbach, K., Selby, J. V., Damberg, C., et al. (1999). Resolving the gatekeeper Conudrum. *JAMA: The Journal of the American Medical Association, 282*(3), 261–266.

Hackman, J. R., & Wageman, R. (1995). Total quality management: Empirical, conceptual, and practical issues. *Adminstrative Science Quarterly, 40,* 309–342.

Harris, R. E. (2013). *Epidemiology of chronic disease: Global persepctives.* Burlington: Jones & Bartlett Learning.

Hroscikoski, M. C., Solberg, L., Sperl-Hillen, J. M., et al. (2006). Challenges of change: A qualitative study of chronic care model implementation. *Annals of Family Medicine, 4,* 317–326.

Huber, D. (2005). *Disease management: A guide for case managers.* Missouri: Elsevier Saunders.

Hung, D. Y., Rundall, T. G., Tallia, A. F., et al. (2007). Rethinking prevention in primary care: Applying the chronic care model to address health risk behaviors. *The Milbank Quarterly, 85* (1), 69–91.

Hunter, D. J., & Fairfield, G. (1997). Managed care: Disease management. *BMJ: British Medical Journal, 314,* 50–53.

IOM [Institute of Medicine]. (2004). *Health literacy: A prescription to end confusion.* Report released 8 Apr 2004, Washington, DC: National Academies Press.

Janus, K. (2003). *Managing health care in private organizations. Transaction costs, cooperation and modes of organization in the value chain.* Frankfurt am Main: Peter Lang.

Jenkins, C., Pope, C., Magwood, G., et al. (2010). Expanding the chronic care framework to improve diabetes management the REACH case study. *Progress in Community Health Partnership: Research Education and Action, 4*(1), 65–79.

Kane, R. L., Priester, R., & Totten, A. M. (2005). *Meeting the challenge of chronic illness.* Baltimore: Johns Hopkins University Press.

Kaplan, S., Greenfield, S., & Ware, J. (1989). Assessing the effects of physician-patient interactions on the outcomes of chronic disease. *Medical Care, 27*(3), Supplement: Advances in Health Status Assessment, 110–127.

Katz, M. (2006). *Health care for less.* New York: Hatherleight.

Kelly, D. L. (2003). *Applying quality management in healthcare: A process for improvement.* Chicago: Health Administration Press.

Kessner, D. M., Kalk, C. E., & Singer, J. (1971). Accessing health quality – The case of tracers. *The New England Journal of Medicine, 288*, 189–194.

Klein, M. (2009). *Patientencoaching, Win-Win-Situation für Krankenkassen und Versicherte,* Presentation on 2 July 2009 on the conference "Versorgungsmanagement" of SkectrumK.

Klusen, N., & Meusch, A. (2009). Vorwort der Herausgeber. In N. Klusen, A. Fließgarten & T. Nebling (Eds.), *Informiert und selbstbestimmt. Der mündige Bürger als mündiger Patient,* Beiträge zum Gesundheitsmanagement Band 24, Nomos, Baden Baden.

Kongstvedt, P. R. (2013). *Essentials of managed health care* (6th ed.). Burlington: Jones & Bartlett Learning.

Krause, D. S. (2005). Economic effectiveness of disease management programs: A meta-analysis. *Disease Management, 8*, 114–134.

Kumar, S., & Snooks, H. (2011). *Telenursing.* London: Springer.

Lattimer, V., george, S., Thompson, F., et al. (1998). Safety and effectiveness of nurse telephone consultation in out of hours primary care: Randomised controlled trial. *BMJ: British Medical Journal, 317*, 1054–1059.

Lattimer, V., Sassi, F., George, S., et al. (2000). Cost analysis of nurse telephone consultation in out of hours primary care: Evidence from a randomised controlled trial. *BMJ: British Medical Journal, 320*, 1053–1057.

Lawrence, D. (2001). Gatekeeping reconsidered. *The New England Journal of Medicine, 345*(18), 1342–1343.

Linden, M., Gothe, H., & Ormel, J. (2003). Pathways to care and psychological problems of general practice patients in a "gate keeper" and an "open access" health care system. *Social Psychiatry and Psychiatric Epidemiology, 38*, 690–697.

Löcherbach, P., Klug, W., & Remmel-Faßbender, R. (2003). *Case management* (2nd ed.), Luchterhand.

McGlynn, E. A. (1997). Six challenges in measuring the quality of care. *Health Affairs, 16*(3), 7–21.

McGlynn, E. A., Asch, S. M., Adams, J., et al. (2003). The quality of health care delivered to adults in the United States. *The New England Journal of Medicine, 348*(26), 2635–2645.

Meltzer, D., Chung, J., Khalili, P., et al. (2009). Exploring the use of social network methods in designing health care quality improvement teams. *Social Science and Medicine, 71*(6), 1119–1130.

Miksch, A., Trieschmann, J., Ose, D., Rölz, A., Szecsenyi, J., et al. (2011). DMP und Praxis: Stellungnahme von Hausärzten und Veränderung von Praxisabläufen zur Umsetzung des DMP Diabetes mellitus Typ 2. *ZEFQ, 105*(6), 427–433.

Moll van Charante, E. P., Riet, G., Drost, S., et al. (2006). Nurse telephone triage in out of hours GP practice, determinants of independent advice and return consultation. *BMC Family Practice, 7*(74), 1–9.

Mullahy, C. M. (1996). Case management and managed care. In P. R. Kongstvedt (Ed.), *The managed health care handbook* (pp. 274–300). Gaithersburg: Aspen.

Mullahy, C. M. (2010). *The case manager's handbook* (4th ed.). Sudbury: Jones and Bartlett.

Mullner, R. M., & Mullner, R. M. (2009). *Encyclopedia of health services research.* California: Sage.

Naylor, M. D., Brooten, D., Campbell, R., et al. (1999). Comprehensive discharge planning and home follow-up of hospitalized elders. A randomized clinical trial. *JAMA: The Journal of the American Medical Association, 281*, 613–620.

NBCH [National Business Coalition on Health]. (2006). *Health risk appraisal at the worksite: Basics for HRA decision making.* http://nbch.kma.net/NBCH/files/ccLibraryFiles/Filename/000000000042/HRA_Updated_080303.pdf. Accessed 21 Feb 2013.

Neuffer, A. B. (1997). *Managed care. Umsetzbarkeit des Konzepts im deutschen Gesundheitssystem.* Dissertation, St. Gallen.

NHS Direct. (2011). NHS direct buisness plan 2011/12 – 2015/16: Out update for 2012/13. http://www.nhsdirect.nhs.uk/about/corporateinformation/~/media/files/freedomofinformationdocuments/otherfreedomofinformationdocuments/nhsd_business_plan_2011_12-2015_16_update2012b.ashx. Accessed 16 Feb 2013.

NHS Direct. (2012). *Facts and figures.* http://www.nhsdirect.nhs.uk/News/FactsAndFigures?name=FactsAndFiguresAboutNHSDirect. Accessed 15 Feb 2013.

Nuovo, J. (2007). *Chronic disease management.* New York: Springer.

O'Connor, A., Stacey, D., & Légaré, F. (2008). Coaching to support patients in making decisions. *BMJ: British Medical Journal, 336*, 228–229.

OECD [Organisation for Economic Cooperation and Development]. (2012). *OECD health data 2012.* http://www.oecd.org/health/health-systems/oecdhealthdata2012.htm. Accessed 23 Feb 2013.

Patlak, M., Micheel, C., & German, R. (2008). *Implementing colorectal screening.* Washington, DC: The National Academies Press.

Pauly, M. V. (1995). Practice guidelines: Can they save money? Should they? *Journal of Law, Medicine & Ethics, 23*, 65–74.

Payne, S., Restuccia, J. D., Ash, A. S., et al. (1991). Using utilization review information to improve hospital efficiency. *Hospital & Health Service Administration, 36*(4), 473–489.

Peytreman-Bridevaux, I., & Burnand, B. (2009). Disease management: A proposal for a new definition. *International Journal of Integrated Care, 9* Letter to the Editor.

Plocher, D. (1996). Disease management. In P. R. Kongstvedt (Ed.), *The managed health care handbook* (pp. 318–347). Gaithersburg: Aspen.

Protzman, C., Meyzell, G., & Kerpchar, J. (2011). *Leveraging lean in healthcare: Transforming your enterprise into a high quality patient care delivery system.* New York: Productivity Press.

Rebscher, H. (2006). *Gesundheitsökonomie und Gesundheitspolitik: im Spannungsfeld zwischen Wissenschaft und Politikberatung.* Heidelberg: Economica.

Remler, D. K., Donelan, K., Blendon, R. J., et al. (1997). What do managed care plans do to effect care? Results from a survey of physicians. *Inquiry, 34*, 196–204.

Reuter, W. (1997). Managed Care und die pharmazeutische Industrie. In M. Arnold et al. (Eds.), *Managed care.* Stuttgart: Schattauer.

Robinson, R., & Steiner, A. (1998). *Managed health care US evidence and lessons for the National Health service.* Buckingham: Open University Press.

Roeder, N., & Küttner, T. (2006). Behandlungspfade im Licht von Kosteneffekten im Rahmen des DRG-systems. *Internist, 47*(7), 684–689.

Roland, M., Guthrie, B., & Thomé, D. C. (2012). Primary medical care in the United Kingdom. *JABFM, 25*(S1), S6–S11.

Rosenberg, S. T., Allen, D. R., Handte, J. S., et al. (1995). Effects of utilization review in a fee-for-service health insurance plan. *The New England Journal of Medicine, 333*, 1326–1331.

Sanofi. (2010). *Managed care digest series – HMO-PPO digest 2010–11.* Bridgewater.

Sanofi. (2012). *Managed care digest series – HMO-PPO digest 2012–2013.* Bridgewater.

Scanlon, D. P., Lindrooth, R., Christianson, J. B., et al. (2008). Steering patients to safer hospitals? The effect of a Tiered hospital network on hospital admissions. *Health Services Research, 43*(5 Pt 2), 1849–1868.

Schäfer, W., Kroneman, M., Boerma, W., van den Berg, M., Westert, G., Devillé, W., & van Ginneken, E. (2010). The Netherlands: Health system review. *Health Systems in Transition, 12*(1), 1–228.

Schlesinger, M., Gray, B. H., & Perreira, K. M. (1997). Medical professionalism under managed care: The pros and cons of utilization review. *Health Affairs,* Jan/Feb 1997, *16*(1), 106–124.

Schlette, S., Knieps, F., & Amelung, V. E. (2005). *Versorgungsmanagement für chronisch Kranke, Lösungsansätze aus den USA und aus Deutschland.* Bonn: KomPart.

Schmid, E., Weatherly, J., Meyer-Lutterloh, K., Seiler, R., & Lägel, R. (2008). Patientencoaching, Gesundheitscoaching, Case Management, Medizinisch Wissenschaftliche Verlagsgesellschaft, Berlin.

Schoen, C., Osborn, R., Trang Huynh, P., Doty, M., Zapert, K., Peugh, J., & Davis, K. (2005). Taking the pulse of health care systems: Experiences of patients with health problems in six countries. *Health Affairs, Suppl Web Exclusive* W5 - 509. www.ncbi.nlm.nih.gov/pubmed/16269444.

Schwaiberger, M. (2002). *Case Management im Krankenhaus.* Melsungen: Bibliomed.

Schwarz, R. (2006). Nutzung uns Akzeptanz von medizinischer Telefonberatung in der Bevölkerung. *Schweizer Ärztezeitung, 87*(36), 1551–1555.

Schwenkglenks, M., Preiswerk, G., Lehner, R., et al. (2006). Economic efficiency of gatekeeping compared with fee for service plans: A Swiss example. *Journal of Epidemiology and Community Health, 60*(1), 24–30.

Shapiro, H. M. (1997). *Managed care beware.* West Hollywood: Dove Books.

Shi, L., & Singh, D. A. (2012). *Delivering healthcare in America: A systems approach* (5th ed.). Sudbury: Jones & Bartlett Learning.

Siren, P. B., & Laffel, G. L. (1998). Quality management in managed care. In P. R. Kongstvedt (Ed.), *Best practices in medical management* (pp. 433–459). Gaithersburg: Aspen.

Solberg, L. I. (2006). Care quality and implementation of the chronic care model: A quantitative study. *Annals of Family Medicine, 4,* 310–316.

Stock, S., Drabik, A., Büscher, G., et al. (2010). German diabetes management programs improve quality of care and curb costs. *Health Affairs, 29,* 2197–2205.

Strickland, P., Hudson, S. V., Piasecki, A., et al. (2010). Features of the Chronic Care Model (CCM) associated with behavioral counseling and diabetes care in community primary care. *JABFM, 23*(3), 295–305.

Sultz, H., & Young, K. (2010). *Health care USA: Understanding its organization and delivery.* Sudbury: Jones and Bartlett.

SVR [Sachverständigenrat zur Begutachtung der Entwicklung im Gesundheitswesen]. (2005). Gutachten 2005, Kurzfassung Nr. 25.

Van der Vinne, E. (2009, August 10). The ultimate goal of disease management: Improved quality of life by patient centric care. *International Journal Integrated Care, 9,* e89.

Vargas, R. B., Mangione, C. M., Asch, S., et al. (2007). Can a chronic care model collaborative reduce heart disease risk in patients with diabetes? *Society of General Internal Medicine, 22,* 215–222.

Wagner, E. H. (1998a). Chronic disease management: What will it take to improve care for chronic illness? *Effective Clinical Practice, 1,* 2–4.

Wagner, E. H. (1998b). More than a case manager. *Annals of Internal Medicine, 129,* 654–661.

Wagner, E. H. (2000). The role of patient care teams in chronic disease management. *BMJ: British Medical Journal, 320,* 569–572.

Wagner, E. H., Austin, B. T., & Von Korff, M. (1996). Organizing care for patients with chronic illness. *The Milbank Quarterly, 74,* 511–544.

Wan, T. T. H., & Connell, A. M. (2003). *Monitoring the quality of health care: Issues and scientific approaches.* Norwell: Kluwer Academic.

Ward, M. D., & Rieve, J. A. (1997). The role of case management in disease management. In W. E. Todd & D. Nash (Eds.), *Disease management. A system approach to improving patient outcomes* (pp. S235–S259). Chicago: American Hospital Association.

Wasem, J., Greß, S., & Hessel, F. (2003). *Hausarztmodelle in der GKV – Effekte und Perspektiven vor dem Hintergrund nationaler und internationaler Erfahrungen.* Diskussionsbeiträge aus dem Fachbereich Wirtschaftswissenschaften Universität Essen, Nr. 130.

Wendt, W., & Löcherbach, P. (2009). *Standards und Fachlichkeit in case management.* Heidelberg: Economica.

Wennberg, J. E. (2010). *Tracking medicine: A researcher's quest to understand health care.* New York: Oxford University Press.

Werner, R., & Asch, D. (2005). The unintended consequences of publicly reporting quality information. *JAMA: The Journal of the American Medical Association, 293*(10), 239–1244.

WHO [World Health Organization]. (2005). *Preventing chronic diseases: a vital investment.* Geneva: WHO.

Wickizer, T. M. (1992). The effects of utilization review on hospital use and expenditures: A covariance analysis. *Health Service Research, 27*(1), 103–121.

Zelman, W., & Berenson, R. A. (1998). *The managed care blues & how to cure them.* Washington, DC: Georgetown University Press.

Zitter, M. (2001). A new paradigma in health care delivery: Disease management. In W. E. Todd & D. Nash (Eds.), *Disease management. A system approach to improving patient outcomes.* Chicago: American Hospital Association.

Evaluation Procedure

12

12.1 Overview

In health science **evaluation** refers to a comprehensive assessment and evaluation of the benefits and costs of healthcare technology. The term "healthcare technology" is very broad and includes the following processes and products:

1. Programmes for the prevention and early detection of diseases (e.g. vaccination programmes or screenings of cholesterol and blood pressure values),
2. Medical procedures to treat certain diseases (bypass operations, minimal invasive operations, heart transplants, rehabilitation programmes etc.),
3. Medications, devices for medical diagnoses and therapies as well as other medical products (such as medicines to reduce cholesterol and blood pressure, computer tomography, pacemakers)
4. Medical care in alternative organisational forms (outpatient or inpatient care of dialysis or stroke patients)
5. New organisational forms of care (→ HMOs, → IDS, → gatekeeping),
6. New management instruments (disease management programmes, patient coaching) and
7. Information technology (telematics).

In practise, different forms of evaluation have become established. They all deal with the basic question: How can health and its changes be assessed?

Moreover, the evaluation procedures reveal many similarities in the definition and assessment of health. However, many of the techniques are separated based on their problem orientation and their theoretical basis (see Fig. 12.1).

In this process it must be clearly emphasised that in practise, the individual methods are not clearly distinguished from one another and are often used in combination.

V.E. Amelung, *Healthcare Management*, Springer Texts in Business and Economics, 219
DOI 10.1007/978-3-642-38712-8_12, © Springer-Verlag Berlin Heidelberg 2013

	Economic Evaluation Procedure	Preference Measurement	Evidence-based medicine (EBM)	Health Systems Research	Health Technology Assessment (HTA)
Characteristics	Consideration of costs and monetary outcome indicators in the evaluation	Inclusion of patient preferences	Analysis of efficacy of a medical technology	Analysis of the relation between structural, process and outcome quality (effectiveness)	Additional consideration of ethical, legal and social factors
Decision Problems	Maximizing benefits and minimizing costs of healthcare technologies	Disclosure of hidden needs and preferences	Selection and evaluation of relevant data	Optimisation of outcomes	Selection and timing of healthcare technologies
Theoretical Basis	Economic welfare theory, decision making theory	Conjoint analysis, discrete choice analysis	Epidemiology, meta-analysis	Donabedian's quality approach, healthcare system research	Assessment of technology effects
Application in managed care	Guidelines, case management	Managed care contracts, disease management, service catalogue	Guidelines, disease managment	Quality management, forms of compensation, disease management	Service catalogue, positive lists

Fig. 12.1 Evaluation procedures

12.2 Health Economic Evaluation

Economic evaluation compares the effects or "outcomes" of a certain type of healthcare technology, usually the improvement of the status of health and the increase in life expectancy of patient collectives, with its costs.

The economic evaluation can be carried out from various **perspectives** and have to be revealed before conducting the evaluation. The most comprehensive of the different perspectives used in health economic evaluation is the societal perspective. Here, the costs and utilities of all members of society involved are included. Other perspectives are those of health insurances, hospitals, providers or patients and their relatives (Schöffski and Graf von der Schulenburg 2008).

What should be distinguished from the social perspective is the benefit of health technology from the perspective of certain institutions, e.g. an MCO, a statutory health insurance, a hospital or a public service purchaser. An institution is naturally only interested in the individual potential costs and benefits of a certain measure (as long as protecting the public public's interest is not included within their range of responsibilities). The spectrum of costs and effects that should be considered is thus narrower than in the evaluation from the societal perspective. Therefore, evaluation has the character of a commercial profitability calculation on this level. However, it should be noted that MCOs are in competition with one another for the insured. Thus, both the benefits and the costs in the care concepts carried only by the insured (e.g. time and travel costs, absence from work or psychosocial costs) should be included in the calculation as well because they could be pivotal in choosing an insurance company from the point of view of the insured.

The economic evaluation procedures differ largely depending on how the effects or outcomes of a type of health technology are measured. In all procedures, the determination of the costs is carried out according to uniform criteria. Figure 12.2 illustrates this relation. We will begin by discussing the cost analysis.

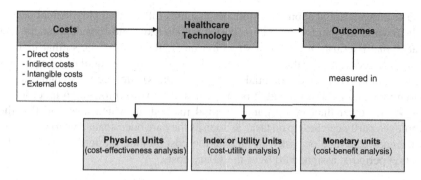

Fig. 12.2 Economic evaluation procedures

Cost Analysis

The production and use of healthcare technologies is linked to an economy's use of resources (work, capital investment etc.). The use of resources valued in prices is referred to as costs. Its amount is determined by the loss of utility of the resources in their next best use which cannot be realised (opportunity cost principle). In economic evaluation studies the costs are systematically categorised according to direct medical costs, direct non-medical costs and indirect costs (Krauth 2010).

Among the **direct costs** are all costs associated with the production and continuous use of a type of healthcare technology. Medical and non-medical costs can also be differentiated. Direct medical costs accrue in the care sector (costs for medical and non-medical personnel deployment, pharmaceutical costs, device costs, administrative costs), while direct non-medical costs comprise healthcare support services (transportation and time costs of the patients as well as support from family members). The prices on the competitive markets are an exact measure of value. As the markets for healthcare services and medical technology are typically monopolised or regulated by the government and even have state-administrated prices, distortions inevitably occur in the relative prices when the actual prices (fee-for-service, nursing rates, drug prices or prices of devices) are used for the cost calculations of the comparable technologies. In the evaluation fictitious competition prices are used if possible (so-called "shadow prices").

The **indirect costs** include production losses as a consequence of morbidity (incapacity to work, disability) and mortality (premature death). From the societal perspective they are determined by human capital or the friction cost approach.

According to the human capital approach, the loss of production potential that accompanies an employee's absence from work is evaluated (Drummond et al. 2005). The indicators for a loss of production are the salary costs (gross income plus additional wage costs such as employer contributions or social security). In the evaluation of human capital via salary costs, possible distortions through gender- and age-specific salaries should be noted.

The human capital approach implicitly assumes full-time employment of people able to work. In contrast, the friction cost approach takes into consideration the fact that in many industrial countries structural unemployment exists, so that indirect costs only accrue in so-called friction periods – periods of time until new employees (from the not yet used potential pool of workers) are recruited and trained (Drummond et al. 2005). In addition, the costs of a loss of production in a friction period are lower than in the human capital method, in which it is said that the employee partly catches up on tasks as soon as they are once again able to work, and colleagues also take on tasks. In the friction cost method the loss of work in the friction period is assigned 80 % of the salary costs.

Cost-Effectiveness Analysis

In the cost-effectiveness analysis the effects of healthcare technologies are measured in physical units. This way the analysis can deal with temporal units (e.g. years of life gained), case numbers or clinical values (e.g. blood pressure values etc.).

The costs of the technologies are calculated as net costs in the cost-effectiveness analysis. That means the costs of illness (which can be partly or completely prevented in the future) are subtracted from the direct and indirect costs which are associated with their use. Information about the costs prevented are provided by illness cost studies in which the direct costs and production losses from illnesses (loss of work, disability, premature death) are calculated (Zweifel et al. 2009).

The net costs are correlated with the outcome measured in physical units, e.g. the costs per year of life gained (cost-effectiveness ratio, CER):

$$CER = \frac{\text{Net costs}}{\text{Years of life gained}}$$

The incremental cost-effectiveness ratio (ICER) serves to compare the costs and benefits of two different options. The cost differences in monetary terms are divided by the effect differences which are often measured in quality adjusted life years. Hence, the ICER can be used for decision-making when rationing of healthcare services becomes necessary (Henderson 2009).

With the cost-effectiveness ratio the cost-effectiveness of a type of technology can be compared with others. Discrepancies can be due to differences in the costs of technology or in effectiveness. Effectiveness should be distinguished between effectiveness under ideal conditions (efficacy) and under real conditions (effectiveness) (Drummond et al. 2005).

Differences between efficacy and effectiveness are due to the fact that specially trained doctors in prestigious academic institutes usually carry out the evaluation of **efficacy** in healthcare technologies for carefully chosen groups of patients. In the evaluation of the efficacy of a certain healthcare technology the economist relies on the outcome of technical and clinical studies ($\rightarrow$ evidence-based medicine).

In contrast, **effectiveness** is influenced by institutional and behaviour-related deviations from the ideal conditions (insufficient quality of devices, organisational and operational problems, incomplete patient compliance, non-compliance with medical treatment standards). The analysis of the relationships between real institutional structures or processes and the outcomes are the subject of $\rightarrow$ health systems research.

The decision-making problem of the cost-effectiveness analysis can be explained as follows: Either those technologies with lower costs and the same level of effectiveness should be chosen, such as in the development of $\rightarrow$ guidelines, or the outcome (e.g. years of life gained, number of cases) or a provided budget must be maximised. The technologies should then be prioritised according to their cost-effectiveness ratio. Certain services, which demonstrate a relatively unfavourable incremental cost-effectiveness ratio, are not included in an MCO's catalogue of services when their costs exceed the budget.

In the context of a cost-effectiveness analysis, however, only technologies whose outcomes were measured with the same (physical) indicator can be compared. Thus, it does not allow for a comparison of measures whose consequences are demonstrated in differing physical units. The values also do not provide any information about how they are subjectively evaluated by concerned and third parties, although for example a year of life gained can indeed demonstrate a different quality of life. The cost-utility analysis tries to resolve these shortcomings.

Cost-Utility Analysis

In the cost-utility analysis the changes brought about by healthcare technology are evaluated on the basis of health-related measurements of quality of life (HRQoL) (Gold et al. 1996; Drummond et al. 2005). The HRQoL measurements classify people according to their health state along a continuum from "least desired" to "most desired", as applied to some or all of the following functions or dimensions:
1. Physical functions: Mobility, physical activity, ability to care for oneself
2. Mental functions: Cognitive, mental, emotional
3. Social functions: Social integration or communication
4. Perception of health: E.g. self-assessment of the patient
5. Symptoms: Pain, discomfort.

The health state can be seen as an aggregated measure of the individual component values and recorded as a measurement. This is called a **health index.** Furthermore, one can also combine the values of individual components or sub-components merely on the dimension level and refer to a **health profile** (Zweifel et al. 2009).

Other procedures refrain from the breakdown of health status into individual components and allow study participants to directly determine their health status on an interval scale, comparable to a thermometer.

Health-related measurements of quality of life are distinguished between measurements developed for certain illnesses (illness-specific measurements) and those which can be applied to various illnesses (generic measurements). Well-known generic HRQoL measurements are the EQ-5D Index and the MOS Short Form, abbreviated as SF-36 (www.sf-36.org; www.euroquol.org; Turner-Bowker et al. 2002).

The **EuroQol** is a health index which was developed to ensure a uniform assessment of health-related quality of life. It is based on the five dimensions of health (mobility, self-sufficiency, daily activities, pain/discomfort, anxiety/depression) which are respectively divided into three levels of impairment. Altogether 243 answer combinations (health states) are possible. The health states were evaluated according to a representative population sample based on the time trade-off method (see below) and transformed into a quality of life index. The **SF-36** is a health profile which was developed for the Medical Outcomes Study in order to measure the state of health using surveys (Schöffski and Graf von der Schulenburg 2008, p. 387ff.). It distinguishes eight health components (physical functions, physical role limitations, emotional role limitations, social functions, pain, mental health, vitality, general health assessment) which are determined using 36 questions. Along with SF-36 there is a shorter version comprised of 12 questions in order to keep the survey time minimal for patients (SF-12). The questions are then combined into two categories (physical and mental well-being).

Two methods are distinguished in the measurement of health and functional states: Psychometric procedures and preference-based procedures (Chapman and Sonnenberg 2003).

The procedure of category scaling is often used in the psychometric methods. In this procedure the different states of health are explained to participants[1] and they are asked to assign these to interval scale values. The "best possible" state is assigned to one end of the scale, either 1 or 100 (= "healthy") and the "worst possible" state is assigned to the other end (0 = "dead") (Drummond et al. 2005). The remaining health states are categorised between these points of reference so that the intervals between them correspond to the subjective differences between the states of health. EuroQol and SF-36 both use psychometric measurement procedures to evaluate the subjective quality of life.

In utility theoretical procedures, which are preferred by healthcare economists, the evaluation of health states is carried out based on the behaviour of study participants in hypothetical decision-making situations. The time trade-off methods are often applied here (Drummond et al. 2005).

In the time trade-off procedure, those surveyed are asked to choose between a certain limited health state (Hj) over a specified period of time (t) and a state of complete health (H*) for a shorter period x ($x < t$). It is assumed for both periods

---

[1] For the evaluation of the state of health, in practise different subjects of evaluation are examined: patients, physicians and nursing personnel, scientists, public representatives or a combination of these groups. This decision is dependant on the perspective of the evaluation.

that they end with death. The period x is varied until those surveyed are indifferent to both alternatives. At this point the evaluation of the state of health is a product of the relation Hj $\approx$ x/t. When x is, for example, 4 years and t is 8 years, 8 years in the state of Hj is equal to 4 healthy years of life. The state of health is thus valued by those surveyed as Hj = 0.5. The more years they are willing to spend in the state of Hj as a "trade-off" for a healthy year, the lower the evaluation of their individual state of health.

As the quality of life becomes more important for the prolonging of life as a goal of medical efforts, it is common to weight years of life gained with quality of life. Thus 3 years of life spent on average with a state of health equivalent to 0.5 correspond to one and a half "quality adjusted life years", QALYs. The QALY measurement is particularly suitable as an evaluation standard when a "trade-off" exists between the prolonging of life and quality of life in a treatment such as chemotherapy.

The cost-effectiveness ratio is calculated in the cost-utility analysis (CUA) as costs per **QALY** gained (Zweifel et al. 2009):

$$CUA = \frac{Costs}{QALY}$$

A higher number of QALYs can thus be based on a prolonging of life and/or an improvement of the quality of life.

The cost-utility analysis enables the comparison of measures with different physical indicators and thus expands the reference spectrum compared to the cost-effectiveness analysis. A cost-benefit analysis serves to measure changes to the state of health and life expectancy in monetary units.

Cost-Benefit Analysis

The theory foundation of the cost-benefit analysis is the welfare theory of the potential Pareto improvement (Drummond et al. 2005). According to this principle, a type of health technology is considered to increase ones welfare when the sum of its monetary benefits is higher than the sum of the costs, so that the benefits outweigh the disadvantages. In this procedure the unit of measurement of the health effects is a change in state of health equivalent to a change in income. The monetary value of the benefits can then be directly compared with the costs. A new technology can be implemented when the monetary value of the benefits is higher than the costs or the cost-benefit relation is greater than 1:

$$Benefits - Costs > 0 \text{ or } > 1$$

There are two common methods to measure the benefit in a cost-benefit analysis: The human capital approach or the willingness-to-pay method (Zweifel et al. 2009).

The **human capital approach** serves as a method for determining the value of life. It measures the contribution of individuals, who are regarded as being capital investments, to the market. These contributions are measured by adding a person's discounted lifetime earnings. Even though this method is widely applied in health economics, it is strongly criticised. Using this method, women, usually earning less than men, are discriminated against men, low wage earners are discriminated against people earning more. Hence, according to the human capital approach, their value of life would be lower. Furthermore, non-market activities, such as raising children or doing any activities not financially rewarded by the society are neglected within this approach (Santerre and Neun 2009).

According to welfare theory the **willingness-to-pay method** is a methodically exact approach. The change in benefit is measured by the highest amount of money a person is willing to pay for an improvement in their health, or the lowest amount they would demand as compensation for a worsening of their health (Drummond et al. 2005).

In order to determine the sums of money, the willingness-to-pay method uses surveys in which those surveyed make evaluations based on fictitious alternative situations (contingent valuation method). Furthermore, the values are indirectly drawn from high-risk market behaviour (consumption behaviour, selection of place of work) of those concerned (revealed preference method).

The advantage of the willingness-to-pay method is that, in principle, all relevant effects of a type of health technology can be determined, including the intangible and the non-health-related effects. Even the effects which a person's change in health have on third parties, such as the effects of a stroke on a patient's relatives, can be measured, unlike with the QALY method.

A fundamental point of criticism of the willingness to pay method is the influence that income and assets have on the willingness to pay. People with higher incomes and assets are willing to pay more for the same improvement in life expectancy and state of health than people with a lower income. In comparison to other economic evaluation procedures, the cost-benefit analysis also has the disadvantage that it is often rejected by non-economists due to its monetary valuation of health. As people are not used to value healthcare decisions in monetary terms and the decisions are merely notional, it is furthermore challenging for those surveyed to attribute monetary values to certain states of health.

Sensitivity Analysis

In the economic evaluation theory there is no common opinion about the treatment of certain problems. It is disputed, for example, to which extent costs that arise after the prolongation of life should be included in the cost calculation. Furthermore, additional treatments for patients whose life was prolonged through the aid of a particular health technology results in additional costs as well. Another point of contention concerns the determination of the rate at which the costs and benefits of a health programme, many of which first occur in the future, should be discounted (discounting problem). Finally, it is unclear how the uncertainty about the extent and duration of costs and benefits should be dealt with.

In these cases it is advisable to carry out sensitivity analyses. A sensitivity analysis assesses how strongly the results of an evaluation react to the variations of the assumptions. On one hand they reveal areas in which further information or regulations are necessary, because the outcome can be greatly influenced by a change in the assumptions. In other areas, however, it may be demonstrated that the outcomes are not significantly changed by a variation in the assumptions (Drummond et al. 2005).

12.3 Preference Measurement

The extension of expert opinions to include the perspective of the patients promotes patient-centred healthcare to thus establish effective structures of care.[2] Patient-centred care is seen as a step to decisively improve the quality of healthcare. This improvement in quality can be attained when the service providers take the needs and preferences of their patients into consideration. In the context of shared decision-making, the consideration of preferences can significantly contribute to an improvement in the patient's quality of life.

In order to implement the desired patient orientation, data which illustrates what the patient actually wants, expects or prefers is necessary. The documentation and analysis of preferences of current and potential patients is thus carried out with the objective of creating a new and improved healthcare.

Patient Benefits and Preferences

When the regulatory bodies (or decision-makers) approve or decide against the medical interventions it is often a decision between multiple options. "Medication A results in a higher risk of side effects in comparison to medication B" or "medication A results in more benefits for the patients than medication B". The decision should be made with consideration of the possible consequences (risks, benefits and economic efficiency) which could accompany the alternatives. The options are implicitly or explicitly evaluated and the decision is made in favour of (or against) an option. More precisely: The authorisation is given (not given) and an additional therapeutic benefit leads (does not lead) to a price premium (maximum amount). The price premium represents the price difference to the competitor's price, which a provider can attain due to their preferability (additional therapeutic value and patient benefit).

---

[2] The following section was written by Prof. Dr. Axel C. Mühlbacher and Susanne Bethge (IGM – Institut Gesundheitsökonomie und Medizinmangement, Hochschule Neubrandenburg).

When the effects of two forms of therapy are compared with each other, a preferential judgement must be made which expresses the relative benefits of the consequences. The preferential opinion says: In view of the effect parameter X, Y, Z, "therapy A" is better than "therapy B" is better than "therapy C". Benefits and preferences are not directly observable; they are instead expressed by evaluative or preferential opinions in expert statements or studies.

In contrast, decision-making is an observable action. The way a patient, physician or expert chooses an option with its consequences can be observed. Under certain conditions one can assume that decisions are based on the judgement of the benefit of consequences (effect parameters). The decision-maker has preferences regarding the consequences which result from the voluntary decision in favour of an alternative. Preferences are thus the basis for choosing an alternative; the benefits of an alternative are the basis for the preference. Stated preferences allow conclusions to be drawn regarding the benefits of available alternatives for the individual.

Preferences (in the widest sense) are referred to when a patient prefers a certain method of treatment or care option over one or more other methods or options. The preference illustrates the relational judgement between different objects. Preferences – as triggers for a voluntary choice – are thus also indicators of a patient's motivation to use services, their demand behaviour and an expression of patient benefits.

Measurement of Preferences

An important foundation for the measurement of preferences is the description of the service to be appraised through one or more characteristics which together depict the entire product or service (Heidbrink 2006). Patients can develop preferences for material products such as medications, homeopathic remedies and other aids, or insurance contracts, but also for services, such as types of care and care concepts (e.g. integrated care).

When measuring patient preferences, two types of method are distinguished: the revealed preference methods and the stated preference methods.

In revealed methods, preference measurement is based on ones behaviour or purchase decisions, in that the sales or prescription statistics are evaluated. Thus, this is an indirect form of preference measurement. The patient/customer is not directly surveyed, but their preferences are derived from so-called secondary data.

After a person has chosen a certain product or service, the decision-maker's preference can be determined (Train 2003; Heidbrink 2006). This type of data analysis provides information about what patients do and how they make decisions. However, it does not allow making conclusions about the reasons for their decisions (Bridges et al. 2007). Thus, it is not possible to determine the relevance of the decision factors.

In stated analyses, individuals' preferences are collected via direct surveys. In this form of determining preferences the respondents appraise a product or service based on various characteristics which are provided for selection in different combinations.

The objective of the stated preference method is to determine which of the characteristics in the selection have the highest or lowest influence (benefit) on the decision (Bridges et al. 2007). When this is known, the types of care can be oriented towards these characteristics. These methods could thus serve to determine preferences and needs for care products, treatment options and also states of health, for patients as well as for service providers.

The Foundational Methods: The Conjoint Analysis (CA)

The term "conjoint" is derived from the words *con*sidered and *joint*ly (Johnson et al. 2007). In an early review about conjoint analyses Green and Srinivasan (1978) demonstrated that they deal with a number of paradigms from different disciplines. They are based, for instance, on paradigms from psychology, economics and marketing, all of which are concerned with the qualitative description of preferences (Green and Srinivasan 1978, 1990).

Conjoint analysis is a statistical method to determine how people (patients) value or evaluate different characteristics of a product. It is considered a method to determine the stated preferences (SP). Preference measurement methods thus serve not only to evaluate the different value of endpoints or the depiction of the differences between them; they can also determine the overall value or evaluation of multidimensional benefits or detriments. The overall benefit or outcome is usually composed of the different weights of individual attributes.

The first conjoint analyses were used in product development, transportation and in other marketing studies. Further developments in the statistical analysis method and the application software also enabled the use of CA in the areas of healthcare and health services research. Conjoint analyses vary in importance in different areas of economics and have become essential in many areas, as they are the only methods which:

1. Conform to the revealed preference data and
2. Model the decisions and not the demand.

The Discrete Choice Experiment

The discrete choice method is a choice-based variation of conjoint analysis which, as already described, was first made possible by the theoretical papers by Lancaster (1966) and McFadden (1974). Instead of a ranking or appraisal of many different therapy characteristics (such as in conjoint analysis), in discrete choice analysis a comparison of different attributes inherent to therapy is carried out and patients (study participants) are required to choose between differently designed therapy options (Ben-Akiva and Lerman 1985).

Through the comparison of pairs, the task is much less complex for study participants, so that this alone ensures better outcomes (Hensher et al. 2005; Johnson et al. 2007; Lancsar and Louviere 2008). The implementation of the discrete choice method also offers practical advantages, so that it has already become an often-used form of conjoint analysis in health economic evaluation (Ryan et al. 2008).

The development and procedure of a discrete choice experiment as well as its evaluation is made up of many stages (Hensher et al. 2005; Bridges et al. 2008): In order to explain patients' decisions in favour of a medical service, a therapy or a certain product (e.g. integrated care) based on its characteristics, the first step is to determine all of the characteristics which are relevant to the decision of the respective survey target group. Applied to integrated care, these could include the waiting time for an appointment with a specialist, access to information, the transparency of the clinical pathway and additionally provided prevention measures, but also the amount of financial incentives (Mühlbacher et al. 2010).

Each attribute is then depicted using different levels. For example, the characteristic "waiting time for an appointment with a specialist" can be assigned the levels "one day", "one week" or "one month". The levels and the attributes are then combined into different options.

Depending on the number of the characteristics relevant for the decision (attribute) and the number of different levels of this attribute, an exponentially increasing number of possible product combinations (therapy products) result. Even in the case of 3–4 attributes with a few levels each, this results in so many product combinations that they could not all be listed as options in a survey. If the study participants were given all of the possible variations, they would be overwhelmed or bored soon, or would react with resistance (Adamowicz and Boxhall 2001), which would lead to useless results.

For this reason a reduced selection is generally used, which however still allows for a reliable calculation of preferences (Telser 2002; Street and Burgess 2007).

The assessment of the benefit function is carried out using the maximum likelihood method. In this approach different appraisal methods (mostly probit or logit estimation) can be used, depending on the distribution function which they are based on (Louviere et al. 2000; Telser 2002; Hensher et al. 2005; Bridges et al. 2008; Ryan et al. 2008).

Case Study 10: Preferences of Overweight and Obese Patients Regarding Long-term Weight Loss: A Discrete Choice Experiment
Background of the Study: Therapy Objective Is a Long-term Change in Lifestyle
Overweight and obesity have reached epidemic proportions in Germany (Antonanzas and Rodriguez 2010). Due to the high prevalence of secondary diseases, prevention and therapy of overweight and obesity represent a great

(continued)

Therapy A	Characteristics	Therapy B
Are communicated, but not implemented in everyday life	**Weight loss strategies**	Are communicated and also trained in everyday life
Selection of different therapy and free time programmes	**Diverse therapy offerings**	Standardised therapy and free time programme
Personal care by personnel	**Type of Advice**	No intensive personal care
Therapy is specified in a standardised way	**Therapy plan**	Therapy is individually tailored to suit you
3 stars, comfort for sophisticated demands	**Hotel and service offerings (infrastructure quality)**	2 stars, standard, medium comfort
Transition into follow-up care is organized	**Coordination and referral**	No follow-up care takes place
Therapy offers group experience	**Social contacts (interaction)**	Group experience not possible in therapy
Not specialised in overweight or obesity	**Specialist competence**	Specialisation in overweight and obesity
	Please choose one option (check one)	

Fig. 12.3 Example of a decision set

Case Study 10 (continued)

challenge for our healthcare system (Stockli and Keller 2002). More than a million deaths can be attributed to overweight and obesity. According to estimates, overweight and obesity are the cause of 5–10 % of the healthcare spending in the United States; in addition it results in at least twice as high indirect costs (through the loss of lives and productivity as well as the income associated with it) (WHO 2006; Tsai et al. 2011).

Although considerable improvements have been made in conventional therapy and rehabilitation, long-term treatment success can hardly be achieved. Preference-based therapy products could increase the level of patient compliance and adherence. Currently there is hardly any information about how patient needs and expectations can be used for successful medical care in rehabilitation. Depending on the measure and method of data collection, insufficient compliance in obesity therapy was recorded among 50–83 % of all patients (Margraf 2002).

If one assumes that patients attempt to maximize their benefits, the consideration of individual motivation is a decisive criterion for the success of treatment. All potential users of healthcare services only maximise their

(continued)

Case Study 10 (continued)

benefits when the healthcare services offered are oriented towards individual needs and consider patient preferences.

The objective of the study is the analysis of therapy characteristics relevant to patients for weight loss and the documentation of patient preferences for weight loss programmes.

Method: Collection of Patient Preferences with the Help of Discrete Choice Experiments

In health economy, patient preferences are increasingly determined using discrete choice analysis (DCE; also discrete choice experiment) (Ryan et al. 2008). The DCE is the selection-based form of conjoint analysis which was made possible on the basis of the theoretical papers by Lancaster (1966) and McFadden (1974). It was these papers which enabled the replacement of the ranking and rating of many different product and service variations by the comparison of pairs, i.e. through a selection decision.

Through the comparison of pairs and the selection based upon it, the complexity is considerably reduced for survey participants and thus more valid survey outcomes are ensured (see Fig. 12.3).

Qualitative methods (analysis of the literature, interview with experts N = 5, focus group surveys N = 44) were systematically used to identify all potentially relevant therapy characteristics. Subsequently 201 overweight and obese rehabilitation patients evaluated the relevant items using a five-point-likert-scale. The psychometric testing and dimensional structuring of 64 items was carried out using exploratory and confirmatory factor analysis and was verified with tests for reliability. Then a DCE was carried out (N = 110 rehabilitation patients in Mecklenburg-Western Pomerania, Germany).

Figure 12.3 shows an example of a decision set from this study.

Outcomes

51.82 % of the 110 respondents in the DCE were male, on average 53.05 years old and had an average Body Mass Index (BMI) of 33.54 kg/m^2 (SD 7.73). All in all, 823 choices were used for the evaluation. The characteristics "coordination of care and referral" as well as "individual therapy planning" attained the highest preference. The characteristic "hotel and service aspects" ("infrastructure") was least preferred by participants in the DCE. Significant values were determined for all attributes.

Overweight and obese patients prefer continual guidance, treatment and follow-up care. These characteristics received the highest values (coefficient: 1.4736; OR 4.365). Most of these patients have a history of "diet careers". Numerous attempts to lose weight based on their own initiative usually failed.

(continued)

Case Study 10 (continued)

In order to attain long-term weight loss, small treatment objectives which build upon one another are necessary. These must be adapted and supplemented depending on the response and rate of success.

Furthermore, it is very important to the patients that their personal situations and conditions are taken into consideration (second most significant characteristic, coefficient: 1.4468; OR 4.249). Consideration of each person's physical activity and nutrition, of everyday habits and individual daily schedules as well as social context conditions are fundamental for successful therapy. It can be concluded that a standard therapy ("same for all") is not desired by those concerned and thus does not contribute positively to motivation in the long term.

In the evaluation of preferences of overweight and obese patients, the attribute hotel and service aspects displayed the smallest coefficient (coefficient: 0.5709; OR 1.769). Thus, it can be assumed that patients are prepared to forego comfort and extras in favour of coordinated, individualised and personal therapy.

Assessment

Decision-makers in healthcare are showing increasing interest in the needs and preferences of all players involved. Furthermore, the methods of preference measurement are gaining increasing importance especially in the policy context, such as the Food and Drug Administration (FDA) in the United States or the European Medicines Agency (EMA) in London, demand proof of the benefits of patient preferences as an additional source of information for the risk-benefit assessment to make decisions about the introduction of new medications as well as their authorisations.

In the area of decisions about medication reimbursements (inclusion in the benefit catalogue of the statutory health insurances) a majority of rating agencies in different countries also require proof of the additional benefit for the patient and the depiction of the patient's perspective (preferences) and their consideration in decisions relevant to them.

In Germany the determination and consideration of the additional benefit for patients is required by law (§ 35b SGB V) and must be considered in decisions regarding new pharmaceuticals. The Federal Joint Committee commissions the Institute for Quality and Efficiency in Health Care (IQWiG) in Cologne with these evaluations. The IQWiG is currently carrying out pilot studies regarding the application and use of different instruments for preference measurement.

Conjoint analyses and discrete choice experiments have proven to be very suitable for application in healthcare and pharmacoeconomics, and are increasingly implemented in these fields. They enable the representation of patient preferences and thus the patient benefit. For example, they were used in cost-effectiveness analyses, in which treatment processes are important, in "contingent valuations", in order to determine willingness to pay or "willingness to accept" or in order to evaluate states of health, quality of life and quality-adjusted years of life. They have also been used for the evaluation of endpoints which are relevant for patients in view of the risk taken in different forms of treatment (O'Brien et al. 1998; Ryan et al. 2003; McIntosh 2006; Johnson et al. 2007; Bridges et al. 2008).

When patient preferences are known and healthcare delivery services or other products are oriented toward these, patients become more active and contribute more to their own treatments. Furthermore, so-called compliance (patient's willingness to participate in therapy) and adherence (along with the willingness simply to participate, also showing initiative to improve one's own health) can be increased. This heightened adherence can, in turn, lead to better treatment outcomes.

With the help of the discrete choice method, the characteristics of a treatment or intervention which are relevant for patients can be documented. These procedures can make a significant contribution to health economy studies in the future. Known preferences enable conclusions to be made about the benefits for individuals.

12.4   Evidence-Based Medicine (EBM)

Evidence-based medicine (EBM) refers to the application of scientific knowledge in clinical care (see Antes et al. 2003). With the words of an exceptional representative of this discipline: "Evidence-based medicine is the conscientious, specific and intelligent use of the best current external scientific evidence for decisions on the medical care of individual patients. The practise of EBM means the integration of individual clinical expertise with the best possible external evidence from systematic research" (Sackett 1998). The ability to identify and evaluate evidence in the scientific literature as well as to apply it in individual cases is the core of evidence-based medicine.

The method is considered as a way to overcome only "opinion-based medicine", which is solely based on the individual experience of a physician or opinion leaders. The attempt to compile and evaluate scientific information in such a way where it can be optimally used by general practitioners to make individualised clinical decisions makes this concept extremely innovative. This includes addressing the desires and opportunities of patients in diagnostic and therapeutic decisions.

The insights of evidence-based medicine can be used as the foundation for evaluation decisions in the healthcare sector as well as by MCOs. The term "evidence-based healthcare" (EBHC) is used primarily for this purpose (Muir Gray 1997). In the United States, HMOs and clinics are increasingly developing internal → guidelines which are weighted according to evidence criteria. For example, evidence-based guidelines exist for obstetrics and neonatology.

The essential characteristics of evidence-based medicine are (Bucher et al. 1996):

1. The identification of evidence-based information is carried out in a systematic way, using medical data banks.
2. The appraisal of established evidence takes place on the basis of epidemiological principles (critical appraisal).
3. The application of scientific evidence must be tested for feasibility in the context of the individual case at hand.
4. The adequacy of medical service must be checked continually in relation to the current level of scientific knowledge and its appropriate application in individual cases.

Evidence-based medicine can be divided into the following process phases (Bucher et al. 1996):

Systematic Acquisition of Information

Meta-analysis is a systematic method of providing information about the effectiveness of a treatment. This is a quantitative method which evaluates the outcome of individual studies with statistical methods. It can be divided into the following steps (Goodman 1996): Specification of the problem, establishment of the criteria for the studies to be included in the analysis, identification of all studies which fulfil the criteria, classification of studies and their results according to methodological attributes and outcomes, statistical analysis of studies with sensitivity analyses as well as the presentation of the outcomes.

Although meta-analysis is a valuable method for evaluating medical measures, the results can be distorted because there is a tendency to not publish studies with negative results as opposed to those with positive results. For this reason, it is critical to investigate which inclusion and exclusion criteria were used and which efforts were made to identify unpublished studies in a meta-analysis.

A good source for meta-analyses is the Cochrane Collaboration, named after the British physician and epidemiologist A. Cochrane (1909–1988). It is a worldwide organisation of specialists which systematically and continually updates reviews on diagnoses and therapies in all realms of medicine. The Cochrane Collaboration's meta-analyses are a source of information evaluated according to evidence criteria. The search for relevant information, however, can also be carried out directly by a commercial provider or online. The most important data banks are MEDLINE, PubMed, EMBASE and INSPEC.

Analysis of the Evidence

The critical appraisal of the quality of a scientific publication is the next step, which should provide the physician with answers for their practical work.

Specialist organisations developed the criteria which serve to assess medical and epidemiological papers, health economic studies, meta-analyses, guidelines and screenings. These criteria should enable distortions of studies (biases) to be

Evidence Level	Type of Evidence
Ia	Evidence based on RCT meta-analyses
Ib	Evidence based on at least one RCT
IIa	Evidence based on at least one other type of well-designed, quasi-experimental study
IIb	Evidence based on at least one other type of well-designed, quasi-experimental study
III	Evidence based on at least one other type of well-designed, non-experimental, descriptive study, such as comparative studies, correlation studies and case control studies
IV	Evidence based on reports from the expert committees or opinions and/or clinical experiences of well-known authors

Fig. 12.4 Levels of evidence for assessing studies (According to Cochrane 2012)

identified as well as to evaluate the possible influence which interferences have on the study outcome (confounding).

The gold standard for the quality of a medical evaluation is the randomised controlled trial (RCT). In these studies patients who could profit from an intervention are divided into an intervention group and a control group according to a random procedure and the outcomes are compared. These two groups only differ in the intervention attributes in a good randomisation.

Case control studies have a somewhat diminished importance. In these studies the people chosen for the control group have the same attributes as those in the intervention group except for the attribute which is being investigated, e.g. a disease (this is referred to as matching). Case control studies are used in the search for the causes of illnesses or in order to determine side effects. Usually these are retrospective studies.

Another type of study is **cohort studies,** in which groups of people are observed over a long period of time and deviations are documented. Cohort studies, which are usually prospective, are always used when RCTs cannot be carried out for ethical or practical reasons.

For the first assessment of the studies it is helpful to systematise them according to **levels of evidence,** in which randomised controlled trials serve as a reference method (see Fig. 12.4).

Application of Evidence Found in Individual Cases

In this last step, the extent to which study results are applicable to the concrete clinical situation or patient group (external validity) must be examined. For this purpose the patient attributes of the study participants must be compared with those of one's own patients. The experience gained can then be integrated into the → guidelines of a hospital or physician's practice.

12.5 Health Services Research

Among the evaluation procedures, health services research is the procedure which investigates the effectiveness of health technologies, i.e. their effectiveness under everyday conditions. The relationships between the structures and processes of healthcare and their outcomes are examined in this procedure. Another important attribute is the patient-centred perspective of the approach. Patient preferences should be given a larger weight in medical decisions.

The results of health services research are relevant for the structuring of → quality management and → disease management as well as for the creation of → pay-for-performance procedures.

The starting point for health services research is the quite broad spectrum of variation in care with healthcare services which apparently has less to do with the patient structure than the respective institutional structures (Anderson and Mooney 1990). Health services research is furthermore based on the experience that limits of capacity and the use of healthcare facilities hardly has a negative effect on the health state of a patient and even less on the health and quality of life of the population (Anderson and Mooney 1990).

Health services research can be defined as a research method which attempts to link the structure or process of providing healthcare with its outcome on the community level, the institutional level or the patient level. Relationships on the institutional level are particularly interesting for MCOs (physician's practice, hospital, internal administration etc.). The distinction in structure, processes and outcome quality is based on the theory of quality from Donabedian, who developed the theoretical basis for health systems research (Donabedian 1966). Donabedian's quality model is based on the central hypothesis that there is a causal relationship between the structural quality of an organisation, the quality of the processes running within it and the quality of its outcomes (see Fig. 12.5).

The term "structure" refers to the administrative, organisational and physical equipment of the facilities in the healthcare system, such as the number of beds and devices, the number of staff, the qualification of the personnel and the technical level of the devices as well as the structuring of the organisation and work flow. The assumption that the use of structural indicators is based on is that providers, which fulfil certain structural standards, also produce better results of care. However, it should be noted that this is not a strictly causal relationship, as the processes are also dependant on factors which are difficult to define or assess, such as the organisational culture, experience and, last but not least, random influences.

The "process" is comprised of the quality of the treatment and administration processes, assessed based on indicators such as the average length of stay, the number of transfers or the existence of guidelines. A superior outcome is expected from compliance with certain process standards.

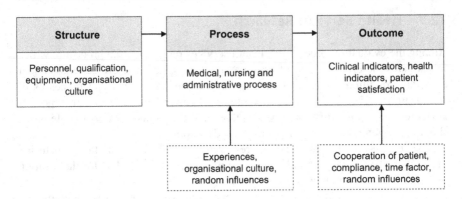

Fig. 12.5 Donabedian's quality model

The "outcome" refers to the change in the state of health and patient satisfaction. The outcomes are assessed using clinical indicators and mortality indicators, health-related indicators of quality of life or through patient satisfaction. Patient satisfaction is an important dimension of outcomes research. It influences the patient compliance and correlates with the clinical and health-related indicators.

The outcome of the processes is also dependant on factors such as the patient's own activities as co-producer of their health and patient compliance with medical advice which can make a causal attribution to the processes within a healthcare facility more difficult.

The procedure for health systems research can be structured in the following way:
1. Identification and selection of the structure, process and outcome indicators
2. Analysis and aggregation of the data
3. Description of the variances in the outcomes and identification of problems
4. Analysis and explanation of variances and
5. Dissemination of results (such as through guidelines).

On the one hand, as with every evaluation procedure, the problems with health systems research are in the assessment of the outcomes as the results apply to multiple dimensions of the state of health and the results are qualitative rather than quantitative. On the other hand, the attributability of the results to the structures and processes represents a problem because the recovery process is dependent on many factors which can only be influenced to a limited extent by physicians, nurses etc. In addition, a clear attribution to certain treatment methods is not always possible and sub-types of a disease display different outcomes. The time factor is also essential. For instance, when should the outcome of a hip implantation be assessed; after a few weeks or a few years?

> **Problems with the Assessment and Attribution of Outcomes**
> 1. The outcomes are multi-dimensional
> 2. Most outcomes are of a qualitative nature
> 3. The outcomes cannot be clearly attributed to one treatment
> 4. The sub-forms of a disease have different outcomes
> 5. The outcomes are dependent on the period of time in which they are observed.

In individual cases it is also difficult to distinguish the process characteristics from the outcomes. Patient satisfaction, for example, is referred to as being an outcome indicator. However, as it influences a patient's compliance and, hence, the treatment outcomes, it could also be classified as a process indicator.

12.6 Health Technology Assessment (HTA)

Health technology assessment (HTA) can be defined as a systematic process through which the direct and indirect consequences of a type of health technology are evaluated (see Gerhardus and Dintsios 2002; Perleth et al. 2008). HTA not only evaluates the effectiveness and the costs, it also evaluates the societal, ethical and legal consequences of a certain technology. Both a new technology and an already-existing technology can be assessed by HTA. The direct consequences include effects which the technology brings about; the indirect or secondary consequences are the unintentional effects of an economic, societal or legal nature. The object of evaluation could include medical technology as well as the remaining healthcare technologies. However, in practise, the evaluation of medical technology is in the foreground.

The definition makes it clear that HTA is a method of evaluation that includes other procedures, namely the cost-effectiveness analysis for assessing cost-effectiveness, evidence-based medicine to assess efficacy and health systems research, to assess effectiveness. Thus, it is the most comprehensive method.

HTA does not only include the implementation of evaluation studies, it is also a management process comprised of the following stages (Goodman 1996):
1. The selection of a technology for a study, in which the level of the burden of disease, the expected improvement potential and the preferences of society play a role (demand analysis)
2. The examination of the security and effectiveness of technology under ideal and realistic conditions, their cost-effectiveness and their ethical, societal and legal effects on the basis of primary studies from different disciplines
3. The synthesis of this information and the compiling of it with available information
4. The dissemination of this information, appraisals and recommendations to the decision-makers in the healthcare system.

HTA can support various types of decisions which can be categorised as follows (Goodman 1996):

1. Technology-oriented evaluation:
   It is geared towards the evaluation of one individual technology with all of its consequences, when for example a pharmaceutical company or a device producer applies for the authorisation of a new medication or device.

2. Problem-oriented evaluation:
   This is concerned with deciding how a certain problem, for which alternative technologies are available, can be best solved; such as the diagnosis of dementia using computer tomography, magnetic resonance imaging or a positron emission tomography.

3. Project-oriented evaluation:
   This concentrates on the introduction of a certain technology within an organisation, e.g. when a hospital must decide whether particular large pieces of medical equipment should be purchased or a new unit of care (e.g. a stroke unit) should be created.

The organisations which carry out HTAs are typically state-owned or partially state-owned authorities and give recommendations for the implementation of healthcare technologies based on HTAs. MCOs can use these recommendations to decide which technologies (which have finished the experimentation stage and are authorised) will be included in their service catalogue, or which already implemented technologies, which have proven to be ineffective, should be removed from the catalogue. In addition, HTA can provide MCOs a basis of information for the establishment of → guidelines and → formularies.

Literature

Adamowicz, V., & Boxhall, P. (2001). *Future directions of stated choice methods for environment valuation.* Conference choice experiments: A new approach to environmental valuation. London.

Anderson, T. F.,& Mooney, G. (1990). *The challenges of medical practice variations.* Houndsmith. London: MacMillan Press Ltd.

Antes, G. (1998). EBM praktizieren. In M. Perleth & G. Antes (Eds.), *Evidenzbasierte Medizin* (pp. 19–26). Munich: Urban & Vogel.

Antes, G., Bassler, D., & Forster, J. (2003). *Evidenz-basierte Medizin.* Stuttgart: Thieme.

Antonanzas, F., & Rodriguez, R. (2010). Feeding the economics of obesity in the EU in a healthy way. *The European Journal of Health Economics, 11*(4), 351–353.

Ben-Akiva, M. E., & Lerman, S. R. (1985). *Discrete choice analysis: Theory and application to travel demand.* Cambridge, MA: MIT Press.

Bridges, J., Onukwugha, E., Johnson, F., & Hauber, A. (2007). Patient preference methods – A patient centered evaluation paradigm. *ISPOR Connections, 13*(6), 4–7.

Bridges, J. F., Kinter, E. T., Kidane, L., et al. (2008). Things are looking up since we started listening to patients: Trends in the application of conjoint analysis in health 1982–2007. *The Patient: Patient-Centered Outcomes Research, 14*(4), 273–282.

Bucher, H. C., Egger, M., Schmidt, J. G., et al. (1996). Evidence based medicine: Ein Ansatz zu einer rationaleren Medizin. *Schweizer Ärztezeitung, 77,* 1660–1667.

Chapman, G. B., & Sonnenberg, F. A. (2003). *Decision making in health care: Theory, psychology and applications*. Cambridge: Cambridge University Press.

Cochrane. (2012). *Von der Evidenz zur Empfehlung (Klassifikationssysteme)*. http://www.cochrane.de/de/evidenz-empfehlung. Accessed 26 Feb 2013.

Donabedian, A. (1966). Evaluating the quality of care. *Milbank Memory Fund Quarterly*, (Pt 2), 166–203.

Drummond, M. F., Sculpher, M. J., Torrance, G. W., O'Brien, B. J., & Stoddart, G. L. (2005). *Methods for the economic evaluation of health care programmes* (3rd ed.). Oxford: Oxford University Press.

Gehardus, A., & Dintsios, C.M. (2002). Der Einfluss von HTA-Berichten auf die gesundheitspolitische Entscheidungsfindung. Eine systematische Übersichtsarbeit. *GMS Health Technology Assessment*. http://bibnet.org/vufind/Record/ccmed957834703. Hannover.

Gold, M. R., Siegel, J. E., Russel, L. B., & Weinstein, M. C. (1996). *Cost-effectiveness in health and medicine*. Oxford: Oxford University Press.

Goodman, C. (1996). A basic methodological toolkit. In A. Szczepura & J. Kankaanpää (Eds.), *Assessment of health care technologies* (Case studies, key concepts and strategic issues, pp. 29–65). Weinheim: Wiley.

Green, P. E., & Srinivasan, V. (1978). Conjoint analysis in consumer research: Issues and outlook. *Journal of Consumer Research, 5*, 103–123.

Green, P. E., & Srinivasan, V. (1990). Conjoint analysis in marketing: New developments with implications for research and practice. *Journal of Marketing Research, 54*(1), 3–19.

Heidbrink, M. (2006). *Reliabilität und Validität von Verfahren der Präferenzmessung. Ein metaanalytischer Vergleich verschiedener Verfahren der Conjoint-Analyse*. Holling: Universität Münster, Philosophische Fakultät.

Hensher, D. A., Rose, J. M., & Greene, W. H. (2005). *Applied choice analysis: A primer*. Cambridge: Cambridge University Press.

Johnson, F. R., Ozdemir, S., Hauber, B., & Kauf, T. L. (2007). Women's willingness to accept perceived risks for vasomotor symptom relief. *Journal of Womens Health (Larchmt), 16*(7), 1028–1040.

Krauth, C. (2010). Methoden der Kostenbestimmung in der gesundheitsökonomischen Evaluation. *Gesundheitsökonomie & Qualitätsmanagement, 15*, 251–259.

Lancaster, K. J. (1966). A new approach to consumer theory. *Journal of Political Economy, 74*(2), 132–157.

Lancsar, E., & Louviere, J. (2008). Conducting discrete choice experiments to inform healthcare decision making: A user's guide. *PharmacoEconomics, 26*(8), 661–677.

Louviere, J. J., Hensher, D. A., & Swait, J. D. (2000). *Stated choice methods: Analysis and application*. Cambridge: Cambridge University Press.

Margraf, J. (2002). *Motivation von Arzt und Patient*. BDA-Manual Adipositas, ifap Service-Institut für Ärzte und Apotheker GmbH.

McFadden, D. (1974). Conditional logit analysis of qualitative choice behavior. *Zarembka, 1974*, 105–142.

McIntosh, E. (2006). Using discrete choice experiments within a cost-benefit analysis framework: Some considerations. *PharmacoEconomics, 24*(9), 855–868.

Mühlbacher, A. C., Juhnke, C., & Bethge, S. (2010). Experts' judgment on patient centered coordinated care. ISPOR 13th Annuale European Congress: Health Technology Assessment. Prague: A European Collaboration.

Muir Gray, J. A. (1997). *Evidence-based health care*. New York: Churchill Linvingstone.

O'Brien, B. J., Goeree, R., Gafni, A., et al. (1998). Assessing the value of a new pharmaceutical. A feasibility study of contingent valuation in managed care. *Medical Care, 36*(3), 370–384.

Perleth, M., Busse, R., Gerhardus, A., Gibis, B., & Lühmann, D. (2008). *Health technology assessment*. Berlin: Medizinisch Wissenschaftliche Verlagsgesellschaft.

Ryan, M., Gerard, K., & Amaya-Amaya, M. (2008). *Using discrete choice experiments to value health and health care* (The economics of non-market goods and resources, Vol. 11). Dordrecht: Springer.

Sackett, D. L. (1998). Was ist Evidenz-basierte Medizin. In M. Perleth & G. Antes (Eds.), *Evidenzbasierte Medizin* (pp. 9–18). Munich: Urban & Vogel.

Santerre, R. E., & Neun, S. P. (2009). *Health economics: Theories, insights and industry studies.* Mason: South-Western Cengage Learning.

Schöffski, O., Schulenburg, Graf v.d., J. M. (2008). *Gesundheitsökonomische Evaluation* (3rd ed.). Berlin: Springer.

Stockli, R., & Keller, U. (2002). From obesity to diabetes. *Therapeutische Umschau, 59*(8), 388–392.

Street, D. J., & Burgess, L. (2007). *The construction of optimal stated choice experiments, theory and methods.* New Jersey: Wiley.

Telser, H. (2002). *Nutzenmessung im Gesundheitswesen: die Methode der Discrete- Choice-Experimente.* Hamburg: Kovac.

Train, K. (2003). *Discrete choice methods with simulation.* Cambridge: Cambridge University Press.

Tsai, A. G., Williamson, D. F., & Glick, H. A. (2011). Direct medical cost of overweight and obesity in the United States: A quantitative systematic review. *Obesity Reviews, 12*(1), 50–61.

Turner-Bowker, D. M., Bartley, P. J., & Ware, J. E. (2002). *SF-36® health survey & "SF" bibliography* (3rd ed.). Lincoln: Quality Metric Incorporated.

WHO [World Health Organization]. (2006). Europäische Charta zur Bekämpfung der Adipositas. In *Europäische Ministerkonferenz der WHO zur Bekämpfung der Adipositas*, Ernährung und Bewegung für die Gesundheit. Istanbul: WHO.

Zweifel, P., Breyer, F., & Kifmann, M. (2009). *Health economics* (2nd ed.). Berlin: Springer.

Part IV

Evaluation of Managed Care

Preliminary Remarks

13

"After a turbulent decade of trial and error, that experiment can be characterized as an economic success but a political failure", stated Robinson (2001, p. 2622), for the United States some years ago. In particular, the question was raised of whether MCOs used "managed care" or "managed costs". Critics emphasise that the second option was indeed the case, and that too little attention was given to the preferences and expectations of the insured as well as those of service providers. This led to the situation that although managed care was considered to be useful in theory, there are considerable problems in its implementation. This is highlighted by the fact that it is unclear to most parties which instruments and organisational forms belong to managed care and that fully accepted methods, such as working according to guidelines or disease management, are not seen in connection with managed care. In general, different objectives and expectations are associated with managed care.

Firstly, the increase in economic efficiency of healthcare provision by reducing costs is doubtlessly the most important goal pursued by managed care. Objectives include the reduction of unnecessary services, prevention of periods of inactivity in the treatment process and the reduction of prices of services purchased.

Secondly, the expectations are oriented towards an improvement in the quality of care. The process and outcome quality are meant to be improved through a standardisation and performance orientation of the care process and an integration of the treatment steps. Healthcare differs from other industries in the fact that, in most cases, better quality goes hand in hand with lower cost (e.g. a well-managed diabetes patient).

The socio-political objective of fair healthcare for the population – with health services independent of a person's income, assets, education or place of residence (Buchanan 1998) – is not a part of the declared objectives of managed care. In our opinion, this goal can only be realised through political interventions, for example compulsory health insurance. However, there is a danger that in a system without general insurance protection, the distribution of healthcare services and access to healthcare facilities will worsen through the use of managed care instruments and institutions. Since the goal of a fair provision of care for the population through

V.E. Amelung, *Healthcare Management*, Springer Texts in Business and Economics, DOI 10.1007/978-3-642-38712-8_13, © Springer-Verlag Berlin Heidelberg 2013

healthcare services has a high value in the health policy target systems, this objective will also be considered in the following evaluation.

Managed care can only fully realise its performance potential when patients, the insured as well as physicians accept it. Thus, along with the aforementioned evaluation criteria, the question should also be raised, to what extent managed care is accepted by patients, the insured and physicians, and how the doctor-patient relationship is changing (Meyer and Denz 2000).

In June 2012 the Swiss population had a referendum concerning managed care. The initiative intended to enshrine integrated care in law but was rejected by more than 75 % of the voters. The objective of this bill was to introduce strong financial incentives for patients participating in integrated care models (MAHP 2012). Since managed care plays an important role in Switzerland, these negative results were surprising and may be explained by the patients' concerns of limited provider choice, a discussion primarily launched by specialist physicians (BDI 2012).

In the following section, the managed care method will be evaluated on the basis of these criteria, by comparing the advantages and disadvantages attributed to this concept with the results of empirical studies. However, it should be emphasised here that it is nearly impossible to make a sound and comprehensive evaluation (Dudley and Luft 2001, p. 1089). In a very established and extensive study Berchtold and Hess (2006) considered and systematically depicted the literature available from studies in Europe. Essentially, it is difficult to make a conclusive evaluation because no real control groups can be formed, as is customary in medicine. This is not only due to the fact that it is nearly impossible to form such control groups – in Switzerland much effort was spent to do so – but because there are other influencing factors which can neither be determined nor qualified. Among these is the intensity of competition in local healthcare markets and the interaction between different instruments. Thus, not only does a great need for research remain, but also for strategic leeway which must be filled by business decisions and action.

Literature

Baumberger, J., & Künzi, M. (2010). 20 Jahre HMO und Managed Care in der Schweiz: Managed Care – Erfolgsgeschichte ohne Wirkung?. *clinicum* 1–10.

BDI [Berufsverband Deutscher Internisten E.V.]. (2012). *Forum Managed Care: Wahl-GAU im Aargau.* http://www.bdi.de/allgemeine-infos/aktuelle-meldungen/ansicht/article/forum-man aged-care-wahl-gau-im-aargau.html. Accessed 12 Dec 2012.

Berchtold, P., & Hess, K. (2006). *Evidenz für Managed Care – Europäische Literaturanalyse unter besonderer Berücksichtigung der Schweiz, Arbeitsdokument* 16, Schweizerisches Gesundheitsobservatorium.

Born, P. H., & Simon, C. J. (2001, March/April). Patients and profits: The relationship between HMO financial performance and quality of care. *Health Affairs, 20*(2), 167–174.

Buchanan, A. (1998). Justice, but not unjustly. *Journal of Health Politics, Policy and Law, 23,* 132–143.

Bundorf, M. K., Schulman, K. A., Stafford, J. A., et al. (2004). Impact of managed care on the treatment, costs, and outcomes of fee-for-service medicare patients with acute myocardial infarction. *Health Services Research, 39*(1), 131–152.

Dudley, R. A., & Luft, H. S. (2001). Managed care in transition. *The New England Journal of Medicine, 344*(14), 1087–1092.

Dudley, R. A., Miller, R. H., Korebrot, T. Y., et al. (1998). The impact of financial incentives on quality of health care. *The Milbank Quarterly, 76*, 649–688.

MAHP [Market Aceess & Health Policy]. (2012). *Managed-Care-Gesetzesvorlage in der Schweiz.* http://www.healthpolicy-online.de/news/schweiz-beschliesst-managed-care-gesetz-zukuenftig-sollen-60-prozent-der-schweizer-in-der-integrierten-versorgung-eingeschrieben-sein. Accessed 12 Dec 2012.

Meyer, P. C., & Denz, M. D. (2000). Sozialer Wandel der Arztrolle und der Ärzteschaft durch Managed Care in der Schweiz. *Das Gesundheitswesen, 62*, 138–142.

Robinson, J. C. (2001). The end of managed care. *JAMA: The Journal of the American Medical Association, 285*(20), 2622–2628.

Cost Effects of Managed Care

14

The influence of managed care on the cost of care is difficult to assess. Only few studies compare the entire cost of MCOs with those of the traditional fee-for-service insurances. Often only certain aspects are investigated, since the complexity would otherwise be impossible to address. Thus, the expenses of hospital services, the use of service providers and the influence on the prices of health services are examined. Due to higher economic efficiency and lower purchasing prices it is also difficult to separate the cost reductions in managed care from the selection effects. At least a portion of the cost advantages of MCOs seems to be due to the more favourable risks in the structure of insured persons in HMOs (Kühn 1997). Shimada et al. (2009) found similar results in their study. They identified that the insured in MCOs demonstrate a better state of health than those in fee-for-service insurances. However, this effect is put into perspective in regions with more competition. In general it must be stated that there is still a lack of established studies (see Sullivan 2000, p. 139) and, to be fair, it must be assumed that such studies will not be available in the near future.

The empirical studies which analyse the differences in expenses between managed care and traditional insurances are largely based on market studies in which markets with differing MCO market shares are compared. They demonstrate that the increase in expenses for healthcare services and the market shares of MCOs, their "market penetration", negatively correlate. The larger the MCO market share, the lower the growth of their expenses. This cost-reducing effect is demonstrated for hospital expenses in most studies (Chernew et al. 1998; Konetzka et al. 2008).

Studies from Switzerland have demonstrated a savings potential of 20–30 %. This is largely attained through the use of managed care instruments such as gatekeeping and budget responsibility (Berchthold and Hess 2006). Another study illustrated that managed care models have a savings in service costs of up to 20 % in comparison to traditional insurances (Baumberger and Künzi 2010). However, even in Switzerland selection effects, both on the supply- and demand-side, play a central role and the actual effects are significantly lower than expected.

Further empirical studies examined the use of health services in MCOs. It can generally be noted that MCOs display a lower frequency of use (Robinson and

V.E. Amelung, *Healthcare Management*, Springer Texts in Business and Economics, 249
DOI 10.1007/978-3-642-38712-8_14, © Springer-Verlag Berlin Heidelberg 2013

Steiner 1998). However, the intensity of the relationship varies based on the respective influencing factors. A close relationship was demonstrated between the reduction in the number of hospital admissions and the number of examinations and treatments carried out. Furthermore, a reduction in the average length of stay was shown, even though it was not very definitive. The influence on the number of doctor visits and medication prescriptions, however, was unclear. The amount of studies which demonstrate a reduction among MCOs is roughly equal to the number of studies that demonstrate high values.

Also, in regard to the use of health services, a tendency is evident that in areas with a high managed care market penetration, the use of a fee-for-service system is lower than in areas with a lower managed care market share (Dudley et al. 1998, Bundorf et al. 2004).

Literature

Chernew, M. E., Hirth, R. A., Sonnad, S. S., et al. (1998). Managed care and cost growth. *Managed Care Research and Review, 55*, 259–288.

Dudley, R. A., Miller, R. H., Korebrot, T. Y., et al. (1998). The impact of financial incentives on quality of health care. *The Milbank Quarterly, 76*, 649–688.

Konetzka, R. T., Zhu, J., Sochalski, J., & Volpp, K. G. (2008). Managed care and hospital cost containment. *Inquiry, 45*(1), 98–111.

Kühn, H. (1997). *Managed Care. Medizin zwischen kommerzieller Bürokratie und integrierter Versorgung. Am Beispiel USA*, Veröffentlichungsreihe der Arbeitsgruppe Public Health des Wissenschaftszentrums Berlin.

Shimada, S. L., Zaslavsky, A. M., Zaborsky, L. B., et al. (2009). Market and beneficiary characteristics associated with enrollment in medicare managed care plans and fee-for-service. *Medical Care, 47*(5), 517–523.

Sullivan, K. (2000, July/August). On the 'Efficiency' of managed care plans. *Health Affairs, 19*(4), 139–148

Quality Effects of Managed Care

15

Linking managed care with poor quality sometimes goes hand in hand. This particularly raises the question of how MCOs may act in extreme situations when a patient is seriously ill. However, what people pay less attention to is how MCOs act in the large amount of normal cases (Reschovsky et al. 2002, p. 354). This once again documents the considerable difficulty of MCOs to build up confidence, also in respect to the general meaning of confidence in healthcare.

The Advisory Council on the Assessment of Developments in the Health Care System in Germany (SVR 2009) could neither confirm significant positive nor negative effects of managed care on quality in its assessment. Using a systematic review of 107 studies, largely originating from the United States, 36 % of the studies were identified which determined a positive or largely positive effect on quality, but 37 % also found negative or largely negative effects. A specification of the quality assessment indicators was not possible due to the great number of parameters.

However, the more recent studies are generally in favour of managed care, while a negative trend was observed in the studies from the 1990s. In examining the individual service areas in the managed care context, in particular medical prevention is seen positively (in 10 of 17 studies). In relation to the different target groups, no differences in quality could be found (SVR 2009, p. 765ff.).

In a somewhat older, comprehensive analysis of the literature of empirical studies regarding the quality of care in MCOs, Robinson and Steiner (1998) in particular evaluated the effects upon the quality of outcomes and processes.

In a total of 25 studies between 1980 and 1996, the quality was determined only once through outcome indicators. These include mortality or survival rate, clinical outcome indicators (e.g. blood pressure values) and health-related quality of life indicators ($\rightarrow$ evaluation procedure). In doing so, the following results were found: In 5 % of the cases (four observations) the outcomes of the fee-for-service system were better than those insured with managed care programmes; in 11 % of the cases (nine observations) the results for the managed care insured were better; and in the remaining 84 % of the observations (67 from 80) there were no significant differences between the two systems.

V.E. Amelung, *Healthcare Management*, Springer Texts in Business and Economics, 251
DOI 10.1007/978-3-642-38712-8_15, © Springer-Verlag Berlin Heidelberg 2013

Among the clinical indicators, 22 from 29 observations displayed no differences. Five of the seven discrepancies related to the cancer treatment of Medicare patients. Here MCOs had better results for the early detection of those cancer types in which good results are attained through prevention and early detection. Other studies showed that in the case of monitoring blood pressure, managed care patients displayed better outcomes 2 years after the initial diagnosis than patients in traditional insurance systems.

Finally, in the area of indicators concerning quality of life, 34 of the 39 observations found no significant difference between those insured with managed care programmes and those insured in the fee-for-service system. Only two observations in one study suggested slightly worse results among managed care patients.

In addition, Robinson and Steiner (1998) also evaluated studies which measure the quality of care using process indicators. Here it was demonstrated that in 22 % of the observations patients in the fee-for-service system received better quality care. In 36 % of the observations managed care patients received better care, and in the remaining 42 % there were no significant differences in process quality. This was particularly true when loose forms of MCO organisations, such as IPA model HMOs, were compared to the traditional insurances. In contrast, the process quality of more strongly integrated MCOs, such as staff MCOs, was higher than in traditional insurances.

The higher process quality of MCOs was particularly due to more comprehensive documentation of the medical history and the risk factors of the chronically ill, through effective monitoring of patient compliance and physicians' adherence to standards (Robinson and Steiner 1998).

With regard to patient satisfaction as a quality indicator, the analyses of Robinson and Steiner revealed that the satisfaction of managed care policyholders (assessed based on process indicators such as style of treatment, communication or waiting times) was consistently lower than that of fee-for-service insured. Out of 37 studies only 16 % favoured MCOs, 32 % found no difference, and 51 % found a higher level of satisfaction among those insured with traditional insurances. The only advantage which managed care policyholders observed was the cost of their insurance. In contrast, they particularly had objections to the scientific and communication abilities of the physicians (Robinson and Steiner 1998).

These results are confirmed in an analysis of the literature by Dudley et al., who included studies which Robinson and Steiner did not consider (Dudley et al. 1998).

In comparison to this, however, there is a correlation between an HMO's financial success and its quality assessment in the HEDIS quality rankings (Born and Simon 2001). In contrast to the initially plausible assumption that economic success is attained through lower quality, the empirical results show the exact opposite. The more successful an MCO is, the higher its score is in the ranking. However, whether it is a non-profit or for-profit system has no influence on the quality (e.g. Scanlon et al. 2005), whereas competition – and here the standard arguments of representatives of economic approaches are confirmed – has a positive effect on the quality ranking. The more competition there is in a market, the higher the average quality (Born and Simon 2001). These statements make it once again clear why it is so difficult to evaluate entire organisational models that are active in different markets.

Literature

Reschovsky, J. D., Hargraves, J. L., & Smith, A. F. (2002). Consumer beliefs and health plan performance: It's not whether you are in an HMO but whether you think you are. *Journal of Health Politics, Policy and Law, 27*(3), 353–377.

Robinson, R., & Steiner, A. (1998). *Managed health care. US evidence and lessons for the national health service*. Buckingham: Open University Press.

SVR [Sachverständigenrat zur Begutachtung der Entwicklung im Gesundheitswesen]. (2009). *Koordination und Integration-Gesundheitsversorgung in einer Gesellschaft des längeren Lebens*, Sondergutachten 2009, Bonn.

Scanlon, D., Swaminatham, S., Chernew, M., Bost, J., & Shevock, J. (2005). Competition and health plan performance – Evidence from health maintenance organization insurance markets. *Medical Care, 43*(4), 338–346.

Access Effects of Managed Care

16

A main point of criticism of managed care is based on the argument that it worsens the care of certain population groups. Robinson and Steiner (1998) also attempted to answer this question in their evaluation of empirical studies. The care of children, women with low income and the elderly were studied. The studies' results showed that the treatment of children by MCOs was just as good or better than that of fee-for-service insurances. Only one study found that children from low-income families had a lower chance of seeing a physician than in the traditional insurance system. In more recent studies no clear results were found. Mitchell et al. (2008) showed that children in MCOs receive a more strongly guideline-oriented treatment than those in traditional insurances. However, while Davidoff et al. (2008) report that chronically ill children in MCOs need less prescriptions than those in fee-for-service insurances, Garrett and Zuckerman (2005) found no difference between fee-for-service insurances and managed care.

Regarding the quality of care among the elderly, Sung et al. (2004) found that elderly people with the indication colon resection had a significantly shorter length of hospital stay and the number of secondary procedures in MCOs was lower. MCOs attained better outcomes in the area of rehabilitation measures as well: 4 months after discharge from a nursing facility their results were better than in fee-for-service insurances (Leach et al. 2001). However, the assessment from the German Advisory Council (SVR 2009) did not provide clear results regarding the quality of care for the elderly.

There is a tendency that physicians involved in managed care have a lower willingness to treat destitute patients than doctors in the traditional insurance system, who have historically assumed this task. In areas with a large MCO market share, this willingness is also lower among physicians who do not work within the managed care system (Cunningham et al. 1999). This development is heightened by the fact that primary physicians, who have a higher percentage of non-insured among their patients, are discriminated against in selective contracting ($\rightarrow$ selective contracting).

V.E. Amelung, *Healthcare Management*, Springer Texts in Business and Economics,
DOI 10.1007/978-3-642-38712-8_16, © Springer-Verlag Berlin Heidelberg 2013

This development made it once again clear that without an adequate governmental framework guaranteeing all population groups the financing of necessary health services, managed care endangers the care of disadvantaged population groups.

Literature

Cunningham, P. J., Grossmann, J. M., St. Peter, R. F., et al. (1999). Managed care and physicians' provision of charity care. *JAMA: The Journal of the American Medical Association, 281*, 1087–1092.

Davidoff, A., Hill, I., Courtot, B., & Adams, E. (2008). Are there differential effects of managed care on publicly insured children with chronic health conditions? *Medical Care Research and Review, 5*(3), 356–372.

Garrett, B., & Zuckerman, S. (2005). National estimates of the effects of mandatory Medicaid managed care programs on health care access and use, 1997–1999. *Medical Care, 43*(7), 649–657.

Leach, L. S., Yip, J. Y., Myrile, R. C., et al. (2001). Outcomes among orthopedic patients in skilled nursing facilities: Does managed care make a difference. *The Journal of Nursing Administration, 31*(11), 527–533.

Mitchell, J. M., Gaskin, D. J., & Kozma, C. (2008). Health supervision visits among SSI eligible children in the D.C. Medicaid program: A comparison of enrollees in fee-for-service and partially capitated managed care. *Inquiry, 45*(2), 198–214.

Robinson, R., & Steiner, A. (1998). *Managed health care. US evidence and lessons for the national health service*. Buckingham: Open University Press.

SVR [Sachverständigenrat zur Begutachtung der Entwicklung im Gesundheitswesen]. (2009). *Koordination und Integration-Gesundheitsversorgung in einer Gesellschaft des längeren Lebens*, Sondergutachten 2009, Bonn.

Sung, J., Wessel, M., Gallagher, S. F., Marcet, J., & Murr, M. M. (2004). Failure of medicare health maintenance organizations to control the cost of colon resections in elderly patients. *Archives of Surgery, 139*(12), 1366–1370.

Acceptance of Managed Care

17

17.1 Acceptance Among the Insured and Patients

The insured and patients tend to be sceptical of healthcare through managed care. Managed care limits the patients'/insured's freedom to choose physicians and possible treatments as well as requiring patients to assume greater responsibility for their own health, which perhaps they do not want. Robinson (2001, p. 2623) aptly remarked: "Consumers experience managed care's cost control strategies in form of barriers to access, administrative complexity, and the well-articulated frustration of their caregivers."

The results already outlined regarding the satisfaction of the insured, which tended to be seen as more negative than the fee-for-service care, suggest a low level of acceptance among the insured in MCOs as far as quality is concerned. However, the considerably lower insurance premiums found significantly higher acceptance. Some complaints about MCOs do not centre on the actual service but rather on the discrepancy between the services provided and those announced in the advertising messages and contracts (Havighurst 2001, p. 11). Generally it can be said that patients fear insufficient care more than they fear a surplus of care (Mechanic 2000, p. 104).

The doctor-patient relationship also seems to be poorer from the patient perspective than in the traditional insurance system. Furthermore, in a study in which patients were asked by MCOs and traditional insurances whether they trust their physicians shows that patients in traditional insurances trust their physicians more (94 %) than patients whose doctors are compensated according to salary (77 %), capitations (83 %) or fee-for-service through MCOs (85 %) (Audiey et al. 1998; IGES 2007).

However, a large portion of the insured does not even know that they are registered in an MCO (Wagner and Kongstvedt 2013). On one hand, this indicates that managed care has slowly conquered the market, and on the other hand that considerable communication problems exist.

V.E. Amelung, *Healthcare Management*, Springer Texts in Business and Economics, DOI 10.1007/978-3-642-38712-8_17, © Springer-Verlag Berlin Heidelberg 2013

17.2   Acceptance Among Physicians

When one considers that the control and standardisation of medical services, along with the transfer of the financial risk to the service provider, are among the essential principles of managed care, it is not surprising that managed care is met with rejection particularly by physicians, who grew up in the traditional insurance system (Deom et al. 2010). This attitude is shared by physician associations.

The criticism particularly focuses on the monitoring by the MCOs, the amount of administrative work, the coordination between different service providers and the ethical conflicts in the doctor-patient relationship (Donelan et al. 1997; Deom et al. 2010; Kongstvedt 2001). This assessment is confirmed in a series of more recent studies.

Studies found that, according to physicians, compensation systems with financial incentives lower the quality of healthcare and their job satisfaction. Even though 84 % of the physicians interviewed believe that financial incentives can positively influence behaviour, actually 67 % said that the incentive does not influence their behaviour. 57 % of those surveyed felt forced to lower the number of transfers. 17 % found that the quality of care suffered from it. Among physicians who received pay-for-performance this percentage was even higher. However, it also became apparent that physicians whose compensation was linked to the quality indicators and patient satisfaction had a higher level of job satisfaction than those who belong to MCOs where compensation is based on indicators of economic efficiency (Grumbach et al. 1998; Teleki et al. 2006).

These results show that the low acceptance by physicians is partly due to insufficient information and experience with managed care. This presumption is confirmed by a study by Deckard (1997), which showed that while the general satisfaction with managed care by those surveyed was low, more specific questions regarding structural deficits which could enable conclusions to be drawn about satisfaction could not confirm this. Improved communication could thus provide the opportunity to heighten acceptance among physicians (Deckard 1997; Kongstvedt 2001).

Literature

Audiey, C. K. (1998). The relationship between method of physician payment and patient trust. *JAMA: The Journal of the American Medical Association, 290,* 178–1714.

Deckard, G. J. (1997). Physician responses to a managed environment: a perceptual paradox. In P. R. Kongstvedt (Ed.), *Readings in managed health care* (pp. 98–103). Gaithersburg: Aspen.

Deom, M., Agoritsas, T., Bovier, P. A., et al. (2010). What doctors think about the impact of managed care tools on quality of care, costs, autonomy, and relations with patients. *BMC Health Services Research, 10,* 331.

Donelan, K., Blendon, R. J., Lundberg, G. D., et al. (1997). The new medical marketplace: Physicians' view. *Health Affairs, 16,* 139–148.

Grumbach, K., Osmond, D., Vranizan, K., et al. (1998). Primary care physicians' experience of financial incentives in managed-care systems. *New England Journal of Medicine, 339*(21), 1516–1521.

Havighurst, C. C. (2001). Consumer versus managed care: The new class actions. *Health Affairs, 20*(4), 8–27.

IGES. (2007). *Internationale Literatur zum Thema "Physician Satisfaction"*. http://www. bundesaerztekammer.de/downloads/InternationaleLiteratur.pdf. Accessed 18 Feb 2013.

Kongstvedt, P. R. (2001). Primary care in open panel plans. In ders (Ed.), *The managed health care handbook* (pp. 105–119). Gaithersburg: Aspen.

Mechanic, D. (2000). Managed care and the imperative for a new professional ethic. *Health Affairs, 19*(5), 100–111.

Robinson, J. C. (2001). The end of managed care. *JAMA: The Journal of the American Medical Association, 285*(20), 2622–2628.

Teleki, S. S., Damberg, C. L., Pham, C., & Berry, S. H. (2006). Will financial incentives stimulate quality improvements? Reactions from frontlines physicians. *American Journal of Medical Quality, 21*(6), 367–374.

Wagner, E. R., & Kongstvedt, P. R. (2013). Types of health insurers, managed health care organizations, and integrated health care delivery systems. In P. R. Kongstvedt (Ed.), *Essentials of managed health care*. Burlington: Jones & Bartlett Learning.

Conclusion

18

It is no surprise that managed care is met with criticism from physicians as well as insured/patients. The traditional system is convincing particularly through its generosity with the available funds and the freedom to choose as well as the decision-making autonomy which it grants. The physicians' and patients' fears regarding a deterioration of quality, however, do not coincide with the empirical studies. Overall, managed care does not represent a lower quality of care. But the expectations of a better quality of care through instruments such as disease management, quality management or the orientation on guidelines have not yet been fully confirmed. However, more recent evaluations of disease management programmes have shown promising results (van Lente 2011).

In contrast, the cost effects are relatively clear. The greatest savings in costs resulted from high priced services, for instance by substituting inpatient services with outpatient services or through the reduction of large-volume services, such as the reduction of doctor visits among the chronically ill with disease management and health promotion measures or patient education. However, selection effects cannot be ruled out at this point.

Managed care organisations and instruments require the corresponding governmental framework to ensure that they are effective. One part of the historical deficits that accompany managed care, particularly in the care of disadvantaged groups in the United States, is due to the lack of a framework, even though intensive state regulation of the managed care sector can be observed in recent years. Countries in which there is a social security obligation thus offer the protection for a socially responsible form of managed care.

Along with monitoring costs in healthcare, managed care provides the chance to preserve and improve the health of the population through cooperation with the public health institutions in the sense of public health management (Schumacher 1998). There are numerous cooperation opportunities, particularly in the area of regional health promotion and the risk assessment of the population.

It has been mentioned multiple times that managed care has come under the crossfire of criticism in the past years. In a market economy environment this automatically leads to adjustment processes. Therefore, we can (and must) realise

V.E. Amelung, *Healthcare Management*, Springer Texts in Business and Economics,   261
DOI 10.1007/978-3-642-38712-8_18, © Springer-Verlag Berlin Heidelberg 2013

today that a considerable number of managed care instruments are no longer or only seldom implemented (e.g. gatekeeping in the United States), or at least in a very watered-down form (utilisation review, capitation). In most cases this may be the correct and necessary decision. It is especially correct and necessary to neither polarise nor to merely consider one side of the coin and act like a "bull in a china shop". This was surely one of the main mistakes of the early managed care protagonists, who acted without regard to losses. However, it should not be forgotten that this also considerably limits the potential of managed care. "As plans move to less restrictive managed care products, they lose their ability to control costs" (Draper et al. 2002, p. 20); or, in Robinson's words (2001, p. 2627): "The retreat from managed care promotes access but also removes the brakes on health care cost inflation." Thus, it is no wonder that the premiums and co-payments of the insured have once again massively increased.

Fox (2001) rightly emphasised that: "Whatever the criticisms of managed care in some circles, a return to an open-ended and unmanaged fee-for-service system that characterized health care financing until a few years ago will not be tolerated by either public or private purchasers." However, it will not only be the health insurances that determine the next steps, for, as Robinson (2001, p. 2627) aptly stated: "Insurers lack the clinical skills and the ethical authority to distinguish the experimental from the accepted therapy, the appropriate from the inappropriate procedure, the qualified from the unqualified physician, or the patient who is truly ill from the worried well".

Literature

Draper, D. A., Hurley, R. E., Lesser, C. S., & Strunk, C. (2002, January/February). The changing face of managed care. *Health Affairs, 2002*, 11–23.

Fox, P. D. (2001). An overview of managed care. In P. R. Kongstvedt (Ed.), *The managed health care handbook* (pp. 3–17). Gaithersburg: Aspen.

Robinson, J. C. (2001). The end of managed care. *JAMA: The Journal of the American Medical Association, 285*(20), 2622–2628.

Schumacher, H. (1998). Public health management. In W. Damkowski & C. Precht (Eds.), *Moderne Verwaltung in Deutschland. Public management in der Praxis* (pp. 282–300). Stuttgart: Kohlhammer.

Van Lente, E. J. (2011). Erfahrungen mit strukturierten Behandlungsprogrammen (DMPs) in Deutschland. In C. Günster, J.Klose, & N.Schmacke (Eds.), *Versorgungs-Report 2011* (pp. 55–82). Stuttgart: Schattauer.

About the Authors

Volker Amelung is Professor for International Healthcare System Research at the Medical University of Hannover, Germany. He is also the president of the German Managed Care Association (BMC), Berlin. In 2011 he founded the private health services research institute inav in Berlin. Volker Amelung is a member of several healthcare associations and internationally affiliated with healthcare management professionals. His research focuses on healthcare policy, managed care and healthcare systems.

Peter Berchtold is a medical doctor by training and worked for more than 20 years in leading positions in hospitals in Switzerland and the United States. He founded college M, a research orientated consultancy company based in Bern, Switzerland, in 2002. Peter Berchtold is also president of the Swiss managed care association "Forum Managed Care".

Dr. Berchtold wrote the case study on Swiss physician networks (case study 2, pp. 65–68).

Susanne Bethge, M.Sc. in Public Health and Adminstration, is research assistant for health economics at the Hochschule Neubrandenburg, Germany. Her research focusses on discrete choice analysis.

Together with Axel Mühlbacher, Susanne Bethge wrote the section preference measurement and the corresponding case study 10 (Sect. 12.3, part III, pp. 225–231).

Anika Brümmer, MPH, is research assistant for health economics and health policy at the Medical University of Hannover, Germany. Her focus of research is on patient reported outcomes.

Anika Brümmer wrote the sections ACO and PCMH (Sects. 3.5 and 3.6, part II, pp. 75–78) and the case study on Wagner's chronic care model (case study 8, pp. 181–184) and contributed to several other parts of the book.

Mirella Cacace is Visiting Professor of regional health economics at the Leuphana University in Lüneburg, Germany. She is a 2008/09 Commonwealth Fund Harkness Fellow at Columbia University, New York. Her main research interest is international comparisons of healthcare systems. Her Ph.D. thesis analyses the changing governance structures in the American health care system.

V.E. Amelung, *Healthcare Management*, Springer Texts in Business and Economics, DOI 10.1007/978-3-642-38712-8, © Springer-Verlag Berlin Heidelberg 2013

Professor Cacace wrote the chapters on Consumer-Driven Health Plans and Health Savings Accounts (Sect. 2.3, Part II, pp. 55–59) as well as the subsection on bundled payments (in section 2.3, Part III, pp. 125–126).

Andreas Domdey, M.D. is a dentist by training and now heading the market access department at Lundbeck, a Danish research orientated pharmaceutical company. He previously worked for a large German sickness fund in Hamburg.

Andreas Domdey wrote the section on disease management and chronic care (Sect. 3.5, part III, pp. 176–180 and 184–185) and contributed the entire chapter on quality management (pp. 200–210).

PD Dr. Christian Krauth is head of the health economics research unit at the Medical University of Hannover, Germany. His research focuses on health economics, experimental economics, health services research and health economic evaluation.

PD Dr. Krauth contributed to the section health economic evaluation (Sect. 4.2, part III, pp. 217–225 and 232–240).

Axel Mühlbacher is professor for health economics and health systems research at the Hochschule Neubrandenburg, Germany. Axel Mühlbacher is a Senior Research Fellow at the Center for Health Policy and Inequities Research at Duke Global Health Institute. He was a 2010–2011 Harkness Fellow from the Commonwealth Fund at the Duke Clinical Research Institute and the Fuqua Business School.

Professor Mühlbacher wrote the section on preference measurement (Sect. 4.3 in Part III, pp. 244–251) and the corresponding case study 10.

Ulla Tangermann, MPH, is research assistant for health economics and health policy at the Medical University of Hannover, Germany. Her focus of research is on international healthcare systems.

Ulla Tangermann wrote the case study on the Quality and Outcomes Framework (case study 6, pp. 138–141) and significantly contributed to several other parts of the book and revised the entire book.

Christoph Wagner is a health economist working at the Institute for Quality and Efficiency in Healthcare (IQWIG) in Cologne, Germany. The IQWIG is a state run agency, providing HTA for the self-governing bodies.

Christoph Wagner wrote the section on patient coaching (Sect. 3.8, part III, pp. 195–200) and contributed to demand management (Sect. 117, part III, pp. 191–195).

Urs Zanoni is a consultant for healthcare projects in Switzerland and has been the CEO of MediX, a physician-driven integrated care organisation. As an economist with a master's degree in Public Health, he has been engaged in the Swiss healthcare system since 20 years.

Urs Zanoni wrote the case study on MediX (case study 7, pp. 153–155).

To a previous German edition Prof. Katharina Janus contributed significantly. The case studies on Kaiser Permanente (pp. 57–60), Leapfrog (pp. 108–110) and IHA (pp. 141–146) are still based on this work.

The entire research project on managed care was started many years ago together with my colleague Harald Schumacher, who passed away far too early in 2002. I tried to keep his way of thinking by continuing the research.

Index